# E Pluribus Barnum

# E Pluribus Barnum

## The Great Showman and the Making of U.S. Popular Culture

Bluford Adams

 University of Minnesota Press

Minneapolis

London

Chapter 5 originally appeared in slightly altered form as "'A Stupendous Mirror of Departed Empires': The Barnum Hippodromes and Circuses, 1874–1891," in *American Literary History*, 8, no. 1 (1996). Reprinted by permission.

Published by the University of Minnesota Press
111 Third Avenue South, Suite 290, Minneapolis, MN 55401-2520
Printed in the United States of America on acid-free paper

**Library of Congress Cataloging-in-Publication Data**

Adams, Bluford.
    E pluribus Barnum : the great showman and the making of U.S. popular culture / Bluford Adams.
        p.    cm.
    Includes bibliographical references (p.    ) and index.
    ISBN 0-8166-2630-8 (hardcover : alk. paper)
    ISBN 0-8166-2631-6 (pbk.)
    1.  Barnum, P. T. (Phineas Taylor), 1810–1891.   2.  Circus owners—
United States—Biography.   3.  Ringling Brothers Barnum and Bailey
Combined Shows—History.   4.  Circus—Social aspects—United States.
5.  Popular culture—United States.   I.  Title.
GV1811.B3A525   1997
338.7'617913'092—dc20
[B]                                                                    96-31754

The University of Minnesota is an equal-opportunity educator and employer.

To Doris Witt, Margaret Welborn Adams, and
L. B. Adams Jr.

# Contents

# Acknowledgments

I have accrued many debts while writing this book. First, let me thank the staffs at the institutions where I conducted my research. I am especially grateful to the staffs of the Library of Congress, the New-York Historical Society, the Robert L. Parkinson Library and Research Center at the Circus World Museum, the Harvard Theatre Collection, and the libraries of the University of Virginia and the University of Iowa. I received valuable research aid and advice from Charles Kelly in the Rare Books Division of the Library of Congress, Marty Jacobs in the theater collection of the Museum of the City of New York, Virginia Smith at the Massachusetts Historical Society, Bryan Benoit formerly of the Harvard Theatre Collection, and Mary Witkowski in the historical collections of the Bridgeport Public Library.

Many generous people provided me with crucial advice and information of various sorts. I would particularly like to thank Yoji Yamaguchi, Philip Kunhardt III, and Fred Dahlinger. I am also grateful to the Riccio, Yamaguchi, and Battle/Bennett families for hosting me so graciously on my research trips.

Throughout this project, I have benefited from interchange with a number of scholars who shared their work and ideas with me. My colleagues in the English Department at the University of Iowa have stimulated my thinking on an array of cultural questions. I also look forward to continued intellectual exchange with Joann Castagna, Janet Davis, Doug Mishler, and Martha Burns. Among the many people who read and responded to parts of this project, I particularly wish to thank Neil Harris, Robert Rydell, and Fred Dahlinger for their valuable suggestions. Another group of scholars aided me with commentary on the entire manuscript; Paul Cantor, LaVahn Hoh, David Roediger, and Peter Buckley all deserve special thanks for their thoughtful response to the work as a whole.

I wish to pay tribute to my teachers, who worked with me on the dissertation from which this book grew. Eric Lott is largely responsible for sparking my interest in popular culture. Throughout the project, he provided incisive criticism and essential advice. He pushed me to understand U.S. culture in its true complexity. I am also enormously indebted to David Levin, who kept me honest with rigorous commentary while keeping me going with moral support. He gave me the confidence to write this book.

I thank my family for sustaining me throughout the project. My grandmothers, my sisters, and my brother repeatedly came to my relief with unstinting humor and sympathy. Angelle Adams, Evelyn Welborn, Margaret Conrad, Welborn Adams, and Courtney Christensen—thanks for everything! I also drew heavily upon my parents, Margaret Welborn Adams and L. B. Adams Jr., for support and advice; they encouraged me to undertake this study and urged me on every step of the way. Finally, I am grateful to Doris Witt for carving out space in her intellectual and emotional life for my Barnum book. I began the project powered by her intelligence and enthusiasm; I end it inspired by her honesty and courage.

# Introduction: "E Pluribus Barnum"

Every community, in the natural course of events, demands an individual who shall take upon himself all sorts of extraordinary achievements in the way of Public Amusements: who will advertise largely in all the newspapers: set great banners flying from the house-top: display enormous pictures of Whales and Giants: who will catch intolerable Anacondas: and nurse unbounded Fat Boys up to the highest mark of heft and rotundity: who will crowd the streets, and distract the walkers therein with Transparencies and Musical Vans: in a word, every community needs a BARNUM: and New York is fortunate in having him.

—Cornelius Mathews, *The Prompter* (1850)

When Cornelius Mathews penned his tribute to the great showman, he never bothered to explain *why* New York, or America for that matter, needed a Barnum. It would probably have seemed a pointless question. By 1850 most Americans were reconciled to having P. T. Barnum, whether they thought they needed him or not. A century and a half later, it may be time to take up the question. This book sets out to explore nineteenth-century America's need not just for Barnum, but for the larger popular culture connoted by his name. Mathews suggests two ways of proceeding with such an inquiry: we can explain the need by studying either the crowd that feels it or the showman whose ads—in the newspaper and on the housetop—help create it. In this book I take both approaches. I examine P. T. Barnum's role as a purveyor of public amusements, and I investigate the social and political forces that produced the need for Barnumesque culture. What I present here is not a narrative of Barnum's career—for that, one must look to his biographers. Instead, this is a series of meditations on nineteenth-century U.S. popular culture that take Barnum as their nodal point.

That may seem a dubious strategy to those familiar with the history of Barnum scholarship: since the 1920s, every generation of biographers, historians, and critics has had its say about Barnum, and the present one is certainly no exception. My own project is heavily indebted to the showman's most recent biographers, as well as scholars of U.S. popular culture working under the rubrics of American studies, cultural studies, social history, ethnic studies, labor history, and women's studies. They have convinced me that Barnum has much left to teach us about the ample slice of the U.S. population that constituted his audience: workers and bosses, blacks and whites, men and women, immigrants and U.S. natives—people from across U.S. society made their way into Barnum's tent. To make sense of what they saw there is to understand more fully who they were.

Mathews to the contrary, one thing Barnum's public most certainly was *not* was a "community." By 1850 it was anachronistic to apply that term to Barnum's class-segmented audience—anachronistic, though not entirely inappropriate, given that Barnum had largely built his career on class-bonding appeals to an audience he called "the Universal Yankee Nation." Scholars have recently begun to excavate the class relations beneath Barnum's populist rhetoric. Some have exposed his early ties to the nation's plebeian amusement culture; others have explored his alignment with the emerging middle class.[1] What needs to be added to their account is a fuller sense of the way the classes collided and collaborated within Barnum's amusements. I argue that Barnum's ties to the middle class were both more numerous and more strenuously opposed than has yet been recognized. To demonstrate this, I have worked to assemble responses to his work from across the nation's solidifying class structure.

The feminized cast of middle-class culture led Barnum to seek patrons among the "ladies"; once the showman had cleared them a space in the popular culture, women were quick to fill it—both as patrons and as performers. The precise meaning of that invasion was, and remains, hotly contested, however. Whereas feminists emphasized Barnum's expansion of women's roles, their opponents stressed his reliance upon traditional images of sentimental womanhood. Barnum attempted to appease both camps, and in the process loaded his amusements with an explosive mixture of feminism and patriarchy. The consequences of his strategy—as the notorious 1855 baby shows demonstrated—could be quite spectacular.

The racial politics of Barnum's work were more clear-cut. From the Joice Heth exhibitions to the Barnum & Bailey Circus, the showman spent the bulk of his career catering to the fears and fantasies of a predominantly white audience. There were, to be sure, some shifts in Barnum's racial ideology: after entering show business as an antiabolitionist Democrat, he gradually aligned his public image—and, to a lesser extent, his amusements—with the Republicans' racial liberalism. By the 1860s, African Americans had finally begun to take a permanent place among his patrons. But Reconstruction would prove as shaky in Barnum's amusements as his new political party. The circuses of his final decades redrew the color line with a vengeance through a series of increasingly elaborate exhibitions of people of color.

The social concerns that I have briefly outlined above are developed across the entire book, but as the following summaries indicate, my emphasis shifts as I turn from one Barnum production to another. Chapter 1 focuses on the class and racial politics of the showman's frequently revised public image. I concentrate on the four Barnums that emerge in his two early newspaper series and his autobiographies, *The Life of P. T. Barnum* and *Struggles and Triumphs*. In 1841, the showman offered his first major self-representation in Barnaby Diddleum, a slaveholding Yankee confidence man with working-class sympathies. From Diddleum's position on the fringe of respectable society, Barnum attacked his enemies in the emerging middle class, especially antislavery ministers and their female allies. Diddleum was largely suppressed by the mid-1840s, when Barnum began recasting himself as the respectable spokesman and entertainer of the "Universal Yankee Nation." Barnum's new persona mythologized his country's classlessness by projecting its social conflicts onto Europe and by escaping into memories of a village childhood. After the Civil War, the reconstructed Barnum of *Struggles and Triumphs* abandoned both his nostalgia and his racism to align himself with the Republican business class. This final, paternalistic Barnum offered his amusements as tools for disciplining the lower classes.

Chapter 2 explores the public image of a woman many perceived as the antithesis of Barnum: Jenny Lind, the Swedish singer whom the showman brought to the United States for an 1850–51 concert tour. In contrast to his own notoriety for relentless self-promotion and enterprise, Barnum packaged Lind as the ultimate sentimental heroine. His efforts to control the meaning and circulation of the public Lind were contested by merchants, feminists, abolitionists, antiabolitionists, and, above all, the singer herself. Although Lind did not hesitate to assert her rights as "a woman of business" and a wealthy philanthropist, she generally helped Barnum position her concerts in the middle of the U.S. cultural hierarchy. Their strategy produced a tour notable for its popularity among the middle class, its mixed reception among elites, and its disruption by plebeian "outsiders."

By the time of the Lind tour, the nation's leading hall of cheap amusements, Barnum's American Museum, was also seeking a patronage in the middle of the social ladder. Chapter 3 traces Barnum's commitment of his Museum to the ideologies and cultural styles of the middle class and their upwardly mobile working-class allies. Barnum's enormous, heterogeneous collection found a coherence of sorts through its promotion of entrepreneurialism, Christianity, domesticity, and temperance. That strategy proved tremendously popular among the respectable families to whom Barnum catered, but it alienated those at the extremes of New York society: patricians attacked Barnum's hall as everything a museum should *not* be, and lower-class looters attempted to dismantle it during the fires of 1865 and 1868.

Chapter 4 explores the relationship between the American Museum's collections and the "moral dramas" presented in its theater, the so-called Lecture Room. It focuses on the period from 1850 to 1861, when Barnum's audience, like the rest of the nation, was split first by conflicts over slavery and temperance, and again by disputes within the antislavery and antiliquor movements over the roles of blacks, women, workers, and radicals. I trace Barnum's effort to negotiate those conflicts through some of the Lecture Room's most popular and controversial moral dramas:

William H. Smith's *The Drunkard,* William W. Pratt's *Ten Nights in a Bar-Room,* H. J. Conway's *Uncle Tom's Cabin* and *Dred,* and Dion Boucicault's *The Octoroon.* I argue that Barnum employed freaks, museum curiosities, and his own celebrity to contain, and at times alter, the meaning of those plays. His goal was to align Lecture Room patrons with temperance philanthropists and liberal slaveholders and against feminists, rebel slaves, and radical abolitionists.

The racial ideologies of Barnum's Museum — and some of the star performers who embodied it — found a second life in the circuses and hippodromes of the showman's final decades. In Chapter 5, I argue that all of Barnum's traveling shows celebrated white, bourgeois manhood under the banners of Christianity and Civilization; but there were differences in the shows' articulation of their social allegiances. The contrast was most obvious in the international racial exhibitions of Barnum's Great Roman Hippodrome of 1874–75 and the Barnum & London Circus of the following decade. The former brought its white patrons in contact with the East through an elaborate pageant built on cross-racial identification; the latter, in contrast, used ethnology to raise a racial barrier between white patron and non-Western performer. I explore this reconstruction of the Oriental for what it can tell us about the status of race as a marker of difference in late-nineteenth-century anthropology and popular culture.

Some of the consequences of the showman's brand of popular cultural ethnology surfaced after his death at the 1893 World's Columbian Exposition. In my conclusion, I use that great amalgamation of high art and commercial amusement to explore Barnum's cultural legacy. When the exposition's directors began "barnumising the Fair" in order to increase admissions, highbrows complained that the showman had saturated not just the White City, but all of U.S. culture. As they debated the showman's lingering impact, those critics echoed half a century of Americans who believed that "'e pluribus Barnum' is a fair reading of our national motto."[2]

# 1

## "All Things to All People": P. T. Barnum in American Culture

I was all things to all people. Studying character, and playing upon the folly and credulity of mankind. I have always made it a point to see how far humbug can possibly be carried, and I have been a leetle astonished sometimes at my own success.
—Barnaby Diddleum (1841)

Although P. T. Barnum is primarily known today for his Greatest Show on Earth, his contemporaries were more apt to praise or condemn him for another mammoth achievement: his celebrity. The *Washington Post* only slightly exaggerated in 1891 when it eulogized him as "the most widely known American that ever lived."[1] Barnum's worldwide fame was no accident. His celebrity was his life's work and his prize possession. He bragged about it, sued people over it, threatened to kill it, but most of all, he reinvented it. First catching the public eye in the 1830s and 1840s as the shady exhibitor of frauds like Joice Heth and the Feejee Mermaid, Barnum lived long and publicly enough to be remythologized as "the Kris Kringle of America" by President Garfield.[2] Between "Mr. Joice Heth" and Garfield's Kris Kringle appeared a series of Barnum personae, which functioned for many Americans as symbols of the nation's burgeoning popular culture. By midcentury, to attack, praise, imitate, or ignore "Barnum" was to take a position in the social and political conflicts being waged through this country's commercial amusements. This chapter focuses on what the public Barnums meant to those struggling over the class politics of those amusements. For much of his career, the showman faced attacks from both ends of the social ladder for his decision to align his amusements and his celebrity with the "middling classes." I argue that the simultaneous emergence of the U.S. middle class and Barnum was no accident: he was the most famous of a generation of entrepreneurs, ideologists, and cultural innovators—many of them the showman's collaborators and friends—who taught the middle class what it meant to be a class. Much of what it meant hinged on U.S. whites' changing attitudes toward African Americans—attitudes that inevitably found their way into Barnum's personae. If the antebellum Barnums tended to equate respectability with whiteness, the postbellum ones advocated a middle-class republic whose "joint owners" were black and white men. Barnum's celebrity was crucial to the formation of a popular culture by and for those "joint owners."

### The Adventures of an Adventurer

There was little in Barnum's first major persona to mark him as a future contributor to middle-class formation. In 1841 the showman introduced himself to New Yorkers as Barnaby Diddleum, the narrator of a pseudoautobiography titled *The Adventures of an Adventurer*.[3] Serialized in the *New York Atlas*, *Adventures* is a fictionalized re-creation of Barnum's entry into show business as the manager of the slave woman Joice Heth. Heth had catapulted to fame in 1835 through exhibitions that billed her as the 161-year-old nurse of George Washington.[4] In view of Barnum's lackluster career in the five years since Heth's death, it isn't surprising that he would return to her as a basis for a public persona. Unlike the circuses and variety acts he had since managed, Heth had been a cultural phenomenon of national proportions. The exhibition of Heth by Barnum and his assistant Levi Lyman drew crowded halls and substantial press coverage in each of the northern towns and cities they visited from August 1835 until her death on 19 February 1836. The exhibitors stoked public interest during the tour by spreading rumors that Heth was actually an automaton or the great-grandmother of living Kentucky slaves. They ignited another journalistic explosion after Heth's death by staging the dissection of her body—an event that exposed their ruse when it revealed her true age to have been no more than eighty.

Barnum, therefore, could count on his New York readers' remembering Joice Heth in 1841. With the savvy that would always mark his self-representations, the showman used *Adventures* to construct a Jacksonian persona out of the remnants of his earliest, and cruelest, effort as a showman.

One of the sources of *Adventures* was Barnum's now lost diary, the form of which Diddleum adopts in the second chapter but drops without explanation in the following installment. The work's greatest debt, however, is to a series of articles on the Heth hoax published in September 1836 in the *New York Herald*.[5] Dictated — according to Barnum — by Lyman, the *Herald* stories are the last of a chain of increasingly preposterous "exposés" appearing in the New York press after Heth's death.[6] They fictionalize the hoax as the brainchild of two unnamed exhibitors, a Virginian and a Yankee. Purchasing Heth from her Kentucky master, the pair forcibly extract her teeth, coach her in religion and the legend of George Washington, and artificially age her on a diet of whiskey and eggs. They then forge documents "proving" her identity and take her on a tour of western and northern cities. The series follows the exhibitors through their triumph over the New York City editors, doctors, and churchgoers, but abruptly breaks off after promising that Heth's career in New England "beats all the past history in droll humbug and exquisite deception."[7]

Four and a half years after the *Herald* stories, Barnum further fictionalized the Heth hoax in *Adventures*. The showman retained the picaresque plot and irreverent tone of Lyman's series, but he replaced the murky, unnamed exhibitors with a megalomaniacal first-person narrator. The change points to a crucial difference between the narratives: whereas Lyman's series focuses on the hoax, *Adventures* is devoted to the hoaxer.[8] Both narratives are efforts to assume fictional control over a bizarre cultural phenomenon for which neither Lyman nor Barnum could claim total responsibility. Barnum and his biographers agree that the showman and his assistant were wholly innocent of originating Heth's performance as Washington's nurse. When the real Barnum purchased the rights to exhibit the infirm slave woman in August 1835, her fame as the hymn-singing nurse of Washington had already been established by exhibitions in Philadelphia. Lyman, however, ignores those shows in order to credit the swindle to his unnamed exhibitors. Barnum goes a step further and attaches Lyman's anonymous fantasy to a thinly disguised version of himself. In *Adventures*, Barnum is out to claim the notoriety that he had passed up during the Heth tour.[9] But notoriety was not all that Barnum was seeking through Diddleum; like all the Barnum personae that would follow, Diddleum was designed with specific cultural and political work in mind.

At first glance it might seem a dubious proposition to read Diddleum as Barnum persona. Indeed, his mania for self-celebration often sets up an ironic distance between him and his creator: "Crown me with fame—erect a monument to my memory—decree me a Roman triumph—I deserve all—I stand alone—I have no equal, no rival—I am the king of Humbugs—the king among princes."[10] Saxon apparently has such effusions in mind when he reads Diddleum as "a nightmarish projection of what Barnum might have become, perhaps even feared he *was* becoming" (*PTB* 88). But instead of the bizarre embodiment of his creator's private demons, I read Diddleum as the first in a series of autobiographical Barnums, personae that were crafted with care, worn for a period, and eventually discarded when their style or politics no longer suited the showman's goals.

As the fictionalized narrator of a very tall tale, Diddleum obviously stands apart from Barnum's autobiographical personae. But Diddleum tells a story that is remarkably similar to the autobiographies. All of them are picaresque first person narratives interspersed with jokes, social commentary, and advice. There are, to be sure, obvious differences between the contents of *Adventures* and its "nonfictional" successors: in the autobiographies, for example, Barnum recounts his management of the Italian plate spinner Signor Vivalla, who is caricatured in *Adventures* as a trick monkey. But at times the "fictional" and "nonfictional" works are virtually indistinguishable: *Adventures* shares with the autobiographies authentic press clippings, actual events, and cameo appearances by New York celebrities who figured in the Heth hoax. If *Adventures* is part fact, it reveals the autobiographies to be part fiction: several of Diddleum's anecdotes reappear in the later writings, reattributed to the showman, his acquaintances, and friends.[11] This recycling of favorite stories suggests the freedom with which Barnum drew on older self-representations to produce their replacements. As I will argue, his revisions often contain valuable clues to his changing politics.

In *Adventures* Barnum's politics are not difficult to discern. Writing in a newspaper owned by the Democratic publishers Anson Herrick, John Ropes, and Frederick West, Barnum adopts one of his most partisan personae, one who rushes into brawls where later Barnums would fear to tread.[12] Granted, the showman's own former career as a Jacksonian editor and spoilsman makes his persona appear almost apolitical: Diddleum never even explicitly declares himself a Democrat. But Barnum clarifies his persona's party ties by identifying him as a political opponent of "the renowned Mrs. Anne R—l, editress to the Washington P—l P—y."[13] Most of Barnum's readers would have recognized this reference to Anne Royall, the pioneering female editor of the *Paul Pry* and outspoken Whig, whom Barnum had met in Washington in 1835. Few would have needed this clue to Diddleum's politics, however. His very existence attests to the need for an imaginary resolution of conflicts within the Democracy. Diddleum is a walking personification of the party's uneasy alliance of North and South, working class and upper class. Through his persona, Barnum works to keep the peace within the Jacksonian phalanx by directing its class and sectional tensions outward against abolitionists, blacks, and women.

Diddleum's utility as a bridge across sectional and class divisions might seem limited at best, given his tendency to crow about his Yankee heritage and wealth. From the first chapter, Barnum explicitly identifies his persona's shrewdness and acquisitiveness with the comic Yankees created by newspaper humorists such as Seba Smith and George W. Arnold. Barnum's creation of a hero able to outsmart, outlie, and outbargain his rivals is his contribution to an explosion of regional humor that had been filling newspapers, magazines, and cheap books since the 1820s. Barnum was experienced in this tradition, having appropriated Arnold's Yankee, Joe Strickland, in advertisements for his lottery parlor in the late 1820s.[14] Diddleum takes up the mantle of Strickland and Smith's Jack Downing by defending the "honor of the Yankees" against all comers.[15] Although Diddleum speaks standard English, he pays homage to his literary forebears by sprinkling his narrative with Down East dialect (as in this chapter's epigraph). He also resembles earlier Yankees in his taste for politics. But unlike the Whig Seba Smith, who used his comic alter ego to mock Andrew Jackson gently while savaging Van Buren, Barnum offers a Yankee with impeccable Democratic credentials.

Four years after Jackson warned against those who were attempting to arouse sectional animosity by "plac[ing] party divisions directly upon geographical distinctions" and by agitating "the most delicate and exciting topics" (Jackson 4), Barnum's Yankee does his part to dampen sectionalism. His strategy is not to avoid that most delicate and exciting topic, slavery, but to rewrite the Yankee as an antiabolitionist slaveholder.[16] Diddleum's ties to the slavocrats are both sentimental and financial. He travels in the South, befriends several southerners, and is once even mistaken for a Mississippian.[17] He acquires Heth while visiting an old acquaintance, a Kentucky planter who pays the Yankee to take the infirm slave woman off his hands. Barnum's decision to make Diddleum the proud owner of a slave ("commanded, at my sovereign will and pleasure") is worth pausing over, as it marks yet another embellishment on the real Heth tour.[18] As Saxon points out, Barnum never actually owned Heth, having merely purchased the rights to exhibit her (*PTB* 21). By making Diddleum a slaveholding Yankee, Barnum was able to personify the trans-sectional economic and social ties that underlay the Democracy.

Diddleum's personal stake in the maintenance of slavery helps justify his glee in duping abolitionists. He deploys Heth against the antislavery movement in the struggle over the legacy of the Founding Fathers. That legacy was contested along the front of virtually every antebellum political struggle, and the conflict over slavery was no exception.[19] During the tour, the Democratic *Boston Morning Post* had recognized Heth's value as a tie to George Washington the slavocrat. Insisting that her biography was "important in many more points than merely the gratification of curiosity," the *Post* reprinted a story on Heth and Washington that Barnum had planted in the New York *Albion*:

> The purity of her character who was thus connected with the
> Washington family, and who performed the first service to the
> first of men, naturally calls to mind the circumstances under
> which he was born, and the school in which those great qualities

were developed which were afterwards devoted to the best interests of man.[20]

In *Adventures* Diddleum even manages to convince his enemies of the centrality of the "school" of slavery to Washington's heroism. In New York he chuckles at the fact that "some of the abolitionists piously believed that the virtue and goodness of Washington might have been, and doubtless was, strengthened by the exemplary piety of this wonderful woman."[21]

Throughout *Adventures*, Barnum satirizes the abolitionists as the dupes of confidence men like Diddleum. Duplicating one of Barnum and Lyman's most vicious moves, Diddleum exploits northern sympathy for slaves by falsely claiming that the proceeds of Heth's exhibition are devoted to the liberation of her enslaved descendants.[22] Barnum's inclusion of this ruse in *Adventures* seems calculated to undermine the efforts by free African Americans to solicit funds publicly for the purchase of their bonded friends and relatives—a practice whose importance to the antislavery movement has been demonstrated by Herbert Aptheker (31–40). But even more damaging was Barnum's depiction of Heth as a willing, even eager, participant in the swindle. In contrast to press accounts that depict the real Heth as the feeble victim of her exhibitors, Diddleum describes her as "an excellent actress."[23] In *Adventures,* Heth lies frequently and fluently about her religion and personal history in order to earn the glass of whiskey that is her nightly reward. The slave soon emerges less as her owner's pawn than as his boozy, profane accomplice. Midway into the tour, Diddleum recalls, "She began to take a great delight in the humbug, which was a profitable one to her."[24] By depicting Heth as a willing partner to his swindle, Barnum helped launch a literary effort to undermine the ex-slave abolitionists— a group whose numbers and power in the antislavery movement were increasing in the early 1840s. The Heth of *Adventures* comes at the beginning of a long line of black literary impostors that would culminate in the ex-slave confidence men in Caroline Lee Hentz's *The Planter's Northern Bride* (1854) and Mrs. G. W. Flanders's *The Ebony Idol* (1860), two of the many proslavery novels that attempted to refute *Uncle Tom's Cabin* (1852).[25] Those works supported the *New York Herald*'s claim that abolitionism preyed on those "who are taken in continually by confidence men of all colors."[26] The consequences of the literary campaign to undermine the credibility of ex-slaves were borne by black abolitionists like William Wells Brown and Frederick Douglass, who were forced to waste considerable effort convincing northern whites of their credibility.

If Diddleum's status as a Yankee slaveholder allowed him to embody one contradiction in the Jacksonian coalition, his status as a rich man with plebeian sympathies personified another. Diddleum is the fit symbol of a party that relentlessly billed itself as the friend of the "common man" while catering to the substantial portion of the U.S. upper class in its ranks.[27] He establishes his knowledge of the bottom rungs of the social ladder by recounting his failure as a country newspaper editor—an episode obviously based on Barnum's experiences in the early 1830s as the editor of the Bethel, Connecticut, *Herald of Freedom*. Diddleum then takes us swiftly over his road to riches. Although he remains somewhat vague as to the extent of his fortune, he leaves no doubt as to his status as a high roller. Recalling his successful exhibition of the trick monkey, he casually mentions "the fifty thousand dollars I made out of the animal, and . . . the forty thousand I lost in handling the gambling game of poker."[28]

Like his standard English, Diddleum's wealth distances him from his plebeian literary ancestors among the Down East Yankees.[29] However, he frequently demonstrates his sympathy for the classes from which he has risen. In one episode suggesting the complexity of his class identifications, Diddleum recalls a game of dare with a group of New York lawyers whom he treats as his social, if not mental, equals. When they decline his challenge to throw their hats into the fire (in lieu of forfeiting bottles of champagne), Diddleum explains their decision in terms of New York City class relations. Estimating that the hats cost six dollars each, he reminisces: "[I]t was in the good old time when tradespeople got good prices, and could afford to spend the money they earned . . . instead of saving it up to satisfy the crazy demands of landlords."[30] Not only does he sympathize with artisans in the bad old times after the Panic of 1837, he pities the female factory operatives he encounters in Providence, insisting that the "many privations" of those women make his exhibition "a glory to them."[31]

Diddleum's sensitivity to the plight of the working class may be a product of Barnum's own financial straits in 1841. As the showman notes in his autobiography, when he published *Adventures* he was "at the bottom round of fortune's ladder," struggling to scrape together a respectable living in an economy still suffering from the aftereffects of the Panic of 1837 (*ST* 110). Barnum had divided the past six years between touring the United States and Canada with small circuses and variety acts and scrambling for a living on the Bowery, New York's center for working-class shops and amusements. In 1839 and 1840, Barnum was a partner in a shady concern that manufactured and sold substances purporting to be blacking, waterproof paste, cologne, and bear's grease from a shop at 101½ Bowery Street.[32] After his partner fled the country, leaving behind a worthless promissory note, Barnum found work writing articles (including *Adventures*) for the Sunday press and clerking for the Bowery Amphitheatre. (Of the latter job, he would recall: "For this I received $4.00 per week! and was thankful for even that" [*Life* 215].) Barnum's financial struggles would have made the wealthy, upwardly mobile Diddleum a wish fulfillment figure. Like the confidence men who slithered through antebellum advice books and novels, Diddleum slips so rapidly across class lines as to make them seem almost nonexistent.[33] Recent critics have read the confidence man's social trajectory as proving the actual or theoretical possibilities for individual advancement in the antebellum United States.[34] But the example of Diddleum suggests that for those, like Barnum, swimming against the tide of a depressed economy, the financial success of the confidence man would have served primarily as a compensatory fantasy.

Given the social gap between the four-dollar-a-week Barnum and his high-rolling persona, one might expect Diddleum to embody not only Barnum's fantasies but also his frustrations. Yet Barnum takes every opportunity to let his hero off the hook. In Providence, for example, Diddleum is never forced to acknowledge his own role in the oppression of the factory operatives. After lamenting their "many privations," he doesn't hesitate to take their money. If Diddleum is able to take his privilege for granted, it is because *Adventures* directs much of its class resentment against the "ladies." This is obvious as Diddleum crows over his portrayal of Heth as the "first person *who put clothes on the unconscious infant* [Washington]." He mocks the "many fine ladies" who "envied the black paws of old Joyce, for the office they had performed."[35] Domesticity is just one of the ideologies of the "fine ladies" that comes under attack in *Adventures*. Diddleum also takes masculinist potshots at other emerging characteristics of middle-class culture, such as sentimentality and moral reform. As critics and historians have documented, that culture was still very much in formation in the early 1840s, but its feminized cast was already becoming obvious.[36] It was obvious, in any case, to Diddleum, who identifies his enemies as the "religious old women of both sexes."[37] Foreshadowing such humorists as George Washington Harris, Johnson Jones Hooper, and Mark Twain, Barnum has his hero reject feminized respectability for the cross-class, homosocial pleasures of the tavern, the card table, and the road. In those male spaces, it was still possible to ignore the conflicts of class and section that would slice across Barnum's party and his persona over the following decades.

## The European Correspondence

In the two decades after *Adventures*, Barnum developed a new public image that embraced much of what Diddleum had reviled. Barnum signaled the shift in encounters with people who blamed him for Diddleum's swindles: some of them apparently believed that Barnum *was* Diddleum. By gradually altering his responses to their accusations, Barnum marked the birth of a new, respectable persona. The transformation was already under way by the mid-1840s, at which point Barnum claimed credit for the Heth hoax, but denied ever having committed one of Diddleum's proudest pranks — impersonating a minister.[38] A decade later, Barnum took another step away from Diddleum in his autobiography by portraying himself as a victim, rather than the instigator, of the Heth hoax (*Life* 155–56). But Diddleum proved difficult to shake.[39] Even his name hung around to plague the showman, as the *John-Donkey* gleefully revealed six years after *Adventures*. The humor

sheet mocked Barnum's failure to land a prize exhibit by bray-
ing, "DIDDLEUM was diddled."[40]

A major phase of Barnum's campaign to shed Diddleum began
in 1844, when he published the first of one hundred letters in
the *New York Atlas* documenting his management of Tom Thumb's
initial European tour. The travel series recalls *Adventures* in its
first-person narration, serialized publication, and episodic contents; but from his opening lines, the Correspondent identifies
himself with, rather than against, middle-class respectability. Unlike his cynical, footloose predecessor, this new Barnum begins
his journey by paying tearful homage to the cult of domesticity.
He orchestrates an emotional departure scene, to the accompaniment of the notorious brass band from his American Museum:

> One of my friends, in giving the parting palm, quietly slipped
> into my hand a keepsake, saying, "Accept this little trifle to
> remember when far from *home*." ... I strove to check the tears,
> and essayed to speak, but the words stuck in my throat. The
> steamer cast off, and the excellent band struck up "Home, sweet
> home." The tears then flowed thick and fast.[41]

Much of the transformation in Barnum's persona is traceable to
his new role as manager of the American Museum, which he had
purchased a few months after publishing *Adventures*. Barnum's
new role as the owner of a family-oriented amusement hall requires him to endorse many of the middle-class proprieties that
Diddleum had flouted, as when he apologizes to his "temperance
friends" for sampling cognac in Bordeaux.[42] He even hails middle-
class True Womanhood in France, telling a group of "brawny-
armed, stout, sun-burnt peasant girls" that in his country "we find
occupations for our females in the house, which is more congenial to their delicate constitutions."[43] Forgetting the hard-pressed
factory operatives of Providence, Barnum offers a portrait of U.S.
gender relations worthy of *Godey's Lady's Book*. The European
Correspondence is his effort to mythologize a uniformly middle-
class "universal Yankee nation" in the act speaking for it—to
French peasants as well as his readership back in the States.[44]

Barnum's new role requires him to revise the regional and political valences of his Yankee persona. Like Diddleum, the Correspondent is eager to defend the honor of the Yankees against
all comers, but whereas Diddleum's foremost challenger is an

Arkansan, the Correspondent takes on various European con artists. These international battles of wits prepare the reader for Barnum's new role as the representative of "all" Americans. The showman also nationalizes his persona by linking it to other
American popular cultural heroes. The Correspondent is especially fond of that legend of the southwest frontier, Davy Crockett—going so far as to emblazon Crockett's motto, "Go ahead,"
on the side of Tom Thumb's miniature carriage. The Correspondent's politics are similarly pluralistic; at one point the Democratic Barnum even has his persona praise those "not cramped
by the trammels of party."[45] The new Barnum would speak not
for a region or party, but for an entire nation.

Barnum confirmed his new nationalism for another figure who
would spend much of his career in search of a broad American
audience, Walt Whitman. In 1846, Whitman recorded Barnum's
impressions of Europe for the *Brooklyn Daily Eagle*: "There every
thing is frozen—kings and *things*—formal, but absolutely *frozen*:
here it is *life*. Here it is freedom, and here are *men*." In response,
Whitman editorialized, "A whole book might be written on that
little speech of Barnum's" (quoted in Brasher 42). Indeed, shelves
of books had already been written around Barnum's thesis. The
European Correspondence was Barnum's contribution to a transatlantic battle of wits being waged by antebellum British and U.S.
travel writers. The most famous players preceding Barnum onto
the field included, for the British, Frances Trollope, Harriet Mar-
tineau, and Charles Dickens and, for the Americans, James Fen-
imore Cooper and Washington Irving.[46] Like the more national-
istic of his predecessors, Barnum dutifully guides his readers
through the natural and historical attractions of the countries
he visits, but he is chiefly interested in them as foils to the great-
ness of his homeland. Sometimes his jingoism takes the form of
comments tacked casually onto his narrative, as when he remarks
of the countryside around Tours, "[I]f it was only removed, with
all its beauties, to America, where it could exist under a *republican* government, it would be a *paradise on earth!*"[47] But when
spurred on by his country's European critics, the Correspondent
spouts paragraphs in celebration of American government, culture, and society. At times, however, the showman's new persona

shows signs of crumbling under the strain of the social and political realities back home that were steadily discrediting his myth
of a white "egalitarian" paradise.

One reality back home that nags the Correspondent throughout his excursion is slavery. Even if Barnum had not been an antiabolitionist Democrat, as an American in Europe in the mid-
1840s he could hardly have avoided taking a position on slavery.
When he disembarked in Liverpool, Barnum was entering a country intensely involved in the U.S. antislavery movement. After
the 1840 World Anti-Slavery Convention in London, the transatlantic traffic of abolitionist speakers, publications, and financial
backing was especially thick.[48] The effects of this coordinated
Anglo-American agitation are obvious throughout the European
Correspondence, not only in the episodes in which Barnum encounters, and debates, British abolitionists, but also in the frequency with which his remarks on Europe circle back to the
dispute over slavery. For example, when an Englishwoman asks
Barnum if Tom Thumb is related to a Native American she sees
in the exhibition room, Barnum compares her thinking to that
of "the white ladies in Massachusetts who petitioned the legisla-
ture for the 'privilege' of marrying negroes."[49] Here Barnum is
slurring the female abolitionists who petitioned to overturn Massachusetts's racist marriage laws.[50] The mental stretch (across
race and geography) required to link the London questioner
with the Massachusetts abolitionists attests to Barnum's preoccupation with slavery while on European soil.

Barnum was not alone in taking slavery as a primary theme of
his travels. Slavery was *the* topic for antebellum Anglo-American
travel writers, especially those who reversed Barnum's course
across the Atlantic. In answer to those writers' attacks on the
hypocrisy of a slaveholding "democracy," Barnum and other antiabolitionists counterattacked with images of European class oppression.[51] Barnum's deployment of this strategy is typified by
his debate with some antislavery Scots he meets on a voyage to
Glasgow. After discharging the standard arguments in the antiabolitionist arsenal (e.g., slavery was a British imposition on
America; southern whites would be endangered by emancipa-
tion), Barnum wheels out his most devastating weapon:

> I thought these philanthropic gentlemen should remember that
> "charity begins at home," and they could talk with more
> consistency against the evil of American slavery when they had
> made the *poor working people* of England, Scotland and Ireland
> half so happy as were the southern blacks.[52]

Barnum's comparison of white European workers and U.S. slaves
is derived from arguments popularized by workers and apologists for slavery. As historians have shown, the two groups developed parallel discourses about the "white slavery" and "wage
slavery" of the working class.[53] Radical workers and slavocrats
put their shared rhetoric in the service of social visions that sometimes overlapped (as in the proslavery position of some unionists) but frequently conflicted: most workers warned of white slavery in order to protest their own subordination to capital; U.S.
slavocrats, on the other hand, used the same vocabulary to argue
for the superiority of their system to any based on free labor.[54]
Barnum's own argument echoes both the slavocrats and the la-
borites: he attacks abolitionists with the fervor of Diddleum, but,
as we shall see, he also supports the expansion of the rights of
white labor in Europe.

The biography of Barnum that the *Atlas* published one year
into his European Correspondence helps explain why Barnum
would sound like a slavocrat. The detailed narrative, which Saxon
argues may well be the work of the showman himself (*PTB* 84),
reveals that in 1838, while traveling with a circus in Mississippi,
Barnum purchased the steamboat *Ceres* and a slave to serve as
his valet. Upon discovering that the "nigger" had stolen his money,
Barnum "gave him fifty lashes, and took him to New Orleans,
where he was sold at auction." Arriving at Opelousas later in the
tour, Barnum traded the *Ceres* and his horses for "cash, sugar,
molasses, and *a negro woman and child.*" Barnum later sold these
slaves in St. Louis. Remarkable in themselves, these revelations
are also interesting for the way they are presented. Given the
laudatory tone of the rest of the sketch, it would appear they are
intended to celebrate Barnum's ties to the slaveholders. By following these revelations with the claim (made without irony)
that "Barnum is a man of liberal principles, and a friend of equal
rights," the biographer fits the showman to the lineaments of

the white male "egalitarianism" in the name of which the Jacksonians had reshaped U.S. politics.[55]

As an ex-slaveholder, Barnum agreed with slavocrats who favorably compared the class relations of the South with those of Britain. As a Yankee entrepreneur, however, he rejected the slavocrats' extension of the comparison to the U.S. North. John C. Calhoun argued that American workers were no different from European ones in their oppression by capital, but Barnum saw U.S. labor as a different story. Abandoning the working-class sympathies of Diddleum, Barnum argues repeatedly that unlike the *"starving workies"* of Europe, wage laborers in America are a happy, prosperous, upwardly mobile group.[56] Consider, for example, his description of Paisley, Scotland, where the local economy has been wrecked by U.S. tariffs, "in consequence of which the thousands of poor factory hands... were thrown almost entirely out of employ, and are now in a state approaching starvation—a case *never* known in America, but of *very frequent* occurrence in the manufacturing towns of Great Britain."[57]

The U.S. lower classes *were* in better shape than their European counterparts in the 1840s, but Barnum embellishes that distinction into a portrait of American classlessness.[58] He insists that, unlike their English counterparts, American workers "can read and write, and have plenty of time to enjoy the fruits of a good education."[59] The Correspondent supports these claims by twice invoking the "periodicals of talent and repute" published by the Lowell operatives.[60] His picture of leisured, contented factory workers is difficult to reconcile with the operatives' massive participation in the Ten Hour Movement, which was taking place as Barnum published the Correspondence.[61]

Like the roots of the shift in Barnum's racial views over the next two decades, the impulses behind his new thinking on class remain nebulous. Part of the explanation may lie in the marginalization of New York City working-class politics in the wake of the Panic of 1837. As Sean Wilentz points out, the decline in wages and employment during the following six years prevented the city's unionists from completing their formation of a broad working-class movement that would extend beyond the male-dominated trades to include women and unskilled laborers (253).

With the trades in retreat, the field was open for the city's manufacturers and small masters to promote their own vision of a classless, free-labor republic built on the mutually beneficial cooperation of employer and worker. A primary source of this entrepreneurial ideology in the mid-1840s was the American Institute, where boosters such as Alexander H. H. Stuart paralleled Barnum's comparisons of a classless America and a proletarianized Britain (Wilentz 302–6). The European Correspondence documents Barnum's interest in the work of the Institute in two letters criticizing its annual fair. Barnum's critique, as I will argue in chapter 3, is partly motivated by his perception of the Institute's fair as a rival to his American Museum. The energy and knowledge that Barnum brings to his attack, however, attest to his genuine devotion to the Institute's mission, "the promotion of American industry," from the standpoint of the employer.[62]

Barnum suggests another explanation for his revised thinking on class in describing his brief return to New York ten months into his tour. Despite being less than five years away from his clerkship at the Bowery Amphitheatre, Barnum discovers that his new wealth opens the doors of the city's upper class. He chuckles at the spectacle of the "codfish aristocracy of New York ... expressing their great delight at seeing me again, although before I left New York those same nabobs would have looked down on me with disdain if I had presumed to have spoken to them."[63] One is tempted to blame Barnum's newfound wealth for the Correspondent's amnesia regarding the hardships of U.S. workers, but the showman works to forestall such a reading. Proudly declaring his artisan roots ("[M]y father was a *tailor*"), he scolds his countrymen for translating inequalities of wealth into social hierarchy.[64] The Correspondent repeatedly portrays such snobbery as a threat to the republic, at one point going so far as to claim, "[T]here is much more starched up, formal, self-conceited aristocracy in republican America than in England." But while the showman abandons Europe to its inherited class system, he retains his faith in the "whole-souled, frank, main body of Americans," whose egalitarian core he claims to embody.[65]

Although Barnum occasionally finds himself at odds with his fellow Americans, he generally succeeds in projecting U.S. social contradictions onto Europe. Throughout the European Correspondence, he excoriates the Old World aristocrats for oppressing the starving lower classes. In Brighton, he resumes Diddleum's satirical pen to savage the "gouty millionaires" and their decadent clergy for banning beggars from the city.[66] In Paris, the Correspondent begins to sound like a radical as he recounts his visit with George Sand, naming her "an ardent friend to the *mass*," who spends nearly all her income "to protect the poor and unfortunate from the oppressions of the rich." Barnum admires this battler for the rights of those "poor fellows," the striking French workers, who were liable to be punished for conspiracy.[67] Noticeably absent is any reference to the American unionists who were subject to the same legal harassment.

As a visitor to what he imagined an alien society, Barnum apparently felt free to extend sympathies to European workers that he denied their U.S. counterparts; at the same time, however, Europe prompted from him some of his most blatant expressions of snobbery. One letter proclaims Tom Thumb the most popular exhibit in the history of London, "[a]nd what is still more gratifying is, that much the largest class of his visitors have been persons of the highest rank and refinement."[68] Another missive boasts that the dwarf's "visitors . . . include but very few of the uneducated class of citizens."[69] Clearly designed to boost the General's popularity among the educated classes back home, such references portend the elitist rhetoric that would creep into Barnum's productions — including his self-representations — over the next two decades. In the 1840s, however, Barnum's guise as the propagandist of a classless America precluded such an open avowal of his own role in U.S. class formation. Calling up both Barnum's old working-class sympathies and his new bourgeois affiliations, Europe functions as the stage upon which he plays out the transformation of his views on U.S. society.

### Barnumizing Young America

Barnum was able to assess the impact of the *Atlas* letters in 1847, when he returned from Europe to find himself famous. He may have begun the decade cannibalizing the notoriety of Joice Heth, but he ended it as famous as any of his productions, including the American Museum. Barnum commemorates this achievement in his autobiographies with an anecdote about a man who enters the Museum's ticket office, buys a ticket, and asks the ticket seller to identify Barnum. The man then stares at the showman for a moment, throws down his ticket, and leaves the Museum, declaring: "It's all right. I have got the worth of my money" (*Life* 293).[70] By the late 1840s, Barnum had taken his place alongside Jack Downing and Davy Crockett as a universally recognizable persona that could be donned by anyone with access to a printing press. The rise of the Barnum impersonators was ironic justice for a showman who launched his lottery business by plagiarizing another humorist's persona. The fake Barnums were especially numerous in the politicized, satirical pages of New York City's humor sheets, most notably the *Yankee Doodle, John-Donkey,* and *New York Picayune.*[71] In the 1840s and 1850s these sheets put Barnum to uses of which, in many cases, he could not have approved.

The European Correspondent's cultural nationalism made him particularly attractive to the clique of New York City writers and critics calling itself Young America. Born in 1836 as the Tetractys Club, literary Young America (not to be confused with political Young America of the 1840s and 1850s) established itself as the torchbearer for a U.S. culture freed from European domination.[72] As Barnum returned from Europe, the literary Young Americans were taking their final stand in their humor sheet, *Yankee Doodle* (1846–47). The sheet frequently appropriated Barnum's celebrity in satirizing its political enemies, who came from both parties, as the Young Americans were anti-Polk Van Buren Democrats. One issue featured a letter from "Barnum" nominating himself for the presidency, on a platform to end Polk's war upon Mexico.[73] The showman appeared repeatedly when *Yankee Doodle* published Herman Melville's series of "Authentic Anecdotes of 'Old Zack,'" a mild satire on America's latest war hero and Whig presidential hopeful, General Zachary Taylor. Melville's irreverence toward Old Zack is often expressed through "Barnum," who appears throughout the "Anecdotes" as an unwitting exhibitor of American mock-heroism. With the aid of Taylor's black "servant" Sambo, Melville's Barnum schemes to acquire and exhibit various bathetic "trophies," including Taylor's tobacco box, pie plate, torn trousers, and, inevitably, Old Zack himself.[74]

Like much of what appears in the irony-drenched pages of *Yankee Doodle*, the sheet's take on Barnum is ambiguous. On the one hand, the Young Americans clearly enjoy ventriloquizing the showman's unabashed jingoism, as when "Barnum" offers to exhibit Queen Victoria:

> America is a large country: it has a great many people in it, and what's better still, they are all friends of BARNUM. Whatever BARNUM does is right. With this commanding feeling in my power, I feel at liberty to write you, as I now do, in the name of the people of the United States, to come to America.[75]

The clique that dared to dream of an American Shakespeare was inevitably drawn to Barnum's cultural nationalism. Throughout the European Correspondence, Barnum had relentlessly promoted the American entertainers, entrepreneurs, and showmen who were defeating the Europeans on their home turf.[76] The showman, however, was too tainted with American popular culture to suit some of the Young American literati. Thus, an issue of *Yankee Doodle* that genially joked about the new attractions at Barnum's American Museum also lashed out with all apparent seriousness at the "Impudent Desecration" of the agent of an unnamed American individual (whom many readers would have known to be Barnum) trying to buy Shakespeare's house.[77] This attack reflects the hostility toward commercial amusements that Peter Buckley has identified as the flip side of Young America's vision of a literary democracy (285–86). For a group of literati trying to fend off their enemies' charges of philistinism, the one thing worse than the absence of an American Shakespeare was the showman's tarring the image of the English one.

One Young American who embraced, rather than fled, Barnum's commercial amusements was Cornelius Mathews. Mathews's notorious limitations as a writer should not be allowed to overshadow his pioneering commitment to the literary possibilities of the city.[78] After the collapse of literary Young America, Mathews continued mapping the social and cultural life of the metropolis in *A Pen-and-Ink Panorama of New-York City* (1853), a work that prefaces its tour of New York with yet another call for an independent American culture worthy of the name. The narrator recalls his quixotic boyhood quest for any sign of "America" in his country's literature, theater, and fashions—all of which are dominated by Britain. In what amounts to the symbolic end of his quest, he shifts to midcentury New York and guides the reader up Broadway to Barnum's American Museum. Here he launches into a hyperbolic biography of the owner, which establishes Barnum's credentials as a spread-eagle culture hero.[79] Born "next door to" Independence Day (41), Mathews's Barnum boasts a personal history entwined with that of his nation. But what makes Barnum especially attractive for Mathews is his cultural power. With a "genius" comparable to his country's "artists, soldiers, and poets," Barnum has the force to turn back the wave of British cultural imports (38). Mathews mimics his subject's hyperbole to present him as "the most successful contriver and caterer of public amusements that ever has lived or ever will live in all the rolling ages of time" (46). In Barnum, Mathews suggests, the United States has found the cultural force that Young America had sought among the nation's literati. Mathews is careful to advance such a claim only through the half-serious tones of Diddleumesque exaggeration. That a remnant of Young America could advance it at all, however, attests to the success of Barnum's efforts at both legitimating U.S. "popular amusements" and establishing himself as the walking embodiment of those amusements.

In invoking Barnum's work in popular culture as an important component of U.S. cultural nationalism, the Democrat Mathews had the endorsement of his Whig rivals at the *American Review*. In March 1852, the *Review* took up the cry for cultural nationalism by claiming that American "literature . . . has more to show for her last thirty years than any other nation whose first century is not yet accomplished" (235). The *Review* proved its point with a pantheon of American literary greats that included novelists, poets, journalists, historians, dramatists, essayists, tragedians, a critic, and "Barnum for showman" (235). Although Perry Miller finds "curious" a catalog that places Barnum in the company of Emerson and Hawthorne (302), those familiar with Barnum's self-representations at midcentury might not have been puzzled. The list attests to Barnum's success at rescripting both the political and cultural valences of his public persona. Having assiduously distanced himself from his Democratic roots throughout the Correspondence, Barnum was ready to be lifted into a Whig pantheon.

More important for my purposes here, however, was Barnum's work at legitimating both the image of U.S. popular culture and his own position as the leading promoter of that culture. It is Barnum's turn to amusement reform that best explains how he could be associated with anything as reputable as "literature."

By 1850, Barnum had begun staking his position as a standard-bearer for U.S. culture on the respectability of his amusements. This was evident in June of that year, when he took the stage at his American Museum to dedicate himself to "rational amusement with a proper sense of virtue and morality." Moreover, he proclaimed, "unless some unforeseen calamity overtakes me, I pledge myself to withdraw into private life, if ever the moment arrives that the great mass of our citizens prefer immoral and vicious, to moral and reformatory entertainments."[80] Here Barnum wagers his very existence as a public figure on the state of popular taste. He is constructing a "mass" audience in the process of reconstructing himself: he can be Barnum because they will always prefer his brand of "moral and reformatory entertainments." Despite the catholicity of taste implied in the word *mass*, Barnum has in mind a more restrictive definition of popular culture — one taken from the liberal clergymen and theater managers who led a movement for amusement reform in the 1840s and 1850s. As David Grimsted and Peter Buckley have documented, clergymen such as Edward Everett Hale and Henry Whitney Bellows struggled to overturn Christians' lingering prejudices against public amusements.[81] Their work was supported by reformist theater and museum managers such as William Niblo, Noah Ludlow, Sol Smith, and Moses Kimball — all associates of Barnum — who seized the chance to add Christian respectables to their audience through "moral" amusements. In 1841, Barnaby Diddleum had mocked the "saints" who flocked to Niblo's, but less than a decade later his creator was preaching amusement reform like the best of the liberal clergymen.[82]

### The Life of P. T. Barnum

The showman's effort to rescript himself as an amusement reformer would culminate in 1854 with the publication of his first autobiography, *The Life of P. T. Barnum*. Although Barnum relies on the work of the liberal clergymen throughout his book, his debts are especially obvious in his concluding chapter. There he diagnoses America's cultural and social ills in terms made familiar by the amusement reformers. Like them, he addresses a broad American audience while leaving no doubt as to his narrower class allegiances. Those allegiances become clear midway through his discussion of amusements, when he begins targeting his remarks to the middle of the social ladder:

> With their traditions and habits, our countrymen, of the middling classes, inherit in too great a degree a capacity only for the most valueless and irrational enjoyments, and their inclination to intemperance and kindred vices has repeatedly and most conclusively been shown to be a natural result of the lamentable deficiency among us of innocent and rational amusements. (399)

In language that he would reiterate for the next four decades, Barnum presents his "innocent and rational amusements" as a necessary therapeutic release for a middle class squeezed between self-discipline and social duty. He is relying on a model that would be fully elaborated by Henry Bellows in his 1857 defense of commercial entertainments, *The Relation of Public Amusements to Public Morality*. Bellows would launch his argument with the rhetorical question: "[H]ow shall humanity do most work, support most anxiety, have the most genuine seriousness?" (6). The answer is through moral amusements, especially the theater, which refresh the "conscience, will, and aspirations," just as sleep does the body (6). Valueless in themselves, amusements in this schema become a necessary outlet for a middle class that, as Barnum indicates, had largely constructed itself on its repressions.

Barnum joins the reformers in defining the significance of amusements by their relation to work. *Life* pays tribute to this reciprocal model by offering Barnum as an authority on both: in his final chapter, he balances his views on amusements with "Barnum's Rules for Success in Business."[83] A combination of the Franklinesque ("Avoid extravagance" [397]) and the Barnumesque ("Advertise your business" [396]), the Rules leave no doubt as to their implied bourgeois audience, particularly in the imperative: "Engage proper employees" (396). Barnum's decision to end his book by appealing to employers (both current and would-be ones) carried obvious risks for a showman who relied on the lower classes for a substantial part of his patronage. That Barnum realized the fine line he was walking can be surmised from his positive treatment of his own experiences with the lower classes. In his preface, for example, he stresses the cross-class nature of his "checkered" career: "I have been a farmer's boy and a merchant, a clerk and a manager.... I have been in jails and palaces; have known poverty and abundance" (iii). *Life* follows through on this summary with what would prove to be Barnum's fullest portrait of his Bowery years. Although those were years of frustration and financial hardship for the showman and his family, he manages to recall them with a good deal of fondness. Recounting the 1835 reception of Signor Vivalla by lower-class New Yorkers, he seems almost wistful: "The applause...was tremendous. It was such as only a Chatham or a Bowery audience could give" (161).

Barnum also appears to be cultivating plebeian readers in *Life*'s selective incorporation of the European Correspondence. His excerpting is both extensive and politically cautious. Wary of the period's foremost political conflict in the wake of the Kansas-Nebraska Act, he carefully omits all of the Correspondent's anti-abolitionist polemics, as well as the *Atlas*'s account of his slave trading. But while remaining mostly silent on race, Barnum eagerly sounds off on class. *Life* includes the Correspondent's stinging indictment of the New York City nabobs and his declaration, "[M]y father was *a tailor*, and... I am '*a showman*' by profession, and all *the gilding* shall make nothing else of me" (274).

As his reference to his father would suggest, Barnum uses his childhood to establish his plebeian credentials. His real childhood was accurately, if somewhat anachronistically, characterized by *Littell's Living Age*: "By both parents he was descended from respectable middle-class people in Connecticut."[84] Although the term *middle-class* would probably not have been used in Bethel at the time of Barnum's birth, it suggests the middling status of the showman's parents: Irena Barnum was the daughter of one of Bethel's largest landowners, and her husband, Philo, was — in addition to a tailor — a farmer, tavern keeper, and store owner. Saxon has shown how the sixteen-year-old Barnum's ties to Irena's father would have shielded him when Philo died insolvent in 1826 (*PTB* 34). In *Life*, however, Barnum relates that Philo's death left

him destitute: "The world looked dark indeed, when I realized
that I was for ever deprived of my paternal protector! I felt that
I was a poor inexperienced boy, thrown out on the wide world
to shift for myself, and a sense of forlornness completely over-
came me" (91). Saxon has also demonstrated how Barnum ex-
aggerates his forlornness in this scene by avoiding any mention
of his grand-paternal protector, and by misrepresenting by a year
the date of Philo's death, apparently to make himself appear
younger and more helpless than he actually was (*PTB* 33–34).[85]
Barnum managed to sell even his enemies on the myth of his
pinched childhood. The *New York Times*, for example, opened
an attack on *Life* by observing, "In this country, more perhaps
than in any other, Success is regarded as the test of worth:— and
BARNUM is the embodiment and impersonation of success. From
being poor and obscure, he has rapidly made himself very rich
and very famous."[86]

As the *Times* indicated, Barnum had succeeded in fitting his
career to the leading model of masculine success in the heyday
of the self-made man. Like the self-made heroes of midcentury
biographies and novels, the Barnum of *Life* climbs from rural
poverty to urban wealth on the strength of Ben Franklin's virtues
of industry, self-discipline, and frugality.[87] Those traditional virtues
distinguished the self-made man from that other midcentury symbol of social mobility, the confidence man. Whereas the self-made
man earned his trip up the social ladder by following Franklin,
the confidence man rose Barnaby Diddleum-style, by duping his
fellows. Barnum often flirts with the image of the confidence
man in *Life*, especially in his gleeful retelling of his greatest humbugs. Throughout *Life*, however, he is at pains to offset those
shams with the "wonderful, instructive, and amusing realities"
of his museums and other enterprises (225). He thus follows his
account of some his most "doubtful" shows with his work as a
temperance reformer (349). But many critics saw *Life* as nothing
but the gloating of a brazen huckster.[88] According to Barnum,
those who labeled him a confidence man missed one of the central lessons of *Life*: far from enriching him, his early humbugs
eventually reduced him and his family to four dollars a week,
whereas his subsequent fortune "was accumulated almost wholly
from enterprises which were undoubtedly legitimate" (quoted in

*PTB* 16). It was a point he would make even more emphatically in his next autobiography by radically reducing the space he devoted to his "doubtful" enterprises.

Barnum's portrayal of himself as a self-made man would have obviously appealed to the middle class, for whom the self-made man was a defining myth. But Barnum may also have had another audience in mind: by establishing himself at the beginning of the book as someone who has "known poverty," Barnum invites plebeian readers to identify with his climb up the U.S. social ladder. This would help explain why Barnum's lower-class patrons steadily vanish from *Life* as the narrative proceeds: after looming large in his account of his Bowery days, they are mostly absent from *Life*'s concluding chapters. Barnum's gentrification of his patronage reveals far more about his aspirations than about his real audience, as the lower classes still bought a hefty portion of Barnum's tickets at the American Museum in 1854. As I will argue, however, the Museum also expected its plebeian patrons to identify upward with its implied middle-class audience.

Whether many working-class readers were taken in by Barnum's gambit is difficult to say. The *New York Times* insisted that Barnum "is watched, admired and envied by hundreds of thousands who are as poor as he was, and who are anxious to be as rich as he is."[89] In his next autobiography, Barnum would devote a chapter to an English reader who accepted *Life*'s invitation to identify up the class ladder. There Barnum describes his 1858 encounter with a man he calls "Wilson" (actually Barnum's future father-in-law, John Fish), who tells the showman, "[O]nly a few years ago I was working as a journeyman, and probably should have been at this time, had it not been for your book" (*ST* 506–7). Inspired by *Life*'s account of Barnum's rise, Wilson has become part owner of a textile mill. In conducting business, he claims to rely solely on "Barnum's Rules for Success in Business." Wilson's faithfulness to the showman's model is evidenced by his nickname, "Barnum," his ability to quote entire pages of *Life* from memory, and his christening of the engines in his mill with the names of the showman and his wife, Charity.

*Life* hints at the difficulties Barnum faced in rallying the lower classes around a middle-class standard. The strains are particularly apparent in the book's account of the Jenny Lind tour. By bringing the singer to the United States, Barnum boasts of giving "to the cultivated and wealthy as well as to the middling classes a larger measure of enjoyment than has ever been derived from the enterprise of any other single individual" (400). Barnum, as we shall see, is on the mark here in his description of Lind's paying audience, but he is ignoring the rowdy lower-class "outsiders" who also attended—and disrupted—many of the concerts.[90] Such lacunae suggest the obstacles that would hinder Barnum in his effort to hold together a cross-class audience over the following decades.

*Life* generally avoids confronting the class fissures that were slicing through Barnum's audience and his persona in the 1850s by directing the reader's gaze backward to a mythologized classless past. Whereas the European Correspondent idealizes America by exporting its social conflicts to Europe, the narrator of *Life* escapes into a nostalgia-tinged America of the early nineteenth century. The embodiment of Barnum's nostalgia is Bethel, Connecticut, the preindustrial, white, pastoral paradise where the Yankees divide their time between swapping tales and playing practical jokes. The emblematic social encounter in this microcosm of republicanism is the aggressive trading that goes on over the counters of the stores where the young Barnum works. In these exchanges, customer and clerk square off with only their wits and self-interest to guide them. Barnum recalls "many a sharp trade with old women who paid for their purchases in butter, eggs, beeswax, feathers, and rags" (28). For both parties to the transaction, the question is not whether, but how, to deceive: "Each party expected to be cheated, if it was possible. Our eyes, and not our ears, had to be our masters" (*Life* 99).[91] Although Barnum occasionally worries about the moral consequences of such hard trading, he generally celebrates the country store as a bastion not of greed, but of spirited, egalitarian competition.[92]

Far from seeking wealth as a means to social status, the inhabitants of Barnum's classless village teach the narrator, and presumably his reader, a lesson about the dangers of inherited privilege. *Life* ironically invokes the threat of patrimony by opening with an engraved portrait of Barnum's grandfather and the words:

PHINEAS TAYLOR WAS my maternal grandfather. I was his first grandchild, and it was suggested that I should perpetuate his honored name. My delighted ancestor confirmed the choice, and handed to my mother a gift-deed, in my behalf, of five acres of land. (10–11)

The deed conveys to the young Barnum the rights to Ivy Island, a worthless piece of swampland that becomes the basis for a remarkable hoax. For "six or eight years" (31), Barnum's family and neighbors tantalize the boy with visions of the estate that will be his upon his twenty-first birthday. Under their flattery, the would-be "nabob" grows increasingly impatient with his life as a farm boy, until the day when he finally visits Ivy Island, accompanied (as if to emphasize the crumbling of his imagined privilege) by his father's Irish hired hand, Edmund. In the wake of his disillusionment, Barnum endures not only the taunts of his parents and grandfather, but also five years of references to Ivy Island from his neighbors, who ask if he still values being "named Phineas" (35).

Cruel as it may seem, the hoax is critical to Barnum's moral posture in *Life*, because it stands as his rite of passage into the white male egalitarianism of Bethel. Stripped of his reliance upon patrimony, Barnum is now prepared to take his place behind the counter of the village store. Moreover, it is from the anachronistic perspective of the Bethel Yankee that Barnum views American culture and society throughout *Life*—a point Barnum emphasizes in justifying his decision to ground the book in the Bethel of his parents and grandparents. He refuses to apologize for "devoting so much space" to his forebears: "I feel myself entitled to record the sayings and doings of the wags and eccentricities of Bethel, because they partly explain the causes which have made me what I am" (105). Having mythologized Bethel as a classless paradise, Barnum can use it as a platform from which to critique his contemporaries for their past and present violation of the lessons of Ivy Island.[93] He condemns his fellows for their "severe and drudging practicalness—a practicalness which is not commendable, because it loses sight of the true aims of life, and concentrates itself upon dry and technical ideas of duty, and upon a sordid love of acquisition" (399). As a recent critic of *Life* has pointed out, Barnum's critique seems ludicrous in a book

that documents *his* drudging practicalness and love of acquisition (Buell 59). Indeed, Barnum follows his jeremiad with an
engraving and description of his gaudiest possession, his mansion, Iranistan. Such contradictions are blatant even by Barnum
standards; they suggest that, to appear as anything but a joke,
the showman's critique must be read in the context not of his
career in show business, but of his childhood in Bethel. To find
America's lost "ideality" we turn our eyes from Iranistan to the
saltbox house of Barnum's youth (399), which graces the book's
first pages.

Barnum's employment of Bethel as a perspective from which
to critique contemporary society can be compared to the strategy of his contemporaries, the writers of the American Renaissance. As Sacvan Bercovitch has argued, those authors attacked
what they saw as their country's betrayal of the agrarian ideology of the early republic (643).[94] Like Barnum, they sometimes
exaggerated the egalitarianism of their country's past in the process of critiquing its class-stratified, materialistic present. But
contemporary commentators were more likely to note the differences than the similarities between Barnum and his literary
counterparts. The *Knickerbocker*, for example, read Thoreau's
*Walden* as the "antidote" to Barnum's *Life*, which was published
in the same year.[95] In the 1850s, Barnum also showed up in the
notebooks and journals of Ralph Waldo Emerson as a symbol of
everything wrong with America. One journal entry contempora-
neous with *Life* listed Barnum under the heading "charlatans"
(*Journals* 378). In his notebook, Emerson would observe: "Men
had rather be deceived than not; witness the secure road to riches
of Barnum & the quacks" (*Topical* 247). Such references leave
no doubt that the Concord sage saw Barnum as a perpetrator,
rather than a fellow critic, of his country's slide from early republican promise into what "The American Scholar" condemned as
"[p]ublic and private avarice" (79).

Emerson's fullest exposition of what Barnum was doing to
America occurred in his essay "Success," which originated as a
lecture he delivered in the late 1850s. As its title implies, the essay stands as Emerson's effort to redefine success in a society saturated by advice literature (some of it written by Barnum) aimed
at aspiring white males. He opens by attacking his culture's reign-

ing notion of success, which he blames on "shallow American-ism": "We countenance each other in this life of show, puffing, advertisement and manufacture of public opinion; and excellence is lost sight of in the hunger for sudden performance and praise" (290). Here Emerson is savaging the cultural phenomenon that was popularly known as "Barnumism."[96] Although the essay never mentions Barnum by name, Emerson's repeated use of the words "show" and "showman" as terms of opprobrium (as well as his thinly veiled reference to Jenny Lind) leaves little doubt as to whom he has in mind.[97] Emerson is not particularly bothered by the effect of this shallowness on U.S. society at large; to the contrary, he strikes an elitist note by dismissing most of his fellow citizens as an obtuse "mob."[98] Instead, he is worried that the disease is also infecting his implied audience of aspiring scholars and artists. Emerson represents the threat in the form of a Barnumesque rival, whom he labels the "showman":

> The time your rival spends in dressing up his work for effect, hastily, and for the market, you spend in study and experiments towards real knowledge and efficiency. He has thereby sold his picture or machine, or won the prize, or got the appointment; but you have raised yourself into a higher school of art, and a few years will show the advantage of the real master over the short popularity of the showman. (294–95)

Although the showman loses out to the Emersonian master in the end, the unsettling fact remains that he has penetrated the nation's most rarefied cultural spaces. This is a worry shared by many of Emerson's peers. In a review of Barnum's *Life*, author/journalist William H. Hurlbert warns that "quackery has invaded the groves of the Academy. Respectable publishing houses borrow the phraseology and imitate the tricks of cheap clothiers and patent-medicine men" (246–47).[99] The explanation for this popular cultural infestation lay in the decline in power of the cross-class group of critics, scholars, and connoisseurs—among them a working-class friend of the author—whom Hurlbert labels the "'mystic aristocracy' of Art" (252). In a well-ordered society, the majority of the people, "the less gifted many," would experience their culture vicariously through "these gifted few" (250). Unfortunately for Hurlbert, the people have begun seeking culture for themselves, which is especially lamentable because

[t]here are many things in regard to which the verdict of the
"people" is quite as likely to be wrong as right, some things in
regard to which it is quite certain to be wrong. Yet the word
"popular," has come to be considered pretty generally, in
America, as a synonyme [*sic*] of "excellent." (246)

Hurlbert blames this triumph of the "popular" over the "excellent" on Barnum and his literary imitators, who have given the
public the trash that it wants rather than the art that it needs.
Hurlbert's anger leads him to betray his egalitarian vision of a
cross-class cultural aristoi: he likens Barnum to, among other
people, "the shabby men who bear placards about the streets" in
an effort to convince us that the showman's philistinism is, at
bottom, plebeian (256).

Hurlbert's classist insult should not be allowed to obscure the
real threat that Barnum posed for the highbrows. In the days
when Barnum bore placards about the streets for the Bowery
Amphitheatre, he was beneath the notice of the elitists.[100] It was
only after he joined in shaping and promoting the midcentury
explosion of middlebrow culture that they began attacking him.
Both traditional elitists like Hurlbert and iconoclastic ones like
Emerson lamented their lack of control over the nation's new culture industries. Barnum served them as an epithet with which to
smear the new middlebrow entrepreneurs and artists.[101] George
Templeton Strong saw him in newspaper editor James Gordon
Bennett; Severn Wallis saw him in novelist Harriet Beecher
Stowe; and E. L. Godkin saw him in story paper editor Robert
Bonner.[102] Barnum would have been flattered to be linked with
Bonner and Stowe, and appalled by the comparison with his arch-
enemy Bennett. But from the point of view of the highbrows, Barnum, Bennett, Stowe, and Bonner all stood for the twofold threat
of the new culture industries: their contamination of high culture with commercialism and their frightening power over their
lower- and middle-class patrons.

The highbrows viewed Barnum and his fellows as dictators
over a benighted million. In 1855, the Brahmin paper of record,
the *Boston Daily Advertiser,* moaned that "Barnum in his way, is a
despot more tyrannical than Emperor or Czar. The public—which
pays heavy taxes to support him in his tyranny—must simply
bow its neck beneath the weight of his decrees."[103] Foreshadow-

ing twentieth-century opponents of mass culture, the elitists exaggerated the power of Barnum and his collaborators by depicting their audiences as docile, uncritical suckers—a conception that reveals far more about the highbrows than about the culture they purported to critique.[104] To contest the cultural "despots," in the post-Civil War decades a group of urban intellectuals, reformers, and artists—among them the New Yorkers whom Thomas Bender has dubbed the "metropolitan gentry" (172)—formulated their own brand of cultural paternalism. Among the most influential of these highbrows were landscape architect Frederick Law Olmsted, Unitarian minister Henry Whitney Bellows, and social worker Charles Loring Brace. Building on the philosophy of the antebellum amusement reformers, the gentry spearheaded the creation of new public cultural institutions, including charities, city parks, libraries, museums, and concert halls. As Iver Bernstein has argued, they were out to create class-binding institutions—social and cultural formations designed for the broadest possible audience, but controlled by elites (154). Charles Loring Brace voices the group's outspoken paternalism in his history of New York's Children's Aid Society, *The Dangerous Classes of New York* (1872). Despite his genuine knowledge of, and sympathy for, plebeian New Yorkers, Brace depicts them as infantilized slaves of their bodies. This is obvious in his praise for the total abstinence movement against lower-class drinking: "It has addressed the working-man—as, in fact, he often is—as a child, and saved him from his own habits, by a sworn abstinence" (67). Brace joined his fellows in viewing public culture as a tool for promoting plebeian self-control. Olmsted praised his own work at Central Park for instilling the "most unfortunate and most lawless classes of the city" with "courtesy, self-control, and temperance" (quoted in Kasson 15). At the Park, as in other gentry-sponsored cultural institutions, plebeian self-control went hand in hand with elite social control. Through their formation and administration of the nation's public culture, the gentry wielded a social power far beyond their numbers or wealth.

Although he symbolized much of what the metropolitan gentry despised about U.S. culture, Barnum viewed himself as their collaborator. By the 1860s, he shared their Republican politics and supported their work in the U.S. Sanitary Commission.[105] In his final decades he would also come to share their elitist conception of culture. He voiced his new views, aptly enough, to the doyen of the metropolitan gentry, British poet and literary and social critic Matthew Arnold.[106] In the winter of 1883–84, Arnold made his first U.S. visit, extending his sway among highbrows through lectures such as "Numbers; or, The Majority and the Remnant." Among Arnold's most openly antidemocratic writings, "Numbers" condemns rule by the majority, who are "unsound," whether in Athens or America (*Philistinism* 149). Arnold argues that cultural and political power should instead reside in a minority of moral truth seekers, whom he styles the "remnant." The lecture showcases Arnold the authoritarian, the man who had called for the suppression of working-class demonstrators in *Culture and Anarchy* (62–66). Barely visible in "Numbers" (but nevertheless present in his hopes of expanding the remnant) is Arnold the liberal, who had spoken out over the previous decades on behalf of public education. Arnold's suspicion of democracy drew the wrath of a large segment of his U.S. audience, but it seems not to have bothered Barnum, who hosted the critic at his Bridgeport mansion the evening after hearing him deliver "Numbers."[107] The following morning, Arnold would write, Barnum "said my lecture was 'grand,' and that he was determined to belong to *the remnant*" (*Letters* 268–69). Barnum did not need Arnold to convert him into a believer in cultural paternalism. Throughout the 1870s and 1880s, the showman framed his circuses as the type of cross-class, "elevating" entertainment the metropolitan gentry prized. His work convinced some elitists to see him not as a threat, but as a fellow traveler: 1886 ads for the Greatest Show on Earth sported endorsements from two figures sacred to U.S. highbrows, William Cullen Bryant and Henry Wadsworth Longfellow.[108] Barnum's success among the gentry is at least partly traceable to the paternalism that had crept into his ads and his persona. In an 1875 manifesto, for example, he dedicates himself to "all the children of men, of whatever age or calling." He pledges

> to bring rational, moral and instructive entertainment, combined with the attractions of wonder and the whole-souled stimulus of innocent mirth, within the reach of the masses and the possibilities of the slenderest purse, and to make them

subservient to Christianity and enlightenment, and auxiliaries of our Public Schools.[109]

Here Barnum foreshadows his emergence as America's Kris Kringle and the Children's Friend—titles that suggest the late-nineteenth-century circus's increasing popularity among children. But the passage also establishes Barnum's paternalistic relation to lower-class adults: it is not their tender ages but their slender purses that make some of those patrons prime candidates for the discipline of "Christianity and enlightenment." To grasp the paternalism of Barnum's final persona fully, however, we must turn from his traveling shows to the book that was largely dedicated to advertising them, his second autobiography, *Struggles and Triumphs*.

### Struggles and Triumphs

Strictly speaking, *Struggles and Triumphs* is not one, but many books: after publishing it in 1869, Barnum regularly issued new editions—updated with appendices and abridgments—for the next two decades.[110] In all its various forms, *Struggles* bears an obvious debt to *Life*: Barnum revised and condensed his first autobiography (incorporating many verbatim passages from it) to form the opening chapters of its successors. *Struggles* also resembles *Life* in presenting itself as a guidebook for young males eager to follow their hero's rise. On the other hand, Barnum does not exaggerate in his preface to *Struggles* when he announces, "[T]his book is new and independent of the former" (vi). In his stance toward black and lower-class Americans, the Barnum of *Struggles* more closely resembles his new cultural and political allies than any of his previous personae.

It is *Struggles's* account of Barnum's rebirth as a Republican that most fully reveals his new social views. The book recounts Barnum's migration into the Republican Party and his service in the Connecticut General Assembly. (He was elected to the terms of 1865, 1866, 1878, and 1879.) *Struggles* attests to the showman's political transformation by reprinting his 1865 speech to the Assembly on behalf of a state constitutional amendment that would have enfranchised literate black males.[111] Drawing on the Republicans' tradition of free-labor rhetoric, Barnum argues for the right of African American men to graduate from "journeymen" to "joint proprietors" in the American democracy (*ST* 625). He cites the cultured, prosperous blacks of Louisiana as proof of the race's ability to fulfill the Republicans' dream of an endlessly expanding, biracial middle class. Barnum's racial egalitarianism is compromised by his reliance upon the racial stereotypes pervading white liberal discourse of the day, yet, given the overwhelming hostility to black male suffrage among his Connecticut audience, his speech stands as a brave call for a Reconstructed North.[112] The man who stood for many Americans as "the embodiment and impersonation of success" had declared his faith in the progress of African Americans.[113] In a career built on public moralizing, this was the moral pinnacle.

In the years after his 1865 appeal, Barnum followed his party's so-called liberal reformers to the right, away from the dream of a free-labor republic. He supported the retreat from Reconstruction in 1872 by publicly endorsing his friend Horace Greeley in his presidential campaign on the Liberal Republican ticket (see Figure 1). Greeley cultivated Democratic support by attacking the southern states' Reconstruction governments and their black constituents (E. Foner *Reconstruction* 502–3). The liberal reformers' support for Greeley foreshadowed their paternalistic attitude toward blacks and lower-class whites in the 1870s and 1880s. By that point many Republicans openly scoffed at the thought of journeymen of any race rising into joint proprietors of the nation's economy or government.

Barnum kept the free-labor rhetoric alive longer than many in his party. In his preface to *Struggles*, he offers his own story of self-made manhood as a model for "the young man, struggling, it may be, with adverse fortune, or, at the start, looking into the future with doubt or despair" (*ST* vi). Like *Life*, *Struggles* beckons lower-class readers to follow its hero's rise.[114] Undermining that impulse, however, is the paternalistic attitude that Barnum occasionally adopts toward his plebeian patrons, employees, and constituents. Consider, for example, the inaugural address (included in later editions of *Struggles*) that he delivered upon taking office as mayor of Bridgeport, Connecticut, in 1875. Speaking

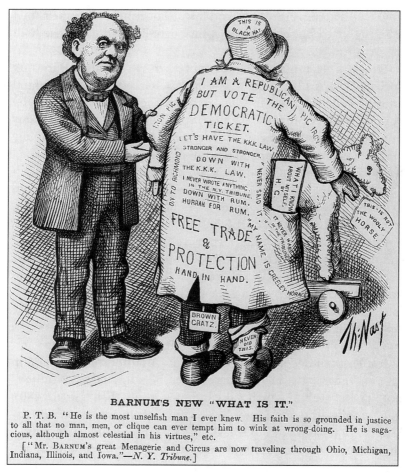

**BARNUM'S NEW "WHAT IS IT."**

P. T. B. "He is the most unselfish man I ever knew. His faith is so grounded in justice to all that no man, men, or clique can ever tempt him to wink at wrong-doing. He is sagacious, although almost celestial in his virtues," etc.

["Mr. BARNUM's great Menagerie and Circus are now traveling through Ohio, Michigan, Indiana, Illinois, and Iowa."—*N. Y. Tribune.*]

Figure 1. Barnum and Greeley, by Thomas Nast. (*Harper's Weekly*)

on behalf of the "industrious and moral portions of our people" (*ST* 1875, 872), he scolds the unemployed for refusing to work. He urges them to quit blaming their problems on the Panic and wasting their time on baseball, billiards, and saloons. The speech resonates with other passages in *Struggles* where the lower classes appear as unruly bodies needing Barnum's discipline.[115] In contrast, the book mythologizes the showman's success at freeing himself from his own body through enormous self-discipline. *Struggles* suggests that by exerting power in both directions—

downward across class lines and inward over himself—the showman is able to launch a celebrity far beyond the limits of the bodily Barnum.

*Struggles* celebrates both types of power by reprinting Barnum's
speech "The Art of Money Getting." Delivered both in England
and the United States, the speech made the showman one of the
period's most popular exponents of the cult of success. Like "Barnum's Rules for Success in Business" in *Life*, "The Art of Money
Getting" exhorts his implied bourgeois audience to Franklinesque
frugality, temperance, and industry. Intimately connected to such
self-discipline, however, is the ability to control others. Barnum
explains how best to discipline one's employees under the heading "USE THE BEST TOOLS." Unwittingly echoing Marx's *Capital*, the showman explains surplus value from the perspective of
the employer: "[T]here is no tool you should be so particular
about as living tools [*sic*]. If you get a good one, it is better to
keep him, than keep changing. He learns something every day,
and you are benefited by the experience he acquires" (*ST* 480).
As Barnum acknowledges, it is because workers are not mindless
tools, but creative thinkers that capitalism has proved so im-
mensely profitable for the bourgeoisie: "An important element in
an employee is the brain. You can see bills up, 'Hands Wanted,'
but 'hands' are not worth a great deal without 'heads'" (*ST* 480).
Yet, while valuing their employees for their heads, Barnum's listeners are encouraged to treat them like interchangeable hands.
Speaking of the "exorbitant" salary demands of some workers,
Barnum observes: "Whenever I have such an employee, I always
discharge him; first, to convince him that his place may be supplied, and second, because he is good for nothing if he thinks he
is invaluable and cannot be spared" (*ST* 480).

If "The Art of Money Getting" teaches Barnum's bourgeois
audience to treat their employees as expendable bodies, it also
teaches them how to transcend their own bodies through commerce. Barnum celebrates the power of advertising to establish
a commercial persona in markets far beyond one's bodily scope.
What is being sold in those markets, Barnum makes clear, is not
so much a good or service as it is celebrity. Barnum's exemplar
of this style of self-promotional commerce is his friend John

Genin, who made a name for himself (at Barnum's recommendation) as the buyer of the first ticket for Jenny Lind's first U.S. concert. Barnum claims that by making his winning bid as "Genin, the hatter," his friend achieved a celebrity that attached itself to his hats all across America. One of those hats belonged to an Iowa man who auctioned it off to the crowd at his hometown post office, which had just received word of Genin's success.[116] Barnum notes that the hat sold for nine dollars and fifty cents even though "it was worn out and not worth two cents" (*ST* 495). For the Iowans, as for their counterparts back East, the value of Genin's hats as clothing paled beside their precious embodiment of his fame.

As Genin's experience demonstrates, the challenge is not only to win fame, but also to commodify it in a hat, a museum ticket, or some other good. Barnum's autobiographies are part of his relentless quest to sell his celebrity. The culminating image of *Life*, Iranistan, suggests the complex interplay among his fame and its commercial embodiments. Barnum built his first mansion in order to cultivate a celebrity that he could "indirectly" exploit through his American Museum (*ST* 262). At midcentury, Iranistan helped make Barnum famous, but by the time of *Struggles* Barnum's amusements were feeding off his superior celebrity. The changing letterheads of Barnum's stationery illustrate this reversal. In the 1850s and 1860s, Barnum typically wrote on business stationery headed with engravings of the American Museum and Iranistan, images calculated to lend him their aura of wealth and power. (Attesting to that aura, Jenny Lind claimed that the Iranistan letterhead convinced her to accept Barnum's proposal of an American tour [*ST* 307].) But in Barnum's final decades, his business stationery was topped by his own portrait (sometimes accompanied by those of his partners). Barnum's letterhead in the late 1880s featured his face in the middle of an elaborate sunburst design, befitting his self-proclaimed status as "The Sun of the Amusement World from which All Lesser Luminaries Borrow Light." Such a celestial celebrity could make even the Greatest Show on Earth pale by comparison: newspaper ads for Barnum's 1879 circus were dominated by a woodcut of his face framed by giant capital letters reading "BARNUM" and "I AM HERE!"[117] The reader must look to the smaller print below to discover that he has brought his circus with him.

Barnum sometimes lost control over his public self once it found its way into the marketplace. As early as the 1840s, we recall, writers and advertisers had already begun adopting his persona for their own purposes. At first, Barnum was flattered by those appropriations. *Life* and *Struggles* both feature positive portraits of would-be Barnums (including, most memorably, a mulatto barber who vows to "come Barnum over de colored people" [*Life* 335]). The showman helped clone himself by training Tom Thumb and Commodore Nutt to talk and dress like miniature Barnums. After the Civil War, however, the real Barnum began to tire of the fake ones. In *Struggles* he complains that other circus owners are hiring men "named, or supposed to be named, Barnum, intending to advertise under the title of 'Barnum's Show'" (*ST* 1873, 758). Here Barnum is facing the fact that, as a commodity, his celebrity is subject to duplication by others. He notes that such appropriations fool the public only in rural areas, where the newspapers do not penetrate. Thus, Barnum depended upon the press not only in creating his public persona, but also in keeping it in his grasp. But his success in commodifying himself required him to spend his last decades proving to the public that "Barnum" was more than a trademark, that there was indeed a person behind the famous name. *Struggles* tells of his refutation of rumors of his death and his suit against the *Philadelphia Sun,* which had claimed that Barnum had merely hired out his name to the circus (*ST* 1889, 321–27). After climbing out of obscurity by making a name for himself, Barnum the man was being overshadowed by Barnum the name.[118]

Barnum's efforts to maintain control over his celebrity can be related to a structuring device in *Struggles* that emphasizes the role society plays in sustaining his public self. The various editions supplement their first-person narrative whenever possible with outside views on the showman drawn from newspapers, speeches, and letters. As a consequence, *Struggles* sometimes bears more resemblance to a series of biographical perspectives on a single subject than to a traditional autobiography written from a stable "I." Barnum's willingness to abdicate the author's role becomes increasingly pronounced in the appendices he attaches to the book's later editions: there "Barnum" emerges as the aggregation of the various views of the reporters, friends, acquaintances, and family members who recorded their encounters with him.[119] This tendency to decenter the autobiographical "I" reaches its culmination with Nancy Barnum's *The Last Chapter*, an account of Barnum's last days and funeral that, as Saxon notes, can be viewed as the conclusion to the autobiographies (*PTB* 22).

Remembering the various voices that bring us Barnum in *Struggles*, one might expect the energized conflict and contradiction celebrated in the poetry of Barnum's contemporary and fellow self-mythologizer Walt Whitman. But whereas Whitman's self is expansive enough to contain conflicting multitudes, Barnum's final persona is vast but uniform. In reading the various versions of *Struggles*, one is struck most of all by Barnum's ingeniousness at getting so many different reporters, celebrities, and politicians to say the same thing about him: namely, that he is a symbol of the American male's potential for unlimited success. The closest thing to dissent in *Struggles* is a pair of anecdotes retained from *Life* in which Barnum's underlings attempt to trace their own labor in the commodity that is "Barnum." The scenes echo other passages in *Struggles*, where the showman engages an unwitting interlocutor in a conversation about "Barnum." As those conversations proceed, Barnum's celebrity momentarily seems to float free of its amused owner. In the encounters from *Life*, that ownership comes under dispute when the showman meets two men who helped construct his public image by painting Iranistan and selling tickets to his speeches. Remaining incognito, Barnum listens as each asserts an insider's knowledge of the "Barnum" he helped construct. The showman is amply compensated for the workers' irreverence by their chagrin at discovering his identity. Noting how each of the now discredited Barnum makers hides from him in shame, the showman revels in his reaffirmed grip on "Barnum."[120]

By silencing such challenges from below, *Struggles* confirms Barnum's status as a spokesman for the post–Civil War business class in the United States. This final Barnum develops *Life*'s preoccupation with the "middling classes" into a thoroughgoing defense of the U.S. marketplace and the men who run it. *Struggles* never flags in its praise of the new American economy, even when the commodification of "Barnum" leaves the public doubting the showman's existence. But, as we shall see, nineteen years before the first edition of *Struggles,* Barnum had demonstrated his ability to mythologize human identity against the market in his promotion of Jenny Lind.

# 2

## The Jenny Lind Tour: "Where's Barnum?"

Have you no poor people in your country? Every one here appears to be well dressed.

—Jenny Lind to Barnum upon viewing the crowd gathered to witness her arrival in the United States (*New York Tribune* 1850)

Even as they celebrate the extension of Barnum's celebrity to an ever broader public, the showman's autobiographies consistently conclude with an inward, domestic turn. In *Life* the narrator winds up "at home, in the bosom of my family," noting contentedly that "'home' and 'family' are the highest and most expressive symbols of the kingdom of heaven" (404). *Life* demonstrates that for much of Barnum's career, incessant travel would have prevented him from experiencing his family on any level other than the symbolic. But as symbols of the cult of domesticity—that emotional and moral nexus central to middle-class formation—home and family figure prominently in many of Barnum's productions, including his own celebrity. For the last forty years of his life Barnum could (and did) tap into this powerful ideological complex by reminding his public of his role in bringing Jenny Lind to America. As the foremost domestic "angel" in the United States before Harriet Beecher Stowe's Little Eva, Lind stood for everything that, in the minds of many Americans, Barnum was not: privacy, artlessness, sensibility, charity, innocence, and piety.

Lind's near-universal reception as the embodiment of sentimental womanhood was the result of a successful collaboration among the singer, Barnum, and the press. Yet, despite a consensus as to who Lind was, there was substantial debate over what her remarkable success meant for U.S. culture. Barnum may have marketed the tour as an escape into the woman's sphere, but he failed to isolate the singer from a host of supposedly "male" concerns. Some of the failure is traceable to Lind's little-recognized success at controlling her public image: as a woman of wealth, fame, and moral authority, the singer had the power to resist male appropriations of her celebrity and to manipulate to her own ends the values she embodied. Although Lind frequently asserted her rights as a woman, she was generally willing to collaborate in Barnum's effort to elevate the tour above its conflicted social context. That they failed to do so speaks to the zeal with which feminists, abolitionists, and their opponents appropriated her celebrity. It also speaks to the way the tour's reception broke down along class lines. Lind and Barnum's effort to position the tour in the middle of the U.S. cultural hierarchy was challenged from above and below: elite critics complained that the singer's repertoire pandered to the tasteless masses, and the lower classes violently protested their exclusion from the concerts. The conflicts sparked by Lindomania undermine commentators—both past and present—who celebrate it as a unique example of "un-commercial, un-political, and un-sectarian excitement";[1] the tour is better understood as a crucial moment in the ongoing struggle over the politics of U.S. commercial amusements.

Given the scale and fervor of Lindomania, it is not surprising that the singer and her manager were sometimes unable to control it. Whether one measures by ticket prices, press coverage, or the "Jenny Lind crowds" that dogged her every move, the singer was a phenomenon unprecedented in the annals of U.S. culture.[2] To be sure, her popularity had waned noticeably before she sailed from New York on 29 May 1852. This was largely a result of her decision to break with Barnum a year before. When she ended their engagement after the ninety-third for-profit concert (they had contracted for 150), she shut down the publicity campaign he had kicked off six months before her arrival.[3] She turned her back on his puff writers, publicity stunts, and orchestrated scenes of public adulation—the machinery that had helped make her "[t]he most popular woman in the world."[4] It was not a role that Lind relished, though it was one she would continue to fill long after her break with Barnum. For the next decade she would remain for many Americans the standard for measuring not just sopranos, or even women artists, but women.

## "Barnum Is Nowhere!"

The Lind tour's symbolic importance to U.S. gender politics was no accident. From the first, Barnum framed Lind, and his relation to her, in terms of the middle class's ideology of separate gendered spheres. At a time when the class's nascent sense of itself depended largely on its gender conventions, the mapping of the spheres was a major preoccupation of midcentury novels, sermons, magazines, advice books, and song sheets.[5] Historians have documented the poor fit between the neatly divided world those works described and the more complicated lives of their authors and readers, but as social theory, the spheres were clearly distinct.[6] They were based on sweeping assumptions about the intellectual, moral, and physiological differences between the sexes. The middle-class female was heralded as the True Woman, a figure of superior morality, sensibility, and piety.[7] She reigned (or was confined, according to early feminists) in the home, where she wielded moral authority, but little legal or economic power. By midcentury, middle-class women had succeeded in stretching the boundaries of the domestic sphere, but when they left their homes to work, petition politicians, or pay charity visits to the poor, they were treading dangerously close to the male sphere. Most Americans still saw the workplace, the hustings, and the street as the rightful domain of "male" rationality and enterprise.

By the time of Lind's arrival in the United States, Barnum was well aware of his own symbolic importance to middle-class masculinity. For many people, the showman's name was shorthand for the American entrepreneur's relentless energy and acquisitiveness: the phrase "Where's Barnum?" had become a standard joke to be cracked upon the appearance of any marketable novelty. In the late 1840s, New York's Burton's Theatre used it as the title of a farce, and newspapers kept it alive in squibs by the score.[8] The *Brooklyn Daily Eagle* even imported the phrase into its weather reports: "Where's Barnum? — There was a white frost on Saturday morning, on the plank road between Bath and West Sandlake in this State."[9] If the real-life showman bargained for Shakespeare's house and Peale's Museum, the *Eagle*'s Barnum was prepared to buy and exhibit the very frost off the ground.

For much of the Lind tour, Barnum offered his reputation for enterprise, energy, and publicity as a foil to the singer's True Womanhood. He framed the tour as an unprecedented moment in American culture when the male sphere was eclipsed by the female. As he declared in a speech after the first concert, Jenny Lind had the power not simply to overshadow him, but to make him disappear:

> LADIES AND GENTLEMEN—I have but one favor to ask of you—and that is, that in the presence of that angel (pointing to the door where Jenny had just passed out) I may be allowed to sink where I really belong—into utter insignificance. If there has ever been a moment when I aspired to have the question generally asked, "Where is Barnum?" that time has passed by forever. I acknowledge frankly, that after such a display as we have had to night, Barnum is nowhere!

But if Barnum was nowhere, it was only because Jenny Lind was so palpably *there*. The showman clarified this point when he proceeded to tell his audience "where Jenny Lind is." This turned out to be not a place, but her resolution to devote all of her earnings from the concert to local charities: Barnum passed on this news despite the fact that "she begged me not to do it."[10]

Barnum's spatial metaphors chime with other instances, both before and after this speech, when he reflects on his celebrity. We recall from *Life* that, at this point in his career, the showman typically invited his audience to join with him in celebrating the ubiquity of the public Barnums: his success at getting people to ask "Where's Barnum?" meant that his name walked around with a life of its own, attaching itself to other people and their work. But in this speech Barnum invokes a perspective from which his purchased, publicized, and endlessly replicated celebrity is "utterly insignificant." That perspective is represented by Lind, who not only plans to give her celebrity-making capital away, but also tries to keep him from talking about it. As if to demonstrate Lind's effect on him, the usually expansive Barnum mimics her humility by refusing this golden opportunity to aggrandize himself with a longer speech.

Barnum would echo his New York remarks after Lind's first concerts in other cities. In Boston he told the crowd, "You can hardly expect a speech from so common an individual as myself, on an occasion like this"; in Philadelphia he insisted, "Barnum's nowhere — nowhere!"[11] The showman was taking some pains to construct the tour as a turning point in the history of his celebrity: the old Barnum of humbug and printer's ink had been annihilated "forever."[12] He had already test-marketed his new persona back in February in a widely reprinted letter to the press announcing his signing of Lind. It depicts her as virtually unmotivated by financial concerns: "Miss Lind has numerous better offers than the one she has accepted from me; but she has a great anxiety to visit America." Having introduced the selfless Lind, Barnum proceeds to mimic her virtues:

> Perhaps I may not make any money by this enterprise, but I assure you that if I knew I should not realize a farthing profit, I would yet ratify the engagement, so anxious am I that the United States shall be visited by a lady whose vocal powers have never been approached by any other human being, and whose character is charity, simplicity, and goodness personified.[13]

As the showman soon discovered, however, his most effective guise would be as Lind's selfish foil, rather than her selfless disciple. The new Barnum thus spent much of the tour playing second fiddle to the old one. This was evident in a conundrum that summed up many Americans' perceptions of Lind and her manager: "'Why is it that Jenny Lind and Barnum will never fall out?' Answer: 'Because he is always for-getting, and she is always for-giving'" (*ST* 338). Whether or not the showman actually originated this saying (as his legal adviser, Sol Smith, suspected), he certainly worked to validate it, particularly in his management of Lind's charity concerts. *Struggles* would document that Barnum inflated the receipts of those concerts by silently paying all their expenses (342–43). When the press responded by contrasting his apparent greed with Lind's altruism, he remained silent — this despite his usual eagerness to defend himself in print.[14] By exaggerating the singer's giving, Barnum encouraged people to overlook the wealthy, powerful woman she was and focus on the poor girl she had been. Like Barnum — but with more validity in her case — Lind was famous for having begun her life in humble circumstances.[15] But whereas a mythologized impoverished child-hood accentuated Barnum's dazzling rise to wealth, it surrounded Lind with a sentimental aura of humility and simplicity that she never lost in the eyes of many Americans. They saw every dollar Lind gave away as confirming her identity with the "poor and plain little girl" of her youth.[16]

Barnum and his collaborators took some pains to ensure that Lind's charities were interpreted as the innocent gifts of an un-worldly girl, but it is at least as plausible to read her U.S. dona-tions as a wealthy philanthropist's endorsement of the public work of her bourgeois sisters. Although the singer undertook the tour to fund her Swedish charities, she also gave more than fifty thousand dollars to U.S. charities.[17] Many of Lind's gifts were targeted to powerful, well-established women's charities, such as the New York Colored Orphan Society and Society for the Re-lief of Poor Widows and the Boston Female Asylum.[18] Other ma-jor recipients, such as New York's Association for the Improve-ment of the Condition of the Poor and Boston's Society for the Prevention of Pauperism, were also staffed largely by bourgeois women volunteers. Through these groups, Lind's gifts financed the efforts of middle- and upper-class women to stretch their sphere beyond the home while bringing relief, Christianity, and moral surveillance to the poor. At a time when the True Woman was idealized for her private acts of kindness, the charities united bourgeois women in a host of new public roles. They also offered a limited degree of cross-class female solidarity. Although never shedding their moralizing view of the poor, the charity ladies were inspired by their experiences to critique male reformers' insen-sitivity to the specific hardships of lower-class women (Stansell 69–72).

But the Lind tour, as far as Barnum and his collaborators were concerned, was not about female power. It was therefore in-evitable that the charity ladies make almost no appearance in press coverage of Lind's philanthropy; when they are depicted, it is as pesky "lady-beggars" whom N. P. Willis skewers for nagging the singer.[19] Lind encouraged the press to ignore her support for women's associational life by delegating the selection of her ben-eficiaries to committees of male philanthropists and politicians. She appears, however, to have charged those committees with finding what she considered to be worthy recipients: Boston committee member Edward Everett noted her preference for organizations "whose object is to relieve those crying natural wants, — food for the hungry & clothing for the naked."[20] She also kept the donations at a substantial size by restricting the number of recipients.[21] Her informed, pragmatic approach to philanthropy was generally ignored by the press, however. Although the bulk of Lind's donations went to large organizations, reporters chose to focus on the singer's spontaneous gifts to deferent, isolated individuals. Those sentimental stories better suited the middle class's notion of the worthy poor, as well as its notion of Jenny Lind.[22]

### "She Sings Herself"

Among the most vocal celebrators of the sentimental Lind were those fixtures of the middle-class parlor, the *Home Journal* and *Godey's Lady's Book*. Praising Lind for remaining "true to the moral instincts of her woman's nature," *Godey's* enlisted her in its ongoing celebration of separate spheres.[23] Its "Editor's Table" spelled out (in terms Barnum would certainly have approved) Lind's significance for U.S. gender relations:

> We thank her for the lesson she reads to all gifted women, that virtue is their highest glory; we thank her for the example she gives to our daughters, that the highest genius can be simple and natural as a village school-girl; we thank her for the sweet pleasure, without meretricious arts, which she confers on the guardians of our country's weal, and on the youth who are our country's hope.[24]

A source of pleasure for U.S. males, Lind is a model for the country's females. Her importance for both hinges on a single set of overlapping terms, all of which mark her otherness to the masculine sphere: girlishness, simplicity, naturalness, and artlessness.[25] These hallmarks of the True Woman dominate contemporary responses to Lind. They appear in descriptions of her appearance and behavior onstage as well as off. They are used to describe not only her character, but also her deportment, voice, clothing, and face. Commentators read her spotless morality in the whiteness of her dress, and her honesty in the "naturalness" of her manners.[26] As Karen Halttunen has demonstrated, the axiomatic transparency of the True Woman was calculated to encourage such "typological" readings: at a time when the middle class valued sincerity above all else, Lind's celebrators could assume an absolute correspondence between her outer life and inner purity.[27]

Perhaps the most striking typological readings of Lind occur in her concert reviews. Many U.S. commentators confidently extrapolated full character studies from the smallest details of her performances. To make this leap they were sometimes forced to ignore what they knew to be the facts of her career. As she sang pieces she had diligently practiced and performed for more than a decade, they found her artless, spontaneous, and unconscious.[28] One reviewer set the tone for such commentary with a description of the singer's first notes in the United States:

> As a bird just alighted upon a spray begins to sing, he knows not why, and pours forth the increasing volume of his voice from an instinct planted within him by that Power which made him vocal,—as flowers unfold their petals to the air, as zephyrs breathe, as rivulets leave their founts, as thoughts flow, as affections rise, as feelings develope [*sic*],—so this wondrous creature sang. It was not Art. It was a manifestation of Nature. Its involuntariness was its charm, its fascination.

Although he proceeded to acknowledge the "cultivation" that lay behind Lind's performance, he still manages to see it as somehow instinctive and untrained.[29]

Lind did her part to encourage such responses through her onstage appearance and repertoire. She typically performed in the unornamented white gowns and head-hugging hairstyles that sentimentalists favored for their supposed accentuation of the body's natural lines (Halttunen 83–88). At a time when *Godey's* advised its readers, "[Y]our dress is a sort of index to your character," the "chastely dressed" Lind wore her virginity on her sleeve.[30] Her clothing and hairstyles set the fashion for her U.S. fans.[31] Like the sincere heroines of sentimental fiction, she was rumored to shun the artificiality of tight lacing.[32] Whether or not that was the case, some of Lind's followers turned to artifice in their efforts to mimic her "natural" look: one barber promised to "furnish hair to customers of the same color as that with which Nature furnished Jenny Lind."[33]

Figure 2. Daguerreotype of Jenny Lind, circa 1850. (Collection of the New-York Historical Society)

Lind's onstage appearance was complemented by concert programs calculated to leave audiences with an impression of her at her most natural: after opening with morceaux from the Italian and German operas on which she had built her European reputation, she typically concluded with folk songs and pastoral ballads such as "Home, Sweet Home," "The Herdsman's Song," and "The Bird's Song." It was apparently these melodies that convinced some U.S. commentators that Lind—who had spent most of her life in European cities—was a former peasant.[34]

But whether she sang the works of Bellini or Henry Bishop, Lind's fabled transparency ensured that reviewers heard in her voice only what they knew about her life. Even when her performances could not be reconciled with her image, her fans persisted in their typological readings. After listening to her sing "Casta Diva" from *Norma*, N. P. Willis complained that the piece was ill suited for "a voice that had formed itself upon her life and character."[35] In her operatic career, Lind had successfully reinterpreted Norma as a figure of love rather than jealousy and revenge, but Willis found it too much to swallow.[36] He insisted that the piece, "to be sung truly, must be sung passionately, and with the cadences of love and sin," and this Lind was simply incapable of doing. It was, in short, "Jenny Lind, and not Norma," whom he had heard.[37] Other reviewers echoed Willis's belief in the identity of Lind's singing and what they knew of her offstage life. The *New York Tribune* observed:

> In JENNY LIND, we still feel that it is not easy to separate the singer from the person. She sings herself. She does not, like many skillful vocalists, merely recite her musical studies, and dazzle you with splendid feats unnaturally acquired; her singing, through all her versatile range of parts and styles, is her own proper and spontaneous activity — integral and whole.[38]

Lind encouraged U.S. audiences to distinguish her from other classical singers by retiring from opera with great fanfare the year before she came to this country. Because many Americans retained a Calvinist prejudice against theatrical performers, and especially against women opera singers, Lind's retirement was interpreted as a casting off of pretension and disguise, a return to the core self.[39] Furthering this impression was the fact that she sang pieces that were often advertised as having been written with her character and vocal talents in mind (e.g., Taubert's "The Bird Song" and Meyerbeer's "Trio for Voice and Two Flutes"). Barnum gave Americans the opportunity to join in the construction of the authentic Lind with his much-publicized contest for a prize song commemorating her coming to the United States.

There were dissenters who attempted to isolate the singer's performances from her offstage reputation. A Boston reviewer complained that many of Lind's enthusiasts had "omitted to *separate* her reputed, and we doubt not her *well-deserved* moral and praiseworthy reputation for benevolence of character — her simple, childlike, unostentatious and bewitching manner and appearance, from the subject of her musical performances, abstractly considered."[40] But Barnum found numerous ways of ensuring that audiences heard the life of Jenny Lind, not Norma, when she sang "Casta Diva." One means of bringing Lind's offstage life into the concert hall was the biographical sketch of the singer (along with sketches of conductor Julius Benedict, baritone Giovanni Belletti, and Barnum) included in the program. But many patrons who refused to pay for a program were already familiar with Lind's biography, as it was available in cheap, well-advertised volumes by George G. Foster and Charles Rosenberg.[41] Shorter versions of her biography appeared in magazines and newspapers across the country.

If the biographies encouraged audiences to agree that Lind "sings herself," many of them also implicitly asked whether, in the dawn of press-constructed celebrity, "Jenny Lind" was not itself a performance. That possibility arises in the biographers' shared quest for a moment in Lind's past when she was at her most girlish, artless, and unknown. Lind's countrywoman Fredrika Bremer focused on the singer's debut as Agatha in Weber's *Der Freischütz*: "We saw not an actress, but a young girl full of natural geniality and grace. She seemed to move, speak, and sing without effort or art. All was nature and harmony."[42] Although other writers dramatize different primal moments, they share Bremer's fascination with the precelebrity Lind. One commemorated the night Lind electrified her audience as an obscure second soprano: "The public had found it out. No previous puffery had brought the girl with a great name to reap a large harvest of scarcely genuine laurels. She had stood amongst them comparatively unknown."[43] By harking to a version of Lind predating the puffery, commentators sought a time when it would have been impossible to conceive of a split between singer and performance, private person and celebrity. In the process, they indicate that as early as 1850 publicists had already saturated the space between famous artists and their audiences. After the journalists, daguerreotypists, poets, merchants, and biographers had done their work, no one could seek the girlish singer without encountering the Barnumized celebrity. But while the fact of Lind's celebrity was undeniable, there was considerable controversy over who controlled its production and circulation. And implicit in that controversy was a debate over the meaning of her success for U.S. gender hierarchy.

Lind's fans went to great lengths to bypass her celebrity. Some attempted to experience her art vicariously through surrogates who were ignorant of her reputation. Biographer Charles Rosenberg, for example, recounted the singer's impromptu performance for a poor English cottage woman who did not recognize her (*Jenny Lind: Her Life* 52). Others were confident that they could distinguish the "real" Lind from her public image. In the *Home*

*Journal,* Willis told of escorting the singer through streets crowded by New Yorkers who did not recognize their idol. "So, do not be sure," he concluded, "that you know how Jenny Lind looks, even when you have seen her Daguerreotypes and heard her sing!"[44] But even Willis's journal acknowledged the difficulties of recovering the undaguerreotyped Lind. In a review titled "Jenny Lind's Impression on a Plain Man's Common Sense," a *Home Journal* critic writing under the Shakespearean pseudonym of "Kent" describes his unsuccessful effort to separate the singer from her press image. So thorough is this mediation that it spoils the concert except for a few brief moments: "Now and then, she produced an effect for which no newspaper had prepared me, and the pleasure, though brief, was intense and thrilling." The pleasure is so brief, in fact, that Kent begins to question the existence of the spontaneous, natural "girl." Even Lind's most nonchalant moves look rehearsed. After delighting in her nervous, hurried entrance, Kent "could not help thinking, that she having entered concert rooms, in exactly the same way, some thousand times, it could not be quite the unconscious, unstudied grace it seemed. No matter, it is very pleasing."[45] He finally abandons all hope of uncovering the "real" singer beneath the performance and resigns himself to the enjoyment of the newspapers' Jenny.

Whereas Kent held Lind partly responsible for her celebrity, many of her supporters strongly disagreed. Central to their celebration of Lind's True Womanhood was the conviction that she lacked both the desire and the ability to control her own public image. Barnum encouraged this view by remarking on numerous occasions that the singer never read the newspapers that were full of her.[46] From the beginning of the tour, Lind's fans credited her with maintaining an aura of informality and familiarity that belied her status as a public figure. In their eyes she had even managed to domesticate that most public of spaces, the concert hall. Musing on her rendition of "Home, Sweet Home," a Cincinnati listener insisted that the song "was breathed forth in notes so sweet, that wherever heard that place is the desired 'Home' forever."[47]

The apparent ease with which Lind's fans reconciled her international fame with her domestic mystique is at least partly attributable to the precedent set by two generations of U.S. women novelists.[48] In the decades bracketing the singer's tour, middle-class authors such as Catherine Sedgwick, Fanny Fern, Grace Greenwood, and Harriet Beecher Stowe achieved fame and financial success by producing the literary equivalents of "Home, Sweet Home."[49] As Mary Kelley and Richard Brodhead have demonstrated, those writers' enormously popular idealizations of domesticity had the paradoxical effect of earning them a public stature enjoyed by few nineteenth-century women. But that fame was contingent upon their privileging the private life of the wife and mother over their own careers as literary celebrities.[50] In her travelogue *Haps and Mishaps of a Tour in Europe* (1854), Grace Greenwood recognized Lind as another woman caught between domesticity and celebrity. Her book recounts a June 1852 voyage from New York to Liverpool that she shared with the newlyweds Otto and Jenny Lind Goldschmidt. The Goldschmidts were returning to Europe after having married in Boston the previous February. Struck by Jenny Goldschmidt's habit of sitting alone, staring out at sea, Greenwood speculated on her thoughts:

> Was it of those perishable wreaths, placed on her brow amid the glare and tumult of the great world, she mused—or of that later crowning of her womanhood, when softly and silently her brow received from God's own hand the chrism of a holy and enduring love? Was it that happy, loving wife, or the great, world renowned artiste, who dreamed there alone, looking out over the sea? (3)

Judging from the U.S. commentary on Jenny Goldschmidt's personal life, there were plenty of people ready to answer these questions. Even before she married, many Americans interpreted her ambivalence about her fame as an affirmation of traditional gender hierarchy. Believing her "more fitted to grace...the domestic circle than to shine on the public arena," they insisted that she really wanted not a career, but a husband.[51] Speculation on Lind's marital prospects was rampant—much of it fueled by a palpable anxiety about her status as a single woman in an era when feminists had begun exposing the oppression structured into marriage.[52] The *Boston Herald* groused: "JENNY LIND was 30 years of age on the 6th of October. Why don't she marry?"[53] Worried that a generation of females was being encouraged to reject the institution altogether, the *Pittsburgh Gazette* interrupted its coverage of the Lind tour for a detailed analysis of six types of "old maids," one consisting of those "tempted into public life as writers, actresses, singers, &c. . . . Such women, if they feel that they can make their love of fame take a place below their love of husband and home, may marry; but on no other conditions."[54] Clearly the lure of female celebrity had the potential of wreaking havoc on American domestic life.

Everyone fearing a rebellion of young women leaped for joy upon the news of Lind's marriage on 5 February 1852. The *Home Journal* saw in Lind's decision a lesson for the country's women:

> [T]here is more than a sisterly well wishing, in the general excitement among her own sex on the subject. The power, in one person, of trying, purely and to such completeness, the two experiments for happiness — love and fame — were interesting enough; but it is strange and exciting to see the usual order reversed — fame first, and love afterwards. To turn unsatisfied from love to fame, has been a common transit in the history of gifted women. To turn unsatisfied from fame to love — and that, too, with no volatile caprice of disappointment, but with fame's most brimming cup fairly won and fully tasted — is a novelty indeed.[55]

The rush to sound the death knell of Lind's celebrity suggests the transgressive potential of the unmarried female performer. A Boston newspaper reported the widespread glee over the annihilation of Lind's name: "The Nightingale is mated; the bird is caged; there's no Jenny Lind now — she's a goner."[56] By no means a radical feminist, Lind did her part to kill off her own celebrity by breaking with the standard practice of famous female singers and performing under her husband's name (Ware and Lockard 127).

As her decision to sing as Madame Goldschmidt suggests, Lind was familiar with the conventions of sentimental womanhood and could deploy them to her advantage. The tears that sprang to her eyes on numerous public occasions may have been spontaneous, but "[s]weet, tearful Jenny" clearly made little effort to stifle them.[57] One newspaper summed up her first days in the United States: "She wept when she saw the American flag — she wept when they serenaded her — she wept nearly all the time, if some of the paper [*sic*] be true, and doubtless fell asleep crying."[58] The London *Atheneum* saw calculation behind Lind's almost too-perfect embodiment of sentimentalism: "Mdlle. Lind seems to do her simplicities with a somewhat suspicious consciousness, and to lend herself designedly to the American sentiment—accepting the altar which they have dressed for her even while she appears modestly to decline it." The writer then proceeded to cite several instances that suggested Lind's complicity in her deification.[59] But skepticism about her persona was not just a British import. The *Richmond Enquirer* speculated that the singer might "be that artless, unsophisticated creature as represented by some. It may be too that she is just *artful* enough to be *artless.*"[60]

Lind's behavior certainly justified a certain degree of cynicism about her public image. As has been amply documented, the singer's personality was particularly ill suited to her sentimental persona. Her combination of ambition and willpower made her more closely resemble Barnum than her wispy, submissive persona.[61] Before and during her tour with Barnum, Lind fought tenaciously to maintain control over her professional life.[62] In patriarchy, however, it was—and is—inevitable that those wise to the real Lind attack her for the same qualities they admire in the showman.[63] The singer encouraged skeptics to read through her sentimental persona by dropping it at strategic moments. When New York City's Mayor Woodhull asked her to sing at a party he was giving in her honor, Lind, according to one observer, "drew herself up to the height of her dignity" and replied, "I would be most happy to sing for you, and I would, perhaps, be offended if you had not asked me, but I have made a contract with Mr. Barnum which prohibits me, and you know, as a man of business, that I must toe the mark as a woman of business in America."[64] Here Lind displays her usual circumspection by simultaneously asserting and surrendering her power over her own voice: as a woman of business she can stand up to one powerful man, but only by reminding him of her professional obligations to another. Lind's quiet insistence upon her rights convinced even the *Home Journal* to soften its strict adherance to separate spheres: Willis at one point interrupted his celebration of Lind the naive girl to praise the singer's "unbending independence and tact at business."[65]

In New York the most striking proof of the fine line Lind was successfully walking was her popularity with both the rabidly antifeminist *Herald* and the feminist *Tribune*. October 1850 saw the *Herald* alternate its praises for that "glorious woman," Jenny Lind, with misogynistic attacks on the women's rights convention taking place in Worcester.[66] The *Tribune*, in contrast, celebrated Lind's success as the promise of a future when women would have the same professional opportunities as men:

> The ovations to the Artist may then, be regarded as in some sort the apotheosis of her sex; and in them we see an emblem of a coming age when society will no longer need, nor seek to be wiser than Nature, and when those spheres of action for which the impulses and powers of soul have been adapted by its Divine Author will be freely opened to every being.[67]

The *Tribune* was not alone in recognizing Lind's value for feminism. The singer figured in the literary criticism of Margaret Fuller and—as Judith Pascoe has argued—the poetry of Emily Dickinson as a powerful symbol of female autonomy and fame.[68] Feminists attempted to put Lind's nonthreatening celebrity to work for her more radical sisters. This was the case on 6 September 1853, when antifeminists shouted down minister Antoinette Brown at a temperance convention being held at New York's Metropolitan Hall. That evening, at a women's rights convention also taking place in New York, William Henry Channing recalled Jenny Lind's markedly different reception in Metropolitan Hall: "[T]he same crowds that greeted Jenny Lind with shouts of applause, when she sings 'I know that my Redeemer liveth,' hiss a strong minded woman who dares to say what the actress sings."[69] Here Channing is out to legitimate the controversial Brown by linking her to the universally popular Lind; to make the connection, however, he must ignore the facts and rescript Lind as a militant feminist.

The *New York Herald* saw nothing similar in Antoinette Brown and Jenny Lind. Angered by Brown's support for feminism and antislavery, the paper chuckled at her suppression. But when it rhapsodized on Lind's value for the northern "races," even the *Herald* could sound feminist. In an elaborate editorial celebrating Lind's first days in the country, *Herald* editor James Gordon Bennett cited her as proof of the inevitable global triumph of the northern Europeans (and their descendants in the United States) over the "races" to the south of them: "[T]he wand of civilization has fallen from the hands of the southern nations, and passed to the hardy northern races."[70] He praised the "power" of a woman who could assume the phallic wand borne by Italian heroes like Raphael and Dante. It is a portrait of Lind that scarcely resembles the shrinking, passive girl of the *Herald*'s own concert reviews.[71]

After circumventing his own gender politics in his meditation on Lind's race, Bennett concludes by affirming his allegiance to male supremacy. His final paragraphs compare Lind not to heroes but to the prophetess Miriam, who pointed the Hebrews "to their future empire." Likewise, Lind heralds the future of the United States, which will be won by men like Barnum: "He is one of our men for the future. He feels it, sees it rushing up to us, and with him the quicker it comes the better."[72] The ease with which the antifeminist Bennett is able to shift his symbolic focus from Lind to Barnum suggests the way True Womanhood could function as a cover for male power. Lind's public image could be appropriated in this manner because she (like the fair heroines of contemporary fiction) occupied a position between white men and their dark female Others. In a society where white manhood depended upon the construction of *some* women as irrational, sexual, earthy, and passionate, the True Woman partook of those characteristics in only the most diluted form (e.g., her sexuality was represented as an innocent flirtatiousness, her passion took the form of silent weeping). This was clear in male reviewers' frequent comparisons of Lind to Italian opera singers. The *Herald* spoke for many in contrasting the styles of the Italians and the Swede: "Theirs was voluptuous and earthly—hers is intellectual and divine."[73] Lind often functions as a surrogate for the male commentator in such comparisons. Despite the pretense to intragender analysis, the relationship driving such commentary is that of the male reviewer and a mythicized dark femininity that both fascinates and repulses him.

Lind's public image mediated white men's fears and fantasies about not only dark women but also other white men. Like their contemporary Nathaniel Hawthorne, Lind's male commentators often appropriated her famous transparency as a vehicle for male power and homosocial desire. Hawthorne employs his fair heroines, especially Phoebe Pyncheon of *The House of the Seven Gables* (1851) and Priscilla of *The Blithedale Romance* (1852), to mediate the relations between his male characters. One might compare Priscilla's role in the erotically charged relationship of Coverdale and Hollingsworth with Lind's position between male audience members and reviewers.[74] The most striking male homoerotic appropriation of Lind was the work of N. P. Willis, who narrated a charged encounter among himself, Lind, and the concertgoing Daniel Webster. Willis eagerly watches as Lind—in the guise of the "herdsman" whose song she sings—stimulates Webster:

> The tone sped and lessened, and Webster's broad chest grew erect and expanded. Still on went the entrancing sound...and forward leaned the aroused statesman, with his hand clasped over the balustrade, his head raised to its fullest lift above his shoulders, and the luminous caverns of his eyes opened wide upon the still lips of the singer.

Willis concludes the scene by revealing the female singer behind the "herdsman" persona, but he persists in seeing her performance as somehow phallic. He credits her with "the sounding of America's deepest mind with her plummet of enchantment."[75]

## Blowing the Bellows

Of all the people most interested in turning the tour into a celebration of male power and pleasure, the post-Lind Barnum was the most blatant. Barnum clearly deserved the lion's share of the credit for Lindomania. Throughout the tour he made ingenious use of standard publicity devices such as the song contest, press puff, street serenade, and ticket auction. His campaign substantially increased Lind's celebrity, though not to the extent that he would claim in his autobiographies. There he depicts the singer as "comparatively unknown" in the United States when he signed her (*ST* 281), although before Barnum thought of bringing her to America, she was already front-page news in New York and the subject of popular farces and burlettas there and in New Orleans.[76] The *Yankee Doodle* took for granted its U.S. audience's familiarity with Lind in the summer of 1847, when an ambitious New York theater manager, George H. Barrett, tried to lure her to America.[77] The humor sheet parodied Barrett's offer:

Perhaps you may modestly tell me you don't think you will be able to please the Americans, who, you have heard are a very nice and refined people. No such thing. Dem it! (excuse me Madam, a way I have,) they're a set of noodles — green noodles.... they take any body that comes along. If you had no voice at all we'd blow the bellowses so for you in advance, that you might go through your part in dumb show, and they'd all swear you were the finest singer of the age.[78]

What "Barrett" has in mind clearly has less to do with music than with audience manipulation. The piece is remarkable for its anticipation of Barnum's account of Lindomania. In Barnum's autobiographies, Lind's audience would appear fully as green as "Barrett" had predicted.

The autobiographies epitomize Barnum's manipulation of Lind's audience in a series of episodes, each of which depicts him standing before an adoring crowd with a woman it takes to be Lind. The first of these occurs as Lind disembarks at a packed Canal Street wharf in New York City. Barnum escorts her to his waiting carriage, but instead of following her inside, he climbs up beside the driver. He explains his action in *Struggles*: "I took that seat as a legitimate advertisement, and my presence on the outside of the carriage aided those who filled the windows and side-walks along the whole route, in coming to the conclusion that Jenny Lind had arrived" (288–89). In what is clearly a pleasant irony for a man trying to shed his reputation for humbug, it is Barnum's presence that authenticates the True Woman's identity. As if to mark the distance he has come since the tour, the showman implies that without him Lind would be nowhere.[79] Moreover, in the narrative of the tour that follows, Barnum has the power to make Lind appear or disappear before her audiences' eyes. He recounts the occasions — several of them confirmed by the tour diary of his daughter Caroline — on which he fooled crowds demanding the singer by appearing with Lind's companion Josephine Åhmansson or Caroline. In Cincinnati, he dupes a crowd gathered at the docks (many members of which had read press accounts of his substitution of Caroline for Lind) by passing off the real Jenny Lind as his daughter.[80] Lest one dismiss these incidents as irrelevant to Lind's relationship with her

Figure 3. Jenny Lind's Mocking-Bird Song. *Humbug's American Museum.*
(Collection of the New-York Historical Society)

musical public, Barnum recalls his daughter's guest appearance
in the choir of a Baltimore church:

> A number of the congregation, who had seen Caroline with me
> the day previous, and supposed her to be Jenny Lind, were yet
> laboring under the same mistake, and it was soon whispered
> through the church that Jenny Lind was in the choir! The

excitement was worked to its highest pitch when my daughter rose as one of the musical group.... Not a note was lost upon the ears of the attentive congregation. "What an exquisite singer!" "Heavenly sounds!" "I never heard the like!" and similar expressions were whispered through the church. (*ST* 309)[81]

Barnum's claim that "we have never discovered that my daughter has any extraordinary claims as a vocalist" further underscores the tenuous relationship between Lind and the tour taking place in her name (*ST* 309). What "Lind's" audience mistakes for heavenly sounds is merely the expectation that the showman has planted in them. And the fact that those sounds are made by a woman the congregation has seen with Barnum means that the determining relationship is between him, not Lind, and the singer's audience.

Barnum's claims to the contrary, Lind's audience was anything but a congregation of suckers. From the moment of her arrival in the United States, segments of the press and concertgoing public contested the showman's efforts to manage her reception. In *Struggles* Barnum presents the tour as a textbook example of press relations: "'[P]rinter's ink' was invoked in every possible form, to put and keep Jenny Lind before the people. I am happy to say that the press generally echoed the voice of her praise from first to last" (302). To prove his point, he includes an "unbought, unsolicited editorial" from his longtime nemesis, the *New York Herald* (*ST* 302). Although much of the commentary on the tour (namely, that which was solicited, if not bought, by Barnum) was devoted to passive puffery, a substantial portion of it was not. Many journalists were skeptical about not only Barnum's machinations, but also their own role in Lindomania. During the singer's first days in the United States, the *Herald* was already insisting that the "one little secret of her success yet untold" was the press.[82] And by the time of Lind and Barnum's split, that paper blamed the break on Barnum's effort "to manage the press, and to stifle criticism."[83]

In an age when critics commonly accepted money, gifts, and tickets in exchange for positive reviews, the Lind concerts sparked numerous attacks on such practices.[84] The tour unfolded as a series of battles between Barnum and the press, with each accusing the other of attempting to control it. The most heated such skirmish occurred during the tour's first swing through Boston: letters reprinted in the local press implied that an unnamed newspaperman was trying to blackmail Barnum. As the story unfolded, the Boston and New York papers printed charges and countercharges regarding the identity of the alleged blackmailer and the authenticity of the letters.[85] Soon after that scandal petered out, the issues it had raised were revived by Walt Whitman (writing as "Paumanok") in the *National Era*. A longtime opponent of puffery, Whitman boldly asserted that "A very large portion of the printed enthusiasm about Jenny Lind's singing is no doubt paid for."[86] When the *New York Evening Post* challenged him to name names, Paumanok replied, "All can be bought, if you make the price high enough."[87] But he added, somewhat contradictorily, that "mere money" could never swerve the editors of the *Evening Post* and *New York Tribune* "one inch from a course they determined on, and considered right, in morals or politics."[88] Whitman may have found it prudent to qualify his claims, but he was far from alone in raising a cry over the showman's misadventures with the press: by the time of Paumanok's letters, even children had begun to taunt Barnum about the alleged blackmailers.[89]

It was not only the press that fought Barnum's effort to manage Lind's reception. Throughout the tour, the showman struggled with those eager to enlist the singer in their social and political causes. Her celebrity was especially coveted by the abolitionists and their foes. Given her famous, if somewhat vague, affiliations with freedom and republicanism (prominently displayed in her apostrophe to the U.S. flag upon her arrival in America), her endorsement was symbolically important for both groups.[90] The *New York Herald* moved quickly after Lind's arrival to put her to work against abolitionism. In its story on Lind's quarters at New York's Irving House Hotel, the paper remarked: "She seemed greatly pleased with the negro servants; they looked so neat and happy, and so different from the miserable objects she had expected to see."[91] But abolitionists were not about to allow the *Herald* to co-opt Lind's celebrity. The *National Anti-Slavery Standard* attempted to call the bluff of the flag-hugging Nightingale. Observing that "Jenny Lind forgot, in the distribution of her charitable donations, the American Anti-Slavery Society," the paper sarcastically wondered "if anybody has told her that 'the flag of

the free' is flapping over three million slaves."[92] Other abolitionists didn't wait for Lind's permission to enlist her in their cause.
The internationally famous Hutchinson Family Singers entertained audiences at antislavery conventions with their "Welcome
to Jenny Lind," which included the verse:

> While the great and honored hear you,
> Let the poor oppressed be near you;
> Then will every heart revere you—
> Jenny sing for liberty. (Hutchinson 267)

While Barnum and Lind apparently approved of the Hutchinsons'
song (the group performed it for her in her hotel suite), they were
careful to remain on the sidelines of the struggle over slavery.[93]
When rumors began to circulate that Lind had donated a thousand dollars to an abolitionist organization, the showman and
singer acted swiftly to refute the charges through a conciliatory
visit and letter to editor Thomas Ritchie of the antiabolitionist
Washington newspaper the *Daily Union*.[94] Armed with Ritchie's
approval, Lind and Barnum took the tour into the deep South free
of any hint of abolition. They thus avoided the controversy that
dogged Scandinavian artists Ole Bull and Fredrika Bremer, who
were attacked for their antislavery politics in the United States.[95]

   That Lind kept out of the fray over slavery is all the more impressive in light of her obvious sympathy for the abolitionists.
She apparently acted on that sympathy only after breaking with
Barnum. A week before leaving the United States, she wrote Harriet Beecher Stowe to praise *Uncle Tom's Cabin* as an important
contribution to "the welfare of our black *brethren*."[96] The singer
also donated one hundred dollars to Stowe's campaign to free
Milly Edmondson and her two enslaved children.[97] More directly
involved than Lind in the struggle over slavery was one of her at-
torneys, John Jay, a man "somewhat known as an abolitionist."[98]
During the singer's last days in America, Jay made the papers by
orchestrating the hairbreadth escape of fugitive slave Nicholas
Dudley.[99] Lind seems to have been more reticent about her antislavery feelings, however. The ineffectuality of the singer's stance
was documented by Harriet Jacobs in her 1861 slave narrative.
She recalls her life as a fugitive (and an employee of N. P. Willis)
in New York City in 1850:

> The great city rushed on in its whirl of excitement, taking no
> note of the "short and simple annals of the poor." But while
> fashionables were listening to the thrilling voice of Jenny Lind in
> Metropolitan Hall, the thrilling voices of poor hunted colored
> people went up, in an agony of supplication, to the Lord, from
> Zion's church. (191)

The press may have celebrated Lind's "deep and heartfelt sympathies for the distressed of every clime," but those sympathies were
apparently not felt in Zion's Chapel, where African Americans
gathered to protest the enforcement of the Fugitive Slave Law.[100]

## The Outsiders

If Barnum and Lind largely succeeded at keeping the struggle over
slavery at arm's length, they found class conflict more difficult
to evade. Throughout the tour, they struggled valiantly to extend
Lind's appeal across class lines. In his autobiographies, Barnum
recalls his efforts to prevent "the 'fashionables' from monopolizing
her altogether, and thus . . . cutting her off from the warm sympathies she had awakened among the masses" (*ST* 290). Those sympathies produced the enormous crowds that swarmed around
Lind in most of the cities she visited—crowds composed, to a
large extent, of lower-class people. In New York, as Buckley has
shown, strategic donations to the Fire Department Fund and Musical Fund Society won Lind the support of the workers who had
led the charge on the Astor Place Opera House the previous year
(532–35). Twenty fire companies escorted the Musical Fund Society to the Irving House for a serenade on Lind's first night in
the country. Later in the tour, she was welcomed by the firemen
of New Orleans and Philadelphia, whom she rewarded with donations. In Philadelphia she shook hands with many in a crowd
consisting largely of firemen, who climbed up to her hotel balcony during a boisterous rally of approval.[101] If male workers
dominated those demonstrations, Lindomania among lower-class
women transformed the shops: *Godey's* noted that in the plebeian
environs of New York's Bowery and Canal Streets and Philadelphia's Eighth and Second Streets, "Jenny Lind plaids, combs,
silks, ear-rings, work baskets, bonnets, and even hair-pins were
advertised and recommended."[102] The proliferation of this cheap

merchandise suggests that lower-class women were as eager to buy into the craze as their moneyed sisters who shopped for Jenny Lind Riding Hats and Pianos on Broadway or Chestnut Street.[103]

Despite the numerous wishful claims to the contrary, plebeian Americans were far more likely to experience Jenny Lind through a hairpin than through a concert ticket. Lind's audiences varied to some degree between cities (depending upon the presence of a fickle upper class), but the one constant throughout the tour was a dearth of lower-class people in her paying audiences. Although everyone agreed that the "desire to see her and listen to her singing seems to pervade all classes," Barnum priced most — though by no means all — of the tickets beyond the means of the lower classes.[104] When the cheapest tickets for the second set of Philadelphia concerts were announced at four dollars, the Harrisburg *Democratic Union* complained: "Miss Lind may express a desire to sing for the people, but if she demands a week's wages to hear her, the *people* will be denied the pleasure."[105] As Kent noted in the *Home Journal*, a Lind concert would exhaust many families' amusement budgets for an entire year.[106] Despite constant protests over the high prices of the tickets, Barnum relented only partly as the tour proceeded.[107] One result of the unprecedented prices was the exclusion from the concert hall of an urban working class famous for asserting its aesthetic tastes in vocal and sometimes violent fashion. So complete was this exclusion that Barnum could assure theater managers Sol Smith and Noah Ludlow:

> I do most heartily detest seeing a set of ragged dirty chaps located right under the eyes & noses of respectable ladies & gents, as is generally the case where there is a *pit*; but as none but decent people generally attend the Lind concerts, it may be best perhaps to still keep the *pit*. (*SL* 53)

In most cities Barnum's ticket pricing created two Lind audiences, segregated along class lines: as the middle- and upper-class ticket holders enjoyed the Nightingale inside the concert hall, huge crowds drawn mainly from the lower classes filled the streets outside, hoping to catch the singer's voice through an open window.[108] If the outside crowd only occasionally surpassed the indoor one in size, the "outside barbarians" almost always surpassed the insiders in enthusiasm.[109] Reporters in several cities noted the effects of the outsiders on the performances: in Philadelphia they "occasionally assisted the [inside] audience in calling for an encore"; in Richmond "a beautiful smile wreathed [Lind's] face, as she heard the applause caught up and re-echoed by the large crowd *outside.*"[110] Some commentators heard an affirmation of bourgeois hegemony in the outsiders' re-echoed applause. A St. Louis reviewer described an outside crowd composed of "the roughest samples of mortality," which amused itself before the concert by "shouting and yelling in a fearful manner." But at the sound of Lind's voice, the outsiders fell silent, listening breathlessly to her every note, "until catching the signal from the audience within the Hall," whereupon they added their "roar" to the applause of the insiders.[111]

Yet at many concerts it was hard to find any deference in the response of the outsiders. The crowd outside the singer's first Tripler Hall performance in New York was so loud that it "tended to agitate the great cantatrice, and to interfere with the enjoyment of the audience."[112] On other occasions, violence erupted during the concerts. At Lind's first U.S. performance (at Castle Garden), a crowd composed of the "hardest kind of looking customers" numbering about five hundred "absolutely besieged the Castle, and made several attacks to force themselves into the garden," only to be repelled by the police.[113] During one of Lind's Boston concerts, rowdies standing on roofs outside Tremont Temple threw pebbles and dirt through the open windows.[114] The situation grew more serious in Cincinnati, where, according to a local reporter, a large crowd gathered in front of the hall before the concert in order "to have a sight at the woman who had gained all hearts. She had, however, arrived two hours before, and the crowd disappointed, actually proceeded to commit acts ... that would disgrace the greatest blackguards of any community."[115] They scaled adjacent buildings, attempted to force open the blinds on the hall's windows, and fought with the police. The brawl climaxed when Barnum's complaints about the noise prompted the police to clear the area with warning shots.[116] In the chaos that followed, the outsiders traded gunfire with the police, leaving a watchman slightly wounded by buckshot—and in the process contradicting Emerson's claim that "Jenny Lind needs no police."[117]

In Pittsburgh Lind had one of her most frightening encounters with those marginalized by Lindomania. Her first concert in the city coincided with payday for the local factory hands. When Lind took the stage, the hall was surrounded by a crowd of boisterous, drunken workers whose shouts overwhelmed the music being performed within.[118] What happened next remains a bit hazy. As one of the more sensationalistic press accounts has it, Lind

> was most grossly insulted by a ruffian crowd, who, while the concert was going on, dashed in stones at the window of her dressing room, and applied to her, that she might hear them, the most shocking and degrading epithets. And when the concert was over, the crowd, which was immense, who had assembled in front of the building, appeared determined not to leave until they would see her.[119]

Other local papers denied that any windows were broken, and insisted that "most of the noise and uproar...were really the manifestations of a rude admonition [*sic*] for the Swedish Nightingale."[120] Whatever the precise details, there can be no doubt that Lind heard admonition, not admiration, in the crowd's disorder. After the concert had ended, she "was too fatigued and too terrified to think of attempting to face the multitude" that remained outside the hall hoping to gaze at her; she vainly waited in the darkened building for the outsiders to disperse, and was finally forced to make her escape through the back door of the hall and down a maze of alleys to her hotel.[121] In what looks like an attempt to offset the outsiders' working-class belligerence, the local press circulated a melodramatic tale of Lind's "rescue" by a loyal drayman who supposedly led her to safety.[122] By the time this story had appeared, however, Lind had already passed judgment on the Pittsburgh outsiders. She left the city on the morning after the debacle, canceling an already advertised second concert. But the victory of the "Pittsburg b'hoys" was short-lived.[123] In the days after Lind's flight, the Pittsburgh *Daily Commercial Journal* labeled her decision to cut short her stay an overreaction that "stains the reputation of Pittsburg [*sic*]." The paper confidently promised: "When Jenny comes again, order will be inforced [*sic*], and ruffianism rebuked and punished."[124] That order was in evidence when Lind returned to the city later that year for a well-received concert without Barnum. On this visit she was presented with diamond bracelets from Pittsburghers apparently wishing to compensate for her earlier scare (Ware and Lockard 114).[125]

## "The Nightingale Uncaged"

The outsiders who disrupted Lind's performances gave the lie to those who hailed the tour as an unprecedented union of "all orders... varied with all colors and ages."[126] But even though few Americans from the lower orders (and even fewer people of color) made it into the concert hall, the Lind tour did stand as a milestone of another sort.[127] The tour marked the emergence of the U.S. middle class as a cultural and commercial force. At a time when the class was still in the process of naming itself, various observers remarked on the prominence in Lind's audiences of the "middle classes," "those of moderate fortunes," and even "the mediocrity."[128] The *New York Herald* dissected the class identities of the patrons at the first Tripler Hall concert:

> The audience consisted for the most part of the middle classes, who are the support of concerts and theatres, and public amusements of every kind. There was also a fair sprinkling of the upper ten, but few or none of the hard-handed working classes. There were a few seats vacant, which doubtless would have been filled by them had the prices of admission been lower.[129]

Other commentators also situated the tour in a broad middle-class cultural landscape of "public amusements of every kind." Among the ablest cartographers of that terrain was N. P. Willis, who charted the social contours of the tour in a *Home Journal* homage "TO THE AMERICAN ARISTOCRACY." He credited Lind with recognizing the country's real center of cultural and economic power:

> The *first* recognition of the fact that THE MANY were the aristocracy of this country — not THE FEW — was made by Jenny Lind. Though a political economist would have long ago told us, that, in a land where every body is tolerably well off, the bulk of the money must be in the pockets of The People — and that The People, therefore, must have the best of everything — no business seemed to be done upon the idea, except in the supply

of *the first wants*—that is to say, by hotels, public conveyances, oyster-cellars, tailors and hatters. Opera-singers persisted in blindly offering their luxuries to the same class as in Europe—to The Few.[130]

Here as elsewhere in his Lind commentary, Willis's populist rhetoric partly disguises his more specific class politics; that he is equating "The People" with the middle class appears, however, in his listing of their "first wants," most of which lay beyond the means of workers. Willis dubs his middle-class constituency "the FIVE-DOLLAR-BILLERS" in honor of their willingness to spend that amount on "the costliest givers of public pleasure." In contrast to the liberality of this class stands the stinginess of its superiors, the nabobs who resent the $1.50 they spend on an Astor Place Opera House ticket.[131] To prove his point about the Five-Dollar-Billers, Willis turned, as he had so often over the past months, to Jenny Lind: her first New York concerts were a milestone because they marked the initial offering "of the highest pleasure of Luxury to its true American market—the first collecting together of the reliable Five-dollar-Billers."[132]

Other commentators agreed that the tour spoke not only to the middle class's cultural dominance, but also to its financial clout. That, according to the *New York Herald*, was the lesson of Barnum's first ticket auction, where hatter John Genin won the first seat with a $225 bid. The paper partly attributed the cheers that met Genin's success to the fact that "the first choice was taken from the upper ten by a tradesman. And here was a capital idea of Barnum's in pitting the people against the aristocracy in a rivalry of dollars."[133] But Genin's bid was soon surpassed by men like Boston singer/composer Ossian Dodge and Philadelphia daguerreotypist Marcus Root, who also made a living selling consumer and cultural goods (many of them bearing the name "Jenny Lind") to urban respectables.[134] Although, as we have seen, cheap Jenny Lind goods were widely available in working-class shops, Genin and his peers won what *Godey's* called a "more legitimate claim to the title" by presenting their wares directly to the singer.[135] In each city, Lind's hotel suites were transformed into showrooms for furniture and piano sellers, florists, and art dealers, with each merchant's contribution to the Nightingale's nest duly noted by local newspapers.[136] Lind's value as a trademark was demonstrated by an apparent surge in piano sales, as well as the persistence to this day of "Jenny Lind" as the name for a style of furniture.[137] The rush to cash in on Lind sparked rumors that she and Barnum were being paid by the hoteliers with whom she lodged, and that the hoteliers had not—as they claimed—purchased the furnishings of her suites, but had merely borrowed them from publicity-hungry merchants.[138] Whatever the truth to those charges, their widespread currency attests to the public's insight into the commodification of Lind: many of those who bought Jenny Lind cigars and handkerchiefs clearly understood what they were purchasing.

More than one critic noticed the obvious contradiction between Lind's lavish surroundings and her reputation for self-sacrifice and modesty. A correspondent for the *National Anti-Slavery Standard* mused on Lind's luxurious suite at Boston's Revere House Hotel:

> Among other circumstances of magnificence, the handle of the lock of her door had the rather equivocally complimentary text engraved upon it, "he that giveth to the poor lendeth to the Lord!" As much to say, if you will give money to the poor the Lord will raise up fools enough to make it worth your while![139]

Equivocal though it was, Lind's reputation for high-living humility made her especially useful to merchants targeting middle-class females. By midcentury those women were becoming increasingly responsible for shopping for their households, a development that prompted some middle-class ideologists to worry about female extravagance.[140] As early as 1844, the *New York Atlas* was warning men of "limited but respectable means" about the lavish tastes of their wives and daughters.[141] During the Lind tour, *Godey's* spelled out the threat more fully in Alice Neal's didactic story: "Furnishing; or, Two Ways of Commencing Life." "Furnishing" centers on two young women, both on the verge of marriage and both charged with purchasing their trousseaux and the furnishings for their first homes. Anne is a country girl of modest means who enjoys stretching her budget at bargain-rate stores. In contrast, her fashionable city cousin, Adelaide, runs up tremendous bills at the toniest shops in town. Although Adelaide is little more than a spoiled child, her profligacy has serious consequences, as it eventually helps bankrupt her merchant father. Adelaide finally learns her lesson, however: she is last pictured nestled in Anne's cozy cottage, having resolved to master the art of good housekeeping and smart consumption under her cousin's tutelage. In the same issue that featured "Furnishing," *Godey's* assured readers that Jenny Lind was no Adelaide. The Editors' Table praised the singer for remaining "[s]imple in her tastes, and true to the moral instinctions of her woman's nature," in the face of enormous temptation:

> Prosperity corrupts; success dazzles; the false is magnified by glitter and tumult, and those who are thus surrounded soon cease to search in the shade for humble merit, or listen for the still small voice of truth. But Jenny Lind has never suffered the love of the false to enter into her heart.[142]

In a society grown increasingly anxious of middle-class women's seduction by the marketplace, Jenny Lind showed how consumption could be both conspicuous and self-effacing.

Lind's aura of humility also helped middle-class enthusiasts rationalize their enjoyment of operatic music. By 1850 grand opera was well established as the property of U.S. elites.[143] This was most obvious in New York, where, even before its 1847 opening, the Astor Place Opera House was widely attacked for its exclusionary dress code, elite backers, and high-priced seats (Buckley 264–66). In 1849 plebeian New Yorkers lashed out against the Opera House in the Astor Place riot, an affray that pitted working-class demonstrators against the supporters of actor William Charles Macready, the police, and the state militia. The riot climaxed on May 10, when the militia fired into a crowd outside the Opera House, killing twenty-two people. In the wake of those shootings, the press largely blamed the predominantly working-class victims, but some papers also charged the Opera House "nabobs" with fomenting class resentment.[144] For many Americans, white kid gloves and opera cloaks had become symbols of a dangerous class pretension—this at the very moment when Lind's middle-class supporters were trying them on for the first time. As they made their way to the dress circle, those fans needed to be reassured that they were not trying to ape the Astor Place nabobs. N. P. Willis told them what they wanted to hear:

[W]hile the Astor Place Opera-house will hold all who constitute
"The Fashion," it would take the Park and all the Squares of the
city to hold those who constitute the rage for Jenny Lind. No! let
the city be as wicked as the reports of crime make it to be — let
the vicious be as thick and the taste for the meretricious and
artificial be as apparently uppermost — the lovers of goodness are
the Many, the supporters and seekers of what is pure and
disinterested are the substantial bulk of the People.[145]

Willis believed he was watching his Five-Dollar-Billers bring their
sincerity to the high cultural ground formerly occupied by the
nabobs. The Lind tour was a final stroke in a quiet revolution by
which opera, that "luxury of the exclusives," had "become a popular taste." It was a cultural transformation with profound social implications, for it demonstrated "the slightness of separa-
tion between the upper and middle classes in our country."[146]

Other commentators agreed that Lind had democratized U.S.
musical culture. Emboldened by her success, they called for the
staging of opera for the masses. Boston critic John Sullivan
Dwight contrasted Lind's success with Max Maretzek's failure to
establish a permanent company at the Astor Place Opera House:
"[T]he fault seems to be that nearly all the operatic experiments
in this country have appealed to fashionable rather than to popular support. Music in America is to be supported by *the people*."[147] But Lind's impact on U.S. cultural hierarchy was more
ambiguous than the singer's fans admitted. Rather than com-
mending her for broadening the audience for classical music,
some attacked her for tainting it with folk songs and popular
ballads. Visiting European performers such as Ole Bull and the
Germania Orchestra had accustomed U.S. concertgoers to such
hybrid programs, but some people demanded more from Jenny
Lind (Hamm 219–20). A few even regretted her performance of
Italian arias in lieu of the "really great music" of Germany.[148]
Complaining that "the programmes have been arranged with a too
timid and exclusive eye to gratifying public taste," the *New York
Tribune* pleaded for the works of Mozart, Handel, and Men-
delssohn.[149] Lind eventually satisfied the *Tribune*, but many reviewers continued to see the tour as a squandered opportunity.
*Holden's Dollar Magazine* pointedly asked: "Is the cause of opera
advanced a jot among us? Are the real prospects of American

music bettered?"[150] By the time Lind left the country, a surprising number of critics were ready to answer no. For them, the tour was the worst of all possible worlds: duping the masses with clap-trap they mistook for art, it denied connoisseurs the opportunity to hear one of the world's greatest singers at her best.[151]

If Lind's effort to stake out a middle ground in the U.S. cultural hierarchy met with mixed reviews, so did Barnum's. On the one hand, the tour served to boost the showman's reputation dramatically among elitists. The most spectacular evidence of this came in 1853, when the gentry at *Putnam's Monthly* nominated Barnum as the manager of the new opera house (soon to be named the Academy of Music) being built in New York City. Of Barnum, the magazine insisted, "He comprehends that, with us, the opera need not necessarily be the luxury of the few, but the recreation of the many."[152] But the showman remained under siege by highbrows who accused him of exploiting Lind and de-grading music. Dwight, for one, celebrated Lind's rupture with Barnum as the "joyful telegraphic whispers of 'the Nightingale uncaged.'"[153] Perhaps the best illustration of the showman's frus-trations at seeking a middle-brow cultural space for the tour came in the contradictory criticism of the *North American Miscellany*. The magazine lauded the lack of musical sophistication in Lind's audiences, gushing over the "[b]looming country lasses" and aged villagers who encored Lind's ballads while ignoring her arias. In their applause, it heard "a more honest compliment than the bravest plaudits of the singing-masters."[154] But there was a line in the U.S. cultural hierarchy below which even the *Miscellany* was unwilling to go. Barnum crossed it when he began using Lind to promote his Great Asiatic Caravan, Museum, and Menagerie. Appalled that he had "introduced the name of the modest, yet wonderful singer, in most shameless contact with his wax im-agery, and men without arms," the *Miscellany* was relieved by the news that Barnum and Lind had parted ways.[155] In the end, Barnum's "instincts" had proved "of too *level* a make for consort with the Nightingale of the North."[156]

By the time of Barnum's rupture with Lind, the complaints of highbrows had combined with lower-class violence to explode the fiction of the singer's "universal" patronage. Within a few years, even Barnum would acknowledge the tour's class-segregated audience (*Life* 400). But even as he acknowledged the social politics of the Lind tour, Barnum was disguising those of his American Museum. As we shall see in the following chapters, his strategy of privileging an audience within, and in some cases antagonistic to, his larger ostensible public was only one of the lessons he gleaned from the Lind tour. Equally important was the necessity of transcending social and political struggle through the rhetoric of patriotism, Christianity, and domesticity. But if Barnum's evasions were frequently exposed during the Lind tour, they were even more vulnerable during his tenure as museum proprietor.

# 3

## Barnum's Long Arms: The American Museum

The seaserpent may have an instinct to retire into the depths of the sea when about to die, & so leave no bones on the shores for naturalists. The seaserpent is afraid of Mr. Owen; but his heart sunk within him when, at last, he heard that Barnum was born.

— Ralph Waldo Emerson, *Journals* (1853)

[N]ow I've seen the babies, and been standing for an hour, I want to see BARNUM, and then I'm ready to go back to old Kentuck.

— overheard from a spectator at the American Museum's baby show, *New York Times* (1855)

Even as he priced the lower classes out of the Lind concerts, Barnum could legitimately claim a popular patronage — bigender, cross-class, multiethnic, and variously aged — at his American Museum, which admitted the million at twenty-five cents the ticket, children half price.[1] In *Life* Barnum distinguished between the audiences of the Lind tour and his museums: whereas the former entertained "the cultivated and wealthy as well as . . . the middling classes," the latter educated "the masses" (400).[2] Lind could have corroborated her manager's point. When she took an afternoon off from rehearsal to visit the American Museum (doubtless at Barnum's urgent request), she was besieged by the plebeian New Yorkers who were largely absent from her paying audiences.[3] Such cross-class encounters were common both at the Broadway and Ann Street Museum, which Lind visited, and at Barnum's second Museum at 539 and 541 Broadway.[4] In decades that saw New York's neighborhoods — and the amusements that catered to them—splinter along lines of class and ethnicity, everybody went to Barnum's. As Peter Buckley observes:

> Barnum managed to house on a single site, forms of exhibition
> and amusement that had previously belonged to different areas
> of the city and that had catered to markedly different "tastes."
> Here was a place that Philip Hone and Mike Walsh could browse,
> if not arm in arm, then at least side by side. (495)

Patricians like Hone and plebeian rebels like Walsh were both welcome at the Museum, but Barnum targeted the classes that fell between them. The Museum privileged the values of its core patronage of middle- and working-class "respectables": entrepreneurialism, temperance, Christianity, and domesticity. The wisdom of this strategy was borne out at the ticket office. Reflecting on the receipts of the Ann Street Museum in the wake of the fire that destroyed it, the *New York Commercial* concluded that "it was the most extensively patronized of any place in the country."[5] But not everyone was happy with Barnum's middle-brow Museum. This chapter examines the critique and competition that the Museum faced from both ends of the cultural ladder: after exploring Barnum's struggle with the highbrows over what a museum—particularly an "American Museum"—should be, I examine his tussle with the Bowery over the class and gender politics of commercial amusements. From either perspective, Barnum's American Museum emerges as a chief site to witness the social and cultural struggles waged over nineteenth-century amusements.

## An Enterprising Museum

When Barnum purchased the American Museum from the heirs of John Scudder in December 1841, he helped bring about a major transformation in the function and cultural stature of the nation's proprietary museums.[6] Over the previous four decades, control over those collections had steadily passed from philanthropists to showmen. Barnum's Museum, like several of its major rivals, had roots in the civic and cultural ambitions of late-eighteenth-century patricians. It was the direct descendant of the museum opened in 1791 by New York's Tammany Society at the urging of merchant/philanthropist John Pintard.[7] Tammany's American Museum sought to provide a core for the city's cultural life by preserving U.S. history, natural history, and art.[8] It resembled Charles Willson Peale's famous Philadelphia collection — also known as the American Museum — not only in its national aspirations, but also in its governing board of "substantial citizens" (Sellers 52). Although the Tammany Society withdrew support from its museum after four years (turning the collection over to keeper Gardiner Baker), wealthy and educated Americans would continue to view museums as agents of cultural and civic progress in the early decades of the nineteenth century. In 1820, Cincinnati physician and civic booster Daniel Drake led the foundation of the Western Museum in a bid to establish the Queen City as a regional cultural center. But after three years of insufficient receipts, Drake's dream was turned over to scientist/showman Joseph Dorfeuille, who made the Western Museum pay by supplementing its natural history collections with sensation, fantasy, and fraud.[9] Dorfeuille's rise portended the explosive growth of museums in Jacksonian America: by the 1840s, showmen from Boston to St. Louis had adopted *museum* as the term of choice for halls featuring a dizzying variety of cheap entertainments. A museum visitor in this period was as likely to encounter freaks and mermaids as Indian relics and animal bones. For many cultural historians, the ultimate symbol of the commercialization of the form was Barnum's purchase of the Peale collections that his museums had helped drive out of business in New York, Baltimore, and Philadelphia.[10] By 1849, when Barnum joined Moses Kimball (proprietor of the Boston Museum) in purchasing the remnants of Edmund Peale's Philadelphia collection, he had established himself as the dominant player in the field. His American Museum would eventually swallow other collections in New York City and Utica; it would also exchange performers and curiosities with smaller museums across the nation. The predominance of Barnum's Museum meant that the day's star attractions (e.g., the Siamese Twins Chang and Eng, the Aztec Children, and the bearded Madame Josephine Clofullia) would all eventually find their way into its halls. Barnum's, therefore, was a distillation of the very best, and the very worst, that the proprietary museum had to offer.

The American Museum was a prime place to experience the variety bordering on chaos that defined the proprietary museum. Barnum's holdings may have been uneven, but they were indisputably varied, especially in natural history. Before the formation of the Central Park Zoo in the mid-1860s, the American Museum was the best place in New York to view exotic animals.[11] The menagerie at the Ann Street Museum included (at various times): tigers, crocodiles, giraffes, anacondas, grizzly bears, a hippopotamus, a sloth, and a manatee. In 1857 the Museum added the nation's first public aquariums, stocked with fish from the tropics and the trout streams of New York State. The living animals were even more numerous after 1866, when Barnum joined with the Van Amburgh Menagerie Company at his second Museum. The Barnum and Van Amburgh Museum and Menagerie Combination—as it was officially known for its last two years— exhibited such exotica as lynxes, kangaroos, and hyenas. The second Museum also revived its predecessor's famous Happy Family exhibit: a collection of predators and prey (e.g., owls and doves, cats and mice) coexisting unhappily in the same cage. In addition to their living animals, the Museums featured ever-expanding collections of mounted mammals, birds, fish, seashells, minerals, skeletons (the final resting place, apparently, of the menagerie), and insects—many of them described with varying degrees of accuracy in the Museum's numerous cheap guidebooks. Casually intermingled among the natural history collections were a vast, motley array of ethnological artifacts, autographs, coins, armor, weapons, shoes, cosmoramic views, daguerreotypes, paintings, sculpture, automatons, waxworks, portraits, and assorted other curiosities.

As these collections grew over the years, so did the space they occupied. Barnum purchased a collection that occupied four 100-foot halls in the Ann Street building. By expanding into the upper stories of adjacent buildings, he more than doubled his exhibition space by 1854 (*Life* 223).[12] Additional enlargements over the following decade gave him a museum that easily dwarfed its U.S. rivals. By 1865 the Ann Street hall boasted six floors of exhibition space: entering the building from the street, patrons encountered ticket offices and the cosmorama room (featuring peep-show views of foreign cities and landscapes); from there, they passed either downstairs to the basement, which held a tank for whales and hippopotami, or upstairs to four floors of exhibition halls jammed with display cases, aquariums, picture and waxwork galleries, and animal cages.[13] When all of this went up in smoke in July 1865, Barnum immediately began rebuilding his empire at his new location. By September he was able to unveil a new collection, which, in turn, was soon spilling out of its five-story home; over the next three years, the Barnum and Van Amburgh Museum also filled up a building next door.

With hundreds of thousands of objects to choose from, even Barnum's harshest critics usually found something to praise in his Museum. No one questioned the value of his Peale portraits, seashells, and tropical fish. But not even those treasures could save the Museum's reputation among highbrows. They seized upon Barnum's as proof of the pathetic inadequacy of U.S. museums vis-à-vis their European counterparts. Perhaps the most devastating attack on the Museum appeared in *The Nation* after the 1865 fire. The anonymous author accused Barnum of, among other things, unscientific exhibitions, disreputable patrons, and profit-driven fakery. His critique is worth examining in some detail, as it stands as a compendium of three decades of elitist complaints about U.S. museums; moreover, it foreshadows the lasting symbolic importance of Barnum's to the patricians who would found the nation's great public museums in the decades after the Civil War.[14]

That *The Nation* would deign to consider Barnum's at all—even to attack it—is a sure sign that the New York gentry had museums on the brain in 1865. With the war just over, city patricians were preparing to fulfill the long-deferred dream of a museum (or, as it turned out, museums) worthy of the nation's cultural capital. In the late 1860s, merchants, bankers, artists, and scientists would come together to found the American Museum of Natural History and the Metropolitan Museum of Art. By the time those institutions opened their doors, Barnum's Museum existed only in memory, the showman's second New York hall having burned in 1868. But Barnum continued to haunt the museum founders as they planned the funding, administration, and mission of the new institutions. The patricians, as Roy Rosenzweig and Elizabeth Blackmar observe, struggled with the legacy of Barnum over "the very definition of *museum*" (353). As they crafted institutions that were public, but not popular, the New York gentry remembered the American Museum as everything they were trying to avoid.

One thing that clearly worried the highbrows about Barnum's Museum was its popular patronage. *The Nation*'s critic reserved his most scathing language for the showman's audience. While acknowledging the occasional presence of respectables in the American Museum, he slandered the bulk of its patronage as "disreputable," "vicious and degraded," and the "worst and most corrupt classes of our people."[15] The classism here is obvious enough: there is no reason to believe that the Museum's predominantly middle- and working-class visitors were any more vicious or corrupt than gentry who published and read *The Nation*. But such hostility to the million was routine among the elite supporters of the city's new museums. Although they relied on the public for land, buildings, and partial funding, the founders of the Metropolitan Museum of Art and the American Museum of Natural History refused to democratize them. They concentrated power in private, elite-dominated boards and, devout Protestants that they were, fought to keep their museums closed on Sunday, the only day of leisure for many of the city's workers (Rosenzweig and Blackmar 353–63).[16] As Lawrence Levine has demonstrated, the story was much the same at public museums founded in other cities after the Civil War (146–58).

Judged by this standard, Barnum's Museum was a bastion of egalitarianism. The *Herald* exaggerated when it claimed that the American Museum's policy was "'a quarter a ticket and no questions asked,'" but Barnum's was far friendlier to the masses than its public successors.[17] Like other New York amusement halls, the American Museum was closed on Sunday, but for the rest of the week its extended hours (sunrise to 10:00 p.m.) and cheap admission put it within the reach of all but the poorest patrons.[18] Moreover, its plain-English displays and guidebooks were accessible even to the barely literate. Barnum's, to be sure, spent almost as much time misinforming the masses as enlightening them, and some of its frauds were anything but innocent. As we shall see, shams like the "What Is It?" would have perpetuated the racist ignorance of white patrons. But there was also a democratic side to some of Barnum's frauds. When the showman challenged the scientists to explain the Feejee Mermaid or the "What Can They Be?" he encouraged a healthy skepticism among his patrons toward institutional authority.[19] Living Barnaby Diddleum's dream of duping "those who pretend to be scientific, but who are but asses in lions' skins," Barnum's Museum alternately revered and ridiculed the "doctors."[20] This was obvious in the winter of 1860–61, when the Museum authenticated its South African tribesmen with a letter from Harvard professor Louis Agassiz; but it also cited its latest frauds, the Aztec Children, as proof of Barnum's stature as a "naturalist" and "man of research."[21] By 1860 those titles were not to be assumed casually. Internationally renowned scholars such as Agassiz and Darwin had established the natural sciences as prestigious disciplines worthy of enshrinement in universities, scholarly institutes, and museums. But Barnum's remained undaunted. The American Museum, as Neil Harris has argued, was a place where laypeople could still take on the experts and win (74–79).

To separate the Barnums from the Agassizes of the world, highbrows increasingly drew the line at the ticket window. By midcentury they had begun condemning proprietary museums for their commercialism. Earlier U.S. museums, in contrast, were expected to conduct themselves like the private businesses that they were. Even a purist like Charles Willson Peale did not hesitate to employ publicity stunts and crowd-pleasing attractions.[22] In his day, such practices were not believed to compromise a museum's integrity. Thomas Bender documents a similar indifference among early-nineteenth-century New Yorkers toward the commercialism of Barnum's predecessor: "No one was at all bothered or uncertain about the propriety of [John] Scudder's commercializing his cabinet. Only later would the presentation of culture become sacred and non-commercial, the project of elite-dominated non-profit organizations" (66).

As cultural hierarchy hardened at midcentury, however, elitists became increasingly wary of the proprietary museum's status as commercial amusement. In 1853 the anticommercial sentiment was strong enough for the New York Times to write Barnum's Museum out of existence. Urging the city to purchase Dr. Henry Abbott's collection of Egyptian antiquities, it flatly stated, "We have no Museums."[23] The *Times* was not the first to call for publicly supported museums; Peale had done so more than half a century before. But as the *New York Herald* demonstrated, it was only after the Civil War that the movement gained much momentum. In 1864 the paper urged Barnum to tear down his Museum and replace it "with one worthy of the city." Otherwise, it warned, rival "capitalists" would beat him to the punch.[24] Two years later, however, the paper derided capitalist "museum mongers"—and Barnum in particular—while insisting, "Private individuals may get up a show, but a museum, to be of any sterling value, must be a public institution."[25] The *Herald's* anticommercial turn suggests the speed at which the city's patricians were gathering support for their plans. It also suggests their success at defining their new museums against their proprietary predecessors.[26]

Barnum would eventually concede that commercialism had weakened his Museum. Writing in response to *The Nation's* critique, he admitted, "[M]y Museum was not so refined or classic or scientifically arranged as the foreign governmental institutions, for mine had to support my family, while those require annually from the government thousands of pounds."[27] But it was unlike Barnum to make such a concession; he appears to have stooped to it in this instance to gain support for the "Free National Museum" that he was vainly trying to start.[28] Throughout his career at the American Museum, Barnum was more likely to celebrate its commercialism than to apologize for it. In 1844, for example, his European Correspondence boldly attempted to rally an audience around the superiority of proprietary museums to public ones:

> I will show the citizens of the Old World that, in good and
> glorious republican America, the aid of the government for such
> a purpose is not required, but that, under our form of
> government, *individual enterprise* can effect what even the
> government itself cannot accomplish in other countries.[29]

If the United States was the land of triumphant enterprise, then a proprietary museum was more nationally representative than a public one—especially a proprietary museum belonging to one of the nation's most enterprising men. Over the next twenty-four years, Barnum's Museum would push this argument to its logical extremes.

Highbrows may have advocated museums as refuges from the marketplace, but the American Museum was a nonstop celebration of trade. After wandering New York City streets vibrant with flags, theatrical bills, and commercial placards, Russian traveler Aleksandr Lakier mused:

> No one better than the American can depict in an advertisement the beauty and sweetness of the most ordinary things. . . . Well, how can one not be tempted, especially when Yankee Doodle rings out from the corner balcony, when it is declared that not for long will New Yorkers have the pleasure of seeing the wonders of Barnum somewhere in some saloon or theater. (67–68)

Barnum also stood for advertising in the minds of many Americans. By the 1850s, the latest innovations in marketing were commonly known as Barnumisms, and most of them were on view at the American Museum.[30] Barnum attracted attention to his hall through a series of ingenious publicity stunts, but the Museum was its own best advertisement.[31] The showman decorated the roof and facade of his Ann Street Museum with flags, paintings, banners, an illuminated color wheel, a Drummond light, a brass band, and gas letters spelling out his name (see Figure 4).[32] Although New York merchants soon adopted many of these gimmicks, Barnum's facade would remain the most garish in New York. The visual (and aural) noise on the Museum's exterior prevented some patrons from appreciating the curiosities within: even after viewing Barnum's collection, British tourist George Borrett was convinced that it occupied "the mere outside shell" of its ad-bedecked hall (279).[33] Inside, the selling was even more intense. Performers hawked their biographies and *cartes de visite*; phrenologists and fortune tellers offered analysis and prediction; craft workers sold ivory carvings, blown glass, and finger rings turned from the beams of Abraham Lincoln's cabin.[34] Also available were cheap copies of Barnum's *Life*, as well as guidebooks, pamphlets, and plays packed with ads for the Museum and city merchants. Any money remaining in visitors' pockets was vulnerable to Barnum's pistol gallery, refreshment stands, Curiosity Shop, and theater, the so-called Lecture Room. In its final years, the Lecture Room featured advertising clocks—displaying a jeweler's name on their faces—and "P. T. Barnum's Improved Mercantile Advertising Drop Scene."[35] A fixture at both Museums in

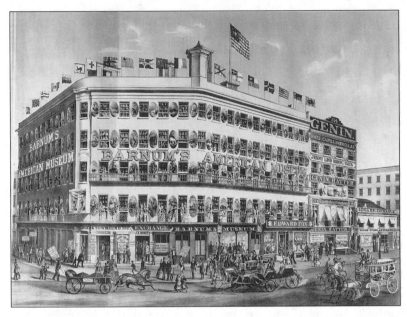

Figure 4. Barnum's American Museum, circa 1851. (Collection of the New-York Historical Society)

the 1860s, the drop curtain was covered with panels bearing the names, addresses, and specialties of numerous city merchants and publishers.[36] For highbrows, it was perhaps the best example of the philistinism that pervaded the Museum. In 1867 *The Nation* culminated a second attack on Barnum and his amusement hall with a satire on his play, *The Christian Martyrs*:

> In the final tableau, Constantine's cross appears in the sky, and
> the Roman empire is converted amidst bursts of applause,
> whereupon the curtain falls and is seen to be covered thickly
> with puffs of "Horse Liniment," "Yahoo Bitters," "Ready Reliefs"
> and "Pain Extractors," and other quack medicines.[37]

Patent medicines were not the only alcoholic fluids to appear on the curtain: Barnum's drop scene also promoted wine and liquor merchants.[38] For the showman to permit such ads in his teetotaling amusement hall—in the theater that had made *The Drunkard* famous, no less—suggests the way entrepreneurialism ruled the American Museum. After a day at Barnum's, few would dispute its claim that "the enterprise and energy of this establishment is surpassed by that of none in the world."[39]

Patrons did not need advertising clocks or curtains to convince them of the Museum's commitment to entrepreneurialism. The Museum's very existence was a testament to "that Spirit of Enterprise incarnate, Mr. P. T. BARNUM."[40] The showman underscored this fact by personally regaling patrons with stories of his latest exploits. In 1860, for example, he celebrated his repurchase of the Museum from its temporary owners, John Greenwood and Henry Butler, by taking to the Lecture Room stage to recount his climb out of bankruptcy.[41] Those who missed Barnum's performance had to settle for a copy of *Life* or the briefer biographical sketches that appeared in various Museum pamphlets. The American Museum offered the chance to experience, and vicariously participate in, all of Barnum's moneymaking schemes, including ones not even remotely connected to it. A popular American Museum poster from the 1860s pictured Museum favorites such as the Happy Family and Tom Thumb alongside unrelated Barnum productions, including East Bridgeport and Jenny Lind.[42] Barnum helped the Museum celebrate the entirety of his career by decorating it with memorabilia from his other enterprises (e.g., a Phillips Fire Annihilator, Jenny Lind and Joice Heth waxworks, and a photograph of his financial adviser, James D. Johnson). For English traveler John Delaware Lewis, however, the American Museum's significance lay less in its Barnumesque icons than in the entrepreneurialism that had brought them there:

> Barnum is not an ordinary showman. He is not one who will be handed down to posterity, only on the strength of the objects which he has exhibited, or the curiosities which he has brought to light. He stands alone. Adopting Mr. Emerson's idea, I should say that Barnum is a representative man. He represents the enterprise and energy of his countrymen in the nineteenth century, as Washington represented their resistance to oppression in the century preceding. (24–25)

Lewis was right to rate the objects in the Museum's collections below the "enterprise and energy" of its proprietor. The American Museum clearly subordinated the former to the latter by spinning what might be called "narratives of acquisition" around many of its exhibits. Those narratives overshadowed all other contexts for their subjects, including aesthetic and scientific ones. Whether the management was promoting its most recently acquired waxwork, animal, or automaton, it was likely to emphasize where it had come from, how it had arrived, and how much it had cost. To be certain, the Museum always retained its strictly nonnarrative patriotic and Christian icons, but Barnum broke with earlier museum proprietors in presenting his collection less as a collection of sacred treasures from his country's past and more as an intersection of stories about its entrepreneurial present and industrial future. In the aftermath of the 1865 fire, it became clear that Barnum's stories were far more important than the objects they supposedly contextualized. The *New York Herald* attributed the showman's decision not to salvage any of his treasures from the Museum's ruins to the fact that "it became rather a difficult matter to identify them or trace their history, as was so carefully marked out while on exhibition."[43] Rather than rewrite narratives around his old curiosities, Barnum apparently found it easier to generate new stories around new objects.

In marketing his attractions through elaborate tales of search and seizure, Barnum defied the conventions of natural history display established by Charles Willson Peale and revived at the American Museum of Natural History in the 1880s.[44] Peale pioneered the exhibition of mounted animals in front of realistic painted backdrops of their habitats (Sellers 19). Whereas his settings were cleared of human intruders, Barnum often foregrounded the processes through which men had killed or captured his specimens. This was obvious in his presentation of his "white whales." The showman announced the arrival of his first pair of belugas with a card in the New York press that invited readers to join him behind the scenes; in it he describes his journey to Labrador in search of the whales, his hiring of thirty-five local men to capture them, his arrangements with steamers and railroads "to convey these leviathans to New-York at the fastest possible speed," and his construction of their "reservoir" in the Museum's basement.[45] The focus of the exhibit was clearly not on the whales, but on the complicated process that brought them to the Museum, a point Barnum underscores in *Struggles* when he casually notes that the whales "soon died" (565), enabling him to send agents back to Labrador to restart the process.[46] In 1865 the Museum symbolically reenacted the acquisition of its eighth and ninth belugas with the performance of "GEORGE, the great WHALE CAPTURER," who entered the whale tank daily.[47]

As its marketing of the belugas indicates, the American Museum's narratives of acquisition would have been impossible without the aid of the press. We have already seen that elitists such as George Templeton Strong and E. L. Godkin likened the cultural crimes of Barnum to those of his journalistic contemporaries.[48] Such comparisons were inspired in part by the symbiotic relationship between the American Museum and the New York City newspapers. In their willingness to publish Barnum's press releases, those papers often functioned as surrogate Museum guidebooks. The New York press also served the Museum as a model—especially in its tendency to foreground the process of news acquisition. Like Barnum, the largest papers plumed themselves on their international reach, and were not shy about calling attention to it. Their stories set a pattern for the American Museum ads that appeared in adjacent columns, especially in headlines that subordinated content to the narrative of acquisition. In 1865 the *Herald* introduced a story on the transatlantic cable in typical fashion:

EUROPE.
Arrival of the Germania Off
Cape Race.
THREE DAYS LATER NEWS.
THE CABLE
The Shore End of the Atlantic
Line Laid....[49]

Once the cable was finished, the phrase "By Telegraph to the Herald" began replacing the names of ships like the *Germania* in the paper's headlines, but the *Herald* continued to foreground the narrative of news acquisition. Also persisting was the ideological effect of such a format. Like the American Museum's stories of train-borne whales, the steamships and telegraphs in the paper's headlines proclaimed it both a chronicler and an agent of U.S. enterprise.

The Museum's closest print analogue, however, was not the metropolitan daily papers, but their pictorial weekly counterparts. The Museum's display of exotic physical artifacts and people alongside the stories of their acquisition closely paralleled the mode of the pictorial newsweeklies that Barnum helped bring to the United States in the 1850s. In 1852 Barnum joined Henry D. and Alfred Ely Beach in founding New York's *Illustrated News* after the pattern of the ten-year-old *Illustrated London News*; both weeklies accompanied stories on news and culture with plentiful oversize woodcut illustrations. From the first, Barnum apparently viewed his pictorial weekly and his Museum as intimately linked in their subject matter. He made the connection in an 1852 letter to Bayard Taylor, who was preparing to leave with Commodore Perry's expedition to Japan. Barnum requested that Taylor send him "drawings & sketches" for the *Illustrated News* and curiosities for the Museum (*SL* 62–63). After devoting much of its existence to the Japan expedition, the Barnum and Beach pictorial folded with its forty-eighth issue, a victim of squabbles between the owners and editors, a shortage of talented illustrators, and the nascent state of printing press technology.[50] Its goodwill and engravings were sold to *Gleason's Pictorial Drawing-Room Companion*.

Barnum could rely on *Gleason's* for friendly coverage of his Museum and traveling shows over the following years, but he was even closer to his pictorial's New York successor, *Frank Leslie's Illustrated Newspaper*. The professional relationship between Barnum and Frank Leslie went back to 1848, when the newly emigrated British illustrator produced a popular catalog for the American Museum (*ST* 268). Over the next five years Leslie would print Jenny Lind concert programs, tour with Barnum and Lind, and direct the art department at the New York *Illustrated News*.[51] By the late 1850s, Leslie had escaped Barnum's shadow to emerge as a self-promoting cultural entrepreneur in his own right. He would eventually supply middle-class America with an array of cheap pictorial magazines featuring fiction, fashion, the arts, and humor. His debt to Barnum was most apparent in his flagship publication, *Frank Leslie's Illustrated Newspaper*, which echoed the American Museum in celebrating its own "energy and enterprise" while documenting that of other Americans.[52] Whether it was reporting on William Walker's exploits in Nicaragua or Matthew Perry's in Asia, *Leslie's* consistently promoted the penetration of the United States into foreign lands and markets. It illustrated its imperialist narratives with woodcuts of bizarre-looking people, plants, and animals, counterparts of the American Museum's Egyptian hippopotamus and South African tribesmen. *Leslie's* acknowledged its ties to Barnum by backing him in his bankruptcy and applauding his Museum. An 1865 story on the showman's latest whales celebrated his "long arms":

> Mr. Barnum's writ runs in all the bailiwicks of nature. Giraffe in South Africa; . . . Python coiling around Javanese forest trees; or White Whale swimming in Arctic seas — are each and all liable to apprehension, by this unresting searcher, or by his "sufficient deputy."[53]

The ideological and professional ties between Barnum's Museum and *Leslie's* were strengthened by similarities of form. Barnum makes this clear in *Struggles* when he recalls his scheme, in his first year as proprietor, of decorating his building's facade with oval paintings of various animals. To depict the building's transformed appearance, he anachronistically invokes a print form virtually unknown in the United States in the early 1840s: "Strangers would look at this great pictorial magazine and argue that an establishment with so many animals on the outside must have something on the inside, and in they would go to see" (141–42).[54] Barnum's comparison of his Museum to a pictorial magazine hinges on their common mode of combining visual exhibit and narrative text. But whereas the reader of *Leslie's* merely looked to the adjacent page for the story, Barnum's patron had to pay a quarter for the "something on the inside." To follow Barnum's comparison, that something was not the living zoological referent of the painting, but the narrative of acquisition that explained its appearance on the building's facade.

The American Museum's intimacy with popular print culture won it no friends among highbrows. Their idea of a museum was not a pictorial magazine, but a library. The *Herald* echoed the city's patricians when it called for a public museum that would be "a library of facts."[55] Although the tie between museums and libraries was metaphoric for the *Herald*, it was literal for many patricians. In the century's last decade, the *Atlantic Monthly* would publish an appeal by Edward Morse titled "If Public Libraries,

Why Not Public Museums?"[56] Inspired by the example of Britain, the metropolitan gentry envisioned libraries as important components of public museums devoted to "[a]ll those valuable things which men do not consume but keep."[57] Barnum's things, however, were valuable precisely because they would not keep: the whales would die, Tom Thumb would leave town, *The Drunkard* would (eventually) close. Judging from its frequency in American Museum bills, Barnum's slogan might have been "THIS WEEK ONLY." The American Museum may have been born of the desire of the Tammanyites to "collect and preserve" U.S. history, but Barnum's was more interested in consuming and selling its past: even Lincoln's cabin was whittled into trinkets.[58] Such practices inevitably revolted those who envisioned museums as temples for sacred treasures; they attacked the American Museum for pandering to its patrons' "most morbid appetite for the marvellous."[59] But for Barnum, as for his journalistic collaborators, nothing was harder to sell than old news.

## A Respectable Museum

Barnum kept his eye on the highbrows, but he was equally concerned with his Museum's relation to the lower rungs of the cultural ladder. In New York, those rungs were occupied by the Bowery, the East Side district of plebeian commerce and amusement. By the late 1830s the Bowery had emerged as the national capital of working-class culture, with its own distinctive fashions, dialects, sports, theater, music, and celebrities.[60] It was a culture complex enough to accommodate an array of plebeian identities: from unionist rebels to hard-drinking traditionalists to upwardly mobile revivalists.[61] The East Side's dominant image, however, was set by the b'hoys, the young white males who gave it a reputation for belligerence, secularism, energy, and plebeian pride. The b'hoys would leave their mark on Barnum's American Museum, both as patrons and as performers. From the first, however, the showman favored his Broadway visitors over his Boweryites. By dedicating his Museum to entrepreneurialism, temperance, domesticity, and Christianity, he targeted a core of middle-class patrons and their "respectable" working-class allies.

In a city growing more class segmented with each year, it would prove a difficult alliance to sustain.

As a center of middlebrow amusements, Barnum's Ann Street Museum could not have been better located. Buckley points out that it stood at the symbolic midpoint of the two routes of mid-century New York culture: the eastern route passing up Chatham Street and the Bowery and the western route traveling up Broadway to the fashionable Fifteenth Ward and—after 1847—the Astor Place Opera House (31).[62] With his professional experience at the Vauxhall Gardens and the Bowery Amphitheatre, Barnum knew how to appeal to an East Side audience. This was obvious in the Museum's Lecture Room, whose repertory in Barnum's first decade consisted largely of the blackface minstrels, impressionists, and comic singers who also performed on the Bowery. In 1848 the Bowery's most famous hero took a turn in the Lecture Room when Pete Morris sang "'I'm one of the B'hoys,' in the character of Mose."[63] Variety performers like Morris would be pushed to the bottom of the Museum's bills after 1850, when Barnum recast his Lecture Room as a home of the "moral drama." The Museum would never fully abandon its Bowery ties, however. East Side minstrels, actors, and comedians would continue to appear in the Lecture Room—especially in the summer—for the rest of its history.

Barnum's reliance on East Side culture encouraged some commentators to view the Museum as an annex of the Bowery. In 1856, that bible of Bowery amusements, the *New York Clipper,* placed Barnum's "on the east side . . . although not literally so."[64] The paper would eventually go so far as to judge the Museum "one point lower" on the city's cultural hierarchy than the New and Old Bowery Theatres.[65] Likewise, the humor sheet *Humbug's American Museum* transplanted Barnum's to the heart of the Bowery in a caricature that populated it with b'hoys, blackface minstrels, and a fire company (Buckley 497). If the Museum belonged on the East Side, critics reasoned, then so did its proprietor. In 1855 the *Boston Courier* spoofed Barnum as a dialect-spouting "Mr. Joyce Heth," who defended his Baby Show with certificates from the Bowery's own Mike Walsh and Captain Isaiah Rynders.[66] The paper invoked the Bowery Barnum to deflate the showman's pose as a temperance philanthropist and amusement reformer. At a time when Barnum aligned himself with the likes of William Ellery Channing, the paper insisted that his real peers were on the East Side.[67]

The real Barnum would carefully limit the East Side's impact on his Museum. Rather than an extension of the Bowery, his Museum often stood as a refutation of it. This was obvious in its celebration of entrepreneurial manhood. The Bowery had its own codes of masculinity, which, as Elliott Gorn explains, were grounded in the notion of honor (142–44). Traditionalist workers believed that to be a man was to fight for one's own honor as well as that of one's family, friends, fire company, political party, and nation. Bowery traditionalists expected all men—whether butchers, prize fighters, or politicians—to assert their manhood with their fists.[68] Broadway, in contrast, idealized a man's power *over* his body rather than *through* it. As Gail Bederman writes, "[M]iddle-class parents taught their sons to build a strong manly 'character' as they would build a muscle, through repetitive exercises of control over impulse" (6). Barnum's autobiographies predictably define what he calls the "elements of manliness in my character" in strictly middle-class terms (*ST* 386). *Life* attests to both his distaste for physical violence and his prodigious self-control.[69] But it is *Struggles* that most directly pits Barnum (and his implied bourgeois reader) against Bowery masculinity. Recalling his first year at the Museum, the showman describes an Independence Day confrontation with two vestrymen from St. Paul's Church, which had the misfortune of facing the Museum across Broadway. The vestrymen are outraged that Barnum has decided to advertise his Museum by tying a string of flags to a tree in their churchyard. They order him to remove it; he responds with calm arguments that only irritate them further. As the case begins to look desperate, Barnum turns to the East Side for help:

> [A]ssuming an angry air, I rolled up my sleeves, and exclaimed, in a loud tone,—
>
> "Well, Mister, I should just like to see you dare to cut down the American flag on the Fourth of July; you must be a 'Britisher' to make such a threat as that; but I'll show you a thousand pairs of Yankee hands in two minutes, if you dare to attempt to take down the stars and stripes on this great birth-day of American freedom!" (137–38)

The success of Barnum's rhetorical foray up the Bowery is registered by a throng of "excited, exasperated men," one of whom warns a vestryman, "[I]f you want to save a whole bone in your body, you had better slope, and never dare to talk again about hauling down the American flag in the city of New York" (138). Barnum codes this "brawny" speaker as plebeian through his slang, as well as his eagerness to fight for the flag. The anecdote also serves to mark Barnum's own manhood as middle-class. His belligerence — like his bared arms and accent — is a performance calculated to whip his listeners into a fighting frenzy. Unlike them, Barnum wishes to keep the flag flying not as a symbol of American honor, but as an advertisement for his Museum.

At the Museum, as in his autobiography, Barnum generally expected male patrons of all classes to identify with his entrepreneurialism — to accept the flag as an ad. The effectiveness of this strategy was acknowledged by English Museum visitor John Delaware Lewis, who noted that Barnum "has endeared himself to the middle and lower ranks of his countrymen, and seems to stand forth proud and preeminent as their model of a speculator and a man" (25). In his second year at the American Museum, Barnum unveiled an ambitious scheme for uniting workers and employers behind his model of entrepreneurial manhood. Addressing himself to "merchants, mechanics, and business men," he offered to display (for a fee, naturally) business cards, art, goods, and inventions in a newly opened hall in the Museum. Dubbed the Perpetual Fair, the hall would be staffed with a clerk to explain the goods and sell them on commission.[70] The scheme was doubtless partly inspired by the exhibits of machinery and inventions popular in early-nineteenth-century museums (Sellers 265–66). As the showman acknowledged, however, his greatest debt was to the annual fairs of New York's American and Mechanics Institutes, where merchants, manufacturers, and inventors displayed and sold their goods to the general public. (The 1838 fair of the American Institute awarded a premium to Barnum and his partner Proler for their molasses-based boot blacking [*Life* 210].) Attracting tens of thousands of visitors, the fairs were the public celebration of the entrepreneurialism that dominated both institutes.[71] In honor of his own effort to turn the commercial fairs into a permanent New York fixture, Barnum rechristened

his collection the American Museum and Perpetual Fair.[72] Hope-
fully observing, "[T]he time is not far distant when that project
of Mr. Barnum's will be looked upon as one of the greatest bless-
ings to men of business," the Museum drew displays from numerous artisans and merchants.[73] When the American Institute
closed its fair in October, Barnum urged exhibitors to bring their
wares over to his hall.[74]

The American Institute seems to have provided Barnum with
not only exhibitors, but also his scheme of combining entrepreneurialism with amusement. The huge crowds at the institute
fairs had long since attracted the attention of showmen: in 1835
Barnum had exhibited Joice Heth to the overflow at the American
Institute's fair, which was then being held at Niblo's Garden. A
decade later, the popular entertainments at that event had grown
to include singers, musicians, blackface minstrels, and freaks.
Annoyed by the rise of a formidable competitor on New York's
amusement landscape, Barnum accused the American Institute's
managers of "making a mountebank show of their concern every
year, instead of devoting it solely to the exhibition of important
specimens of American industry."[75] Claiming that the fair's entertainers had donated their services for free, Barnum charged the
managers with "resorting to clap-trap, in order to catch a few
more coppers."[76] Barnum was on shaky ground here, given that
his own recently closed Perpetual Fair featured its share of clap-
trap. Its headlining exhibit had been French's Rotary Knitting
Loom, which supposedly manufactured "stockings, gloves, and
every article of wearing apparel to measure, all whole, complete
and seamless!" Better yet, "The whole operation of knitting IS
PERFORMED BY A DOG!"[77] Barnum puffed this exhibit despite
the fact that, as he acknowledged to Moses Kimball, it had "so
much more *poetry* than *reality* about it."[78]

Notwithstanding the best efforts of French's knitting dog, Barnum's fair proved less than perpetual. In 1844, while Barnum
toured with Tom Thumb in Europe, it silently disappeared from
the American Museum's bills and its name.[79] Clearly, Barnum had
overestimated the number of "business men" in his patronage.[80]
But he would preserve his fair's legacy of cross-class entrepreneurialism at the Museum over the following decades. The Museum could look for ideological support to the American and

Mechanics Institutes, which were the leading promoters of the harmony of interests between New York employers and workers. Workers who attended the institutes' lectures and fairs were taught that their success depended upon their diligence, temperance, and self-discipline.[81] It was an ethos that obviously conflicted both with the rebel unionists' critique of the wages system and with the Bowery traditionalists' disdain for middle-class respectability, but it found an eager audience at the Museum.[82] As Bruce McConachie argues, Barnum targeted the same workers who supported the institutes, ones who believed that success was "a matter of respectability and individual effort, not working-class solidarity" (*Melodramatic* 165). Labor historians have dubbed those working-class respectables "revivalists" and "loyalists"—terms that convey their evangelical Protestantism and deference to the middle class.[83] The "aristocrats" of the trades, they were mostly white, native-born, skilled, and well paid. They embraced popular movements for temperance and nativism, but shunned unions. They would have endorsed the success advice spelled out in a Museum pamphlet: "Prosecute faithfully, as Mr. Barnum has done, the duties that fall to your lot; be vigilant, active, and industrious, as he has been; and, with the smiles of Fortune, you will find your highest hopes crowned with success."[84]

As Alan Dawley and Paul Faler have explained, this catalog of virtues—the core of what they call the "industrial morality"—was shared across class lines (468). Employers, rebel unionists, and loyalists all prized vigilance, activity, and industry. At the American Museum, however, the industrial morality was the sole property of loyalists and their middle-class allies; the rebels were nowhere in sight. Barnum cultivated recruits for the loyalist cause by positioning patrons above those who stood outside the industrial morality: the laziness and intemperance of blacks, Indians, and Irish were popular themes in both the Museum and its Lecture Room.[85] In the case of the Irish, however, the Museum was forced into a twofold strategy: while Irish peasants were mocked as preindustrial primitives, assimilated Irish Americans were invited to take their place among the Museum's loyalists. Barnum's split response speaks to his reliance upon the Irish as both subjects and objects of his entrepreneurial rhetoric. In his years as manager, Barnum witnessed the transformation of New York's working class from native-born to immigrant, and the Irish were easily the largest group of immigrants.[86] Irish Americans were prominent at the Museum even before the first waves of Great Famine immigrants. *Struggles* demonstrates this with a famous anecdote from St. Patrick's Day in 1843 in which Barnum lures his brogue-speaking patrons out the Museum's back door with a sign reading, "To the Egress." (They believe it identifies an animal.) The showman prefaces the story by explaining that he had been informed by "some of the Irish population that they meant to visit me in great numbers" on the holiday (*ST* 139). But Barnum pursued Irish Americans far more aggressively than this would suggest. St. Patrick's Day was often celebrated as a "Grand Gala Day" at the Museum, with special attractions suggested by an 1848 ad:

> ST. PATRICK'S DAY—Irishmen will remember that their countryman, Mr. MALONE RAYMOND, will this afternoon and evening give his celebrated illustrations of Irish life, wit, humor, anecdote, repartee, stories of the peasantry... assisted by Mrs. MALONE RAYMOND, and his three daughters, who sing the melodies of their native land. It is expected that hundreds of the sons of Erin will support their countryman on this anniversary of their Patron Saint.[87]

When it wasn't St. Patrick's Day, Barnum continued to spotlight the sons and daughters of Erin with Irish performers, plays, and exhibits.[88] Many of those attractions praised immigrants for adopting the values of the U.S. middle class. Thus, the Museum celebrated Irish American temperance with a waxwork of Father Theobald Mathew (who reciprocated with a visit to the Museum) and Irish industriousness in John Brougham's *Temptation; or, The Irish Emigrant*.[89] But the dominant image of the Irish at the Museum—and throughout midcentury U.S. culture—was the comic peasant. In the Lecture Room, farces like James Pilgrim's *The Limerick Boy; or, Paddy's Mischief* depicted the Irishman as the brawling, hard-drinking, comic antithesis of the Museum's respectables. On the stage, Irish rusticity was the stuff of patronizing comedy, but on the street, it was the weapon of nativists: in the mid-1840s the American Republicans rode to power in New York by accusing Irish Americans of violence, superstition, and drunkenness. The party's popularity among middle-class and revivalist natives helps explain why the Museum lent it a cautious endorsement in 1844.[90] Over the following decades, however, Barnum's usually depicted the Irish immigrant as a figure to be pitied, not reviled. Consider an exhibit described in an 1850 American Museum guidebook:

> An African War Horn, made from the tusk of an elephant, is placed by a pair of Irish Brogans, which, like poor Paddy himself, are soiled and hard worn. It is easy to give a history to them; the property of some peasant of the Emerald Isle, they have frequently borne him over his own roads and up to his own hill tops; but Paddy is denied even his usual potatoes at home, and wishes to emigrate to America.... arriving here, he finds a market for his labor. Paddy can, and now he has the chance, *will* work; good wages and good food soon make a different man of him; his worn hat, his frieze coat, and his "brogans" must be changed for other and better necessaries of the outward man.[91]

Here the Museum tries to merge its two images of the Irish. On the one hand, it commends "Paddy" for his eager assimilation of the industrial morality: with his steady work habits, the immigrant is ready to take his place among Barnum's loyalists. On the other hand, the Museum is also stroking the prejudices of its native-born patrons, especially in its condescending tone and its strategic juxtaposition of the brogans and the African war horn. The pairing would have found a receptive audience among nativists who routinely smeared the Irish with the same epithets they applied to blacks (Roediger 133). In this Museum that mythologized Africa as the home of everything primitive, few of Barnum's patrons could have missed the point: work as he might, "poor Paddy" would always remain closer to the preindustrial African than to the Museum's native-born respectables.

## Family Amusements, Baby Shows, and Strong-Minded Women

The American Museum's effort to unite its middle- and working-class patrons behind the industrial morality was bolstered by its devotion to Christian families. Taking his cue from some of the day's leading Protestant clergymen, Barnum blended entrepreneurialism with religion.[92] Patrons were urged to imitate not only his industry, temperance, and vigilance, but also his Christianity.[93]

The Museum began cultivating ties to the church in Barnum's first year as manager, years before many liberal clergymen would join the movement to Christianize amusements. Its pious attractions would eventually include Lecture Room dramas such as *The Christian Martyrs* and *Joseph in Egypt*, "SCRIPTURE DISSOLVING VIEWS" of Holy Land sites, and, from the Mount of Olives, the trunk of "one of the trees under which the Disciples sat and conversed on the new Gospel dispensation."[94] After the Museum's 1850 renovation, patrons passing through its front door were accosted by waxworks depicting the life of Christ, with scenes of the Nativity, Trial, and Last Supper. The Museum's saturation with Christianity is the context for Barnum's anecdote about a pious Maine "spinster" who mistakes a Lecture Room performance of *Charlotte Temple* for religious "services" (*ST* 155). In *Struggles* the showman remembers chuckling at the woman's naïveté, but even an experienced observer was liable to make the same mistake: on Sundays in the 1860s Barnum regularly turned over his Lecture Room to New York's Christian Alliance for religious services. "The curiosities," he promised, "will not be visible."[95] The Museum's worship services would have pleased Barnum's respectables, but they would have won him little support on the Bowery. With a few exceptions, East Side amusements were thoroughly secular.[96]

As Bruce McConachie and Robert Allen have pointed out, the Museum's Christianity underwrote its effort to cultivate an audience among families.[97] This marked another major departure from an East Side that catered chiefly to single white males. That Barnum saw a family patronage as a middle-class one is obvious in the idealized illustrations of museumgoers that appear in guidebooks and on posters: they depict his audience as well-dressed white couples, often accompanied by children (see Figure 9). Such images clearly misrepresent the cross-class nature of Barnum's public, but they accurately convey his popularity among families. Barnum lured parents by promising to exclude "anything calculated to corrupt the mind or taint the juvenile imagination," and he won over their children by catering to their tastes and lifestyles.[98] On holidays, the Museum urged students to take a break "from the cares and duties of life, and the dull monotony of the school-room."[99] Relief took the form of fairy-tale dramas,

Punch and Judy shows, afternoon matinees, half-price tickets, and such irresistible ads as "NOTICE TO BOYS—1000 living mice wanted for the Baby Anacondas."[100] The popularity of these juvenile attractions was obvious at the ticket office. In 1850, the Museum asserted that children composed "fully one third" of its audience—a claim Barnum would reiterate in the wake of the fire at the Ann Street Museum.[101] Speaking of himself in the third person, he insisted: "Barnum has been made rich by catering for *the children*. The youth of America regard the loss of Barnum's Museum as a loss irreparable. Fathers & mothers mourn its destruction on account of their children" (*SL* 140). The prominence of children in Barnum's patronage was also recognized by many of his contemporaries.[102] Horatio Alger clearly knew what he was doing when he made the Museum one of the favorite haunts of his boy heroes.[103] As Buckley has observed, Barnum was the first U.S. entrepreneur to tap fully the juvenile market for commercial amusements (493).

To justify its claim to the title of "the special place of FAMILY AMUSEMENT IN THE UNITED STATES," the American Museum appealed as energetically to women as it did to children.[104] Scholars have recently pointed out how Barnum feminized his audience by rigorously policing its morals.[105] His Museum was a morally sanitized space for unescorted women; this at a time when many Americans assumed that any single woman in a theater was a prostitute. In 1845 the Museum was already recruiting the "right" kind of woman by excluding the "wrong" kind: "No Admittance for FEMALES OF KNOWN BAD CHARACTER, or other improper persons, so that Ladies and Families will be perfectly safe, and no more exposed to evil companions than in their own Parlors."[106] Over the following decades, genteel rhetoric pervaded the Museum's appeals to women; they were typically addressed as parlor-dwelling "ladies," even though many of them were farm- and tenement-dwelling workers. Barnum thus encouraged the same sort of upward identification among his plebeian female patrons as he did among their male counterparts. Lower-class women were expected to share their bourgeois sisters' commitment to the cult of domesticity, and to view female workers—represented at the Museum by the starving seamstresses of Lecture Room melodramas—as objects not of solidarity, but of pity.

The American Museum's attitude toward plebeian women is perhaps best exemplified by its 1855 baby show, which remains among the most poorly understood of Barnum's major productions. Despite stiff competition from his poultry, dog, cat, bullfrog, and beauty contests, his first baby show in June 1855 was the most popular participatory event in the history of the Museum.[107] That exhibit established most of the defining features of the baby shows staged over the following decades by Barnum and other showmen. The 143 "babies" were actually children ranging in age from a few months to five years (except for those competing to be the "fattest child under sixteen years of age") (see Figure 5). They vied for $1,100 in cash premiums and titles including "finest twin," "finest triplet," and "finest baby" in various age categories. The children were typically framed by various bonus entertainments: rounding out the attractions at the Museum's 1855 show were Sylvia Hardy (the Maine Giant Girl), oversize waxwork and painted representations of babies, local politicians and celebrities, and, as presenter of premiums, Barnum himself. The combination proved irresistable. The 1855 show's first four days packed the dusty, sweltering Museum with a reported 60,920 patrons.[108] Immense crowds repeatedly forced Barnum to stop the sale of tickets; on the second day, he stood at the door, "waving back

Figure 5. *New York Picayune* on Barnum's baby show. (Collection of the New-York Historical Society)

the multitude that held up their quarters — 'Back, back, gentle-men,' said he, 'it ain't no use a-trying — you can't come in — the old Museum will burst if I let in another one.'"[109] Public interest remained intense as Barnum and Philadelphia museum owner J. H. Wood staged "Barnum and Col. Wood's Grand National Baby Shows" in Boston, Philadelphia, Albany, and Pittsburgh.[110] Despite nonstop attacks from the press, baby shows were all the rage during the summer and early fall of 1855 (see Figure 6). The na-tion's leading newspapers and magazines ruminated on the mean-ing of the craze for America, its babies, and its women.[111] Mean-while, would-be Barnums staged exhibits in Buffalo, Rochester, and Doylestown, Pennsylvania, and took the phenomenon to Lin-colnshire and Withernsea in England.[112] But in October the Bar-num and Wood juggernaut was stopped in its tracks in Cincin-nati by a few anonymous letters to the local press. When less than a quarter of the registered children showed up on opening day, Barnum and Wood were forced to postpone the Cincinnati exhibit indefinitely and drop plans for shows in other cities. Barnum would revive the baby show at his American Museum and Boston Aquarium in the 1860s, and other showmen would keep the form alive in the United States and England well into this century. For many Americans, however, baby shows had been permanently shoved beyond the pale of respectability.[113]

Cincinnatians viewed their suppression of a national craze as a matter of civic pride; a local wag went so far as to satirize Bar-num and Wood as latter-day Macbeths:

> Great PHINEAS T. all obstacles may scorn,
> Until he comes *where babies are not born*
> *For public show*: Then, farewell to his "HUMS,"
> And 'BARNUM'S WOOD a *Dunce*-inane' becomes!"[114]

Despite the boasts of the Queen City Macduffs, the demise of Barnum's 1855 baby shows had less to do with babies or with Cincinnati than with their representation of women. Although Barnum's appeals to patrons and exhibiting parents were gender-neutral, everyone took for granted the shows' female empha-sis — obvious at a glance in the exhibition halls, where many of the exhibiting parents, and most of the judges and patrons, were women.[115] Women also ran the shows' nursery department and

Figure 6. Song sheet inspired by Barnum's baby show. (Harvard Theatre Collection, the Houghton Library)

hawked baby paraphernalia and trinkets. After eavesdropping on street conversations and wandering through the crowds of women at the Museum's show, a *New York Times* reporter insisted that Barnum and the babies were the subject of conversation "wherever two or more females were gathered together."[116] The shows were calculated to appeal to women in what historians have documented as the heyday of middle-class maternity. By midcentury, as Mary Ryan has pointed out, the U.S. middle class's doctrine of separate spheres had shifted virtually the entire burden of child rearing onto the shoulders of women. Sentimental culture trained women to pride themselves in a maternity that was domestic, Christian, affective, and natural (155–65, 192–93). Barnum tapped this ideology by comparing his show to "an Eden of living, blooming, heavenly flowers!" and its babies to Jenny Lind.[117]

Barnum's sentimental rhetoric could not disguise the fact that his baby shows violated most of the middle class's deepest beliefs about maternity. From his first call for contestants in New York to the moment when he threw in the diaper in Cincinnati, Barnum was attacked as a desecrator of "the sanctities of home and of life."[118] Critics accused him of leading an enormous, motley mob of amusement seekers into the heart of the woman's sphere. Author/lecturer Elizabeth Oakes Smith vented the outrage felt by many: "There is something intrinsically revolting in this attempt to force aside the veil which screens and protects the chaste matron, where she and her 'pretty brood' within the sanctuary of home are exempt from the rude gaze of a prying curiosity."[119] That the baby show could prompt a feminist like Smith to fall back on the clichés of True Womanhood speaks to its transgressiveness. As one might imagine, the attacks from middle-class conservatives were even more heated. Most divided their barbs between the showman and the mothers who filled his platforms. A Bostonian printed a twelve-page pamphlet in rhyming couplets linking the show to the fall of America into a Hell of sectionalism, feminism, atheism, Mormonism, materialism, and free love. But he saved his most scathing censure for the female exhibitors:

> Weep, women of America, weep this day
> "Of trouble and rebuke and blasphemy;"
> Weep for your sex polluted and debas'd,
> Who have the names of "Mother," "Wife," disgrac'd;
> Who prostituted Heaven's choicest boon—
> The offspring of their body,—to a base buffoon. (F.J.N. 4)

As middle-class conservatives rallied against the baby shows, Barnum turned for help to the middle-class health reformers who were advocating a more public, rationalized, and scientific notion of motherhood. The showman's work as a temperance lecturer had put him in contact with a health reform movement founded in the 1830s by Sylvester Graham and William Alcott. By 1855, the movement embraced an ever-expanding array of reforms, including vegetarianism, phrenology, hygiene, physiology, and the water cure.[120] Many of the leading advocates of these causes also embraced women's rights. Feminists such as Mary Gove Nichols, Lydia Fowler, Harriot Hunt, and Paulina Wright Davis lectured, wrote, and organized on behalf of the education of women in the laws of physiology and hygiene. By establishing women's medical schools and advocating new theories about sexuality, pregnancy, and child rearing, they sought to restore to middle-class females some measure of control over their bodies. The popularity of their ideas inspired Barnum to hitch his baby shows to their movement. When the attacks on his exhibit began to mount, he published letters from reformers and ads attesting to the "Important physiological facts" about pregnancy and child rearing that his exhibit would establish.[121] The facts would be collected through a questionnaire filled out by the exhibiting parents. It asked about each mother's age, diet, exercise habits, and family size, as well as her child's dietary, hygienic, and exercise habits.[122] Although some newspapers duly noted the responses of the winning exhibitors, most scoffed at the show's pretensions to health reform. They found its "science" as fraudulent as the pseudoscientific manner (complete with notebook and inquisitive air) that Barnum affected in his appearances on the exhibition platform.[123]

There was, as we shall see, ample reason to suspect that physiology was not the primary concern of the questionnaire. On the other hand, Barnum did recruit the support of some of the leading feminist health reformers: although Elizabeth Oakes Smith rebuffed his invitation to serve as a judge, Harriot Hunt and Lydia Fowler both accepted.[124] Hunt and Fowler were among the nation's first women physicians, but they were even better known as feminists.[125] The radical Hunt was famous for her annual one-woman tax protest against the city of Boston. Less than a week after judging the Boston baby show, she would give the opening address at a women's rights convention in the same city. Fowler's more moderate brand of domestic feminism earned her an invitation from Barnum to speak at the shows in Boston and at the

American Museum. At the Museum she disappointed the *Tribune* when she took the Lecture Room stage in a dress rather than the costume designed by her friend Amelia Bloomer.[126] But her speech (spoofed by one paper as "Woman's Rights and Babies' Wrongs") was a cautious attempt to exploit the baby show for feminism.[127] She mingled sentimental platitudes about babies and motherhood with a call to "agitate the various reforms," especially those concerning the education of women.[128] True to her domestic feminism, Fowler subordinated a woman's right to education to her duty as a mother: "[A]s everybody says that the mother is the prime mover in exerting influence in the early years of childhood, therefore woman's education should be more thorough and scientific. . . . it should embrace at least a correct knowledge of the laws of life."[129] Fowler's privileging of maternity over women's rights (as well as her willingness to defend the baby show against its critics) would have endeared her to Barnum, whose genuine interest in feminism was always overshadowed by his wariness of political controversy.[130]

Barnum would also have liked Fowler's assumption of a middle-class audience — obvious in her remarks about the family: "While the father, especially in our cities, is out of doors engaged in active business," the mother is "the queen-bee of the household."[131] Such invocations of separate spheres were routine among Fowler's peers. The health reformers, as Regina Morantz-Sanchez points out, promoted a model of intensive, full-time motherhood that was infeasible for many working women (43). It was probably also infeasible for some of Fowler's listeners at the Museum, given that many of the exhibiting parents were lower-class immigrants.[132] To take a prize at the Museum, however, those parents would have needed to fit themselves to Fowler's ideal — or, to be more precise, Charity Barnum's ideal, as the showman's wife seems to have taken on the task of eliminating unsuitable families. An unnamed woman identified by the *New York Herald* as "one of the exhibitors" claimed that Mrs. Barnum was grilling patrons well beyond the limits of the questionnaire:

> Mrs. Barnum asked me what country I was from. That was none of her business, as my baby was born here in New York. What difference did it make if I did come from Ireland? She asked me what kind of a looking man my husband was, and I told her she

might go to him if she liked, and see for herself. Only for her I would have got a prize. She thought I was poor, because my child and myself were not dressed as fine as some who were there, and that is another reason why my baby was rejected.

Although the exhibitor identified herself as the wife of a propertied man, she felt her plebeian appearance and her immigrant status had doomed her baby's chances.[133] Irish Americans certainly were at a disadvantage in a show that praised its winning babies "especially on the crowning merit of their being genuine original American stock."[134] But the Museum's anxiety over the nationality of the contestants was inseparable from its preoccupation with their class affiliations. As the Museum demonstrated in its presentation of the champion "baby," Charles Orlando Scott, Americanness in this show was coded middle class. The *Herald* recorded the speech of Scott's exhibitor along with the response of the patrons:

> "This," said he, "is the prize boy. (Sensation) He is an American boy, he is. (This important fact was received in silence.) He is one of Sam's boys. (Faint applause) His mother brought him up — she didn't leave him in the care of a domestic."[135]

The exhibitor struggles to fit Scott to the Museum's social and national aspirations: not only is he one of Uncle Sam's boys, but he is also apparently middle-class, because his mother could have left his rearing to a domestic. Yet Master Scott's mother may not have had this option, as her husband was a coachman — an Irish coachman, according to one source.[136] Unable to come up with a prize child with genuine middle-class credentials, Fowler and the other "ladies of respectability" judging the show apparently went for the likeliest plebeian.[137] But the *Boston Courier* was not impressed. "Master Scott," the paper sniffed, "looks like a butcher's bruiser."[138]

The baby shows' plebeian participants were obviously marginalized by ads boasting of "the first ladies and gentlemen" who judged and attended the exhibits.[139] But the lower classes were not wholly ignored by the Barnum and Wood camp. When attacked by middle-class critics, the showmen occasionally fell back on their plebeian contestants and patrons.[140] Barnum printed a response to Elizabeth Oakes Smith's critique by "An American Woman" who defended the show as plebeian culture:

> Barnum has not appointed his show for the children of the refined and sickly "aristocracy," a scion of which the parents might disdain to have vulgar eyes look upon — but for the sturdy working class, the bone and sinew of the country, who are not ashamed to show their blooming little ones at churches or fairs, or on any public occasion.[141]

This stands as one of the few times the American Museum ever attempted to speak to workers in their traditional rhetoric of artisan republicanism.[142] Rather than being heralded as their country's bone and sinew, Barnum's working-class patrons were more accustomed to identifying with his "first ladies and gentlemen." That the Museum chose this moment to address workers as workers speaks volumes about the attitude of its respectables toward the upcoming exhibit. Having just registered his one-hundredth baby, Barnum had apparently reconciled himself to his show's plebeian cast.[143]

Despite the Museum's rhetoric, the egalitarian possibilities of the baby show were most fully realized not by Barnum's exhibits, but by the "colored" baby shows that followed them across the country. Those shows appear to have originated a month before the Museum's exhibit in a waggish open letter to Barnum in the *New York Tribune*. Someone writing as "Wallace" asked the showman if in "the coming contest between the infantile members of the community, those to whom nature has given a dark exterior will be admitted . . . [?]"[144] Barnum replied that his Museum would feature only "the finest white babies," but that he would also be willing to stage "a similar exhibition of the finest colored ones." Among Barnum's conditions for staging the event was that it occur "at such a (suitable) place as I may select."[145] This would suggest that he viewed the prospective contest as potentially *un*suitable for his Museum. Barnum may have been worried about the baby show's tendency to blur the boundary between performer and patron. By the 1850s, African Americans routinely performed at the American Museum as freaks, dancers, and musicians, but only once — for half a day in 1849 — had they been invited inside as patrons.[146] Barnum's thus honored the midcentury "social us-ages" that excluded blacks from virtually all places of commercial amusement, except for the upper tier at theaters.[147] It was not until the 1860s that "the PEOPLE'S FAVORITE" permanently opened its doors to African Americans on an unsegregated basis.[148]

As readers of the "Wallace"-Barnum exchange might have predicted, no colored baby show ever took place under the showman's name at the American Museum or anywhere else; but, as we shall see, he did support such exhibits when they were sponsored by other showmen. To Barnum's credit, he did *not* publicly support the first attempts to exploit his exchange with "Wallace": the blackface National Baby Show at Josiah Perham's Burlesque Opera House and Lea's Nigger Baby Show at the infamous Franklin Museum. Perham's minstrels opened their parody of the American Museum's baby show two weeks before its start; the following month, George Lea's minstrels lampooned Barnum's physiological pretensions with "FAT NIGGER BABIES, WHO ARE FED & WEIGHED every night in presence of the audience."[149] Lea's rabidly racist burlesque barely resembled the colored baby shows that would follow. In Boston, shoe merchant Horatio Bateman fulfilled Barnum's idea of a black duplicate of his white baby show. Bateman's Colored Baby Show matched Barnum and Wood's Boston exhibit down to the smallest details, including premiums for babies in various age categories, piano accompaniment ("by a colored young lady"), and special attractions, including Mother Boston, a storytelling, centenarian ex-slave.[150] While Mother Boston implicitly competed with the memory of Joice Heth, Bateman's show explicitly challenged Barnum's current exhibit. The colored show boasted that "the neatness and good manners of the children and their mothers could not be exceeded by the best class of Saxon blood."[151] Apparently inspired by Bateman, minstrel manager Josiah Perham took on Barnum and Wood with his own colored baby show in Philadelphia. He even duplicated Barnum's physiological rhetoric—claiming that the Boston colored baby show had "defined laws of nature too often disregarded, and, in fact, yielded to science new and valuable developments."[152] Although Perham claimed to be staging a "RIVAL BABY SHOW," the African American exhibits are best understood as Barnum and Wood's collaborators.[153] Like other rigged contests throughout Barnum's career, the "rivalry" between the black and white shows raised public awareness to a level beneficial to all parties.[154] Barnum acknowledged this when he put in an appearance at Perham's Philadelphia exhibit.[155] Recognizing Barnum's interest in the colored baby show, the *Boston Daily Advertiser* went so far as to dismiss it as "one of the clever schemes of the great showman to increase the excitement."[156]

But Barnum was not the only beneficiary of the colored baby shows. Perham boasted of his exhibit's tendency "to overcome idle prejudices against the colored race, and . . . demonstrate happily the intellectuality of that large portion of our people."[157] This overstated the exhibit's value to African Americans; and yet any show that could inspire such rhetoric from a manager of blackface minstrels clearly had antiracist potential. That potential was most fully realized by the colored baby shows' exhibitors. They seized the opportunity to take center stage in a culture that usually restricted them to the upper balcony. A white British patron of Bateman's exhibit observed:

> The mothers and relatives in charge of the babies were attired in habiliments of great style, and decked out in all the colours of the rainbow, — the children being mostly dressed in white — some in brighter colours; — and we may add, that the parents universally appeared quite delighted and proud at the public notice and exhibition of their offspring. (Pairpoint 44)

What looked to British eyes like an impressive show of black respectability might well offend an American racist. Middle- and upper-class blacks had long been favorite targets of white U.S. rioters, minstrels, and print satirists.[158] To judge from the press response, the black respectables in the colored baby shows aroused a similar hostility among many whites: reporters reconciled themselves to the exhibit by rescripting it as an ethnological "museum," full of black "specimens," or a minstrel show, whose "'niggers,'... were really the funniest of the two displays."[159] Their mockery is perhaps the best evidence of the radicalism of the colored baby shows. Having recently penetrated high culture by means of singer Elizabeth Greenfield ("The Black Swan") and pianist Augustus Luca ("The Ethiopian Thalberg"), African Americans were ready to seize a place in the nation's popular culture as well.

The colored baby shows' racial transgressions clearly contributed to the form's notoriety, but they do not fully explain Barnum's debacle in Cincinnati. Indeed, Perham took some pains to avoid offending a border-state audience: his ads in the Cincinnati papers promised novelty and humor, rather than racial equality.[160] But as Barnum and Wood discovered, the baby shows' gender transgressions were more difficult to disguise. When the Cincinnatians began their inevitable assault on Barnum and Wood's exhibit, the showmen replied with their standard mixture of health reform and sentimentalism.[161] But this time it didn't work. On the eve of the exhibit, a local critic, writing under the aptly patriarchal pseudonym "Pater Familias," delivered the death blow. His article, titled "Prostitution," accused the show's mothers of exploiting their children and their own maternity.[162] As we have seen, there was nothing new about this sort of attack. Pater Familias's success at making it stick seems attributable less to his language than to his timing. His article closely followed two other events that had been filling the Cincinnati newspapers: the police raid on the Free Love Society in New York City and the women's rights convention in Smith & Nixon's Hall, which was the planned site of Barnum and Wood's show. Calling itself the Progressive Union Club, the Free Love Society was a Fourierist association of socialists and marriage radicals that met for lectures, conversation, and dancing in a Broadway hall. The society dissolved after a raid that resulted in the arrest of its most famous member, Albert Brisbane, and in salacious press reports about the promiscuity of its members, particularly its female ones.[163] Although Cincinnatians immediately began linking the "strong-minded" women of the local women's rights convention to their counterparts in the Free Love Society, there were important differences between them.[164] Both saw marriage in its existing form as a fundamental social evil, but the free lovers attacked it for distorting "passional affinities" between couples, whereas the feminists blamed it for subjugating women to their husbands. For the Cincinnati conservatives, however, the feminists and free lovers stood for the same thing: an outside threat to the city's Christian patriarchy. As newspapers ridiculed the demands of the feminists, rumors spread that Cincinnati had been selected as the "headquarters of the [free love] movement in the

United States."[165] At the center of the rumors were health reformers and free love advocates Thomas and Mary Gove Nichols, who
denied—somewhat disingenuously, as it turned out—that they
had come to town to found a free love society.[166] Local conservatives nevertheless warned that "hundreds" of gullible Cincinnatians would rush to become "the disciples of the charlatan and
the dupes of the empyric [*sic*]."[167] The city, therefore, was on the
alert when Barnum and Wood showed up with their own mixture
of charlatanism and empiricism. As Pater Familias thundered,
"There was a time when I believe such things would not have
been *tolerated* in this community," Cincinnatians stayed home in
droves: although eighty-three children were registered for the
show, only twenty ("mainly from the 'rural districts'") appeared
on opening day in a hall largely empty of patrons.[168] Barnum was
left with no recourse but to postpone the show indefinitely, jetti-
son his just-announced plans for a Cincinnati museum, and file
a libel suit against the paper that had published Pater Familias's
letter.[169] Over the following weeks, Barnum and Wood abandoned
an already advertised Baltimore show and dropped plans for
exhibits in "Chicago, Washington and all other large cities."[170] A
Cincinnati editorialist gleefully read the baby show's last rites:
"The bantling is dead!"[171]

### Citizens and Strangers

Barnum demonstrated the lessons he had learned in his first
round of baby shows when he revived the form in the early 1860s
at the American Museum. Having met with decidedly mixed results in his alliance with the reformers, he set to work making
the exhibit safe for middle-class conservatives. At the Museum's
later baby shows, there was no hint of physiology, feminism, or
racial equality. Instead, the showman devoted his 1862 ads to the
"throng of the very best class of both citizens and strangers" who
supposedly visited the exhibit; the following year he claimed that
"MANY OF OUR BEST FAMILIES" had placed "THEIR HOUSE-
HOLD DARLINGS on exhibition to compete for the prizes."[172]
Given that there is no reason to believe that *any* elite children
were on Barnum's platform in 1863, this genteel rhetoric tells us
less about his contestants than about his aspirations for his

amusement hall. Barnum would appeal to the city's "BEST FAM-
ILIES" with increasing desperation in his final decade at the
American Museum. As New York respectables migrated steadily
up Manhattan away from the Barnum's and its lower-class neighbors, the showman was sorely tempted to pack up and follow
them.

Barnum's years at the American Museum coincided with what
historians have documented as the splintering of New York City's
neighborhoods along the lines of class and ethnicity. The march
of the middle and upper classes up the island left the Museum
surrounded by newspaper offices, stores, warehouses, and, a few
blocks east, crowded neighborhoods of lower-class people, many
of them recent immigrants.[173] After the theaters and concert halls
had followed the respectables uptown, the American Museum
was widely understood to be stranded at an unfashionable address. Rumors began circulating as early as 1856 that the Museum would be torn down and replaced by "two elegant warehouses," with the collection finding a home in a new structure
to be built "up Broadway."[174] This proved false, but it registered
the management's genuine dissatisfaction with the Museum's location. In 1858 Lecture Room stage manager Harry Watkins
noted the general surprise at the success of his play *The Pioneer
Patriot*, as "[n]obody expected that money could ever be made at
the Museum again—too far out of the way" (229). Two years later,
the *New York Evening Post* called the American Museum "the
only down-town place of amusement that has successfully with-
stood the uptown movement."[175] Barnum had reconciled himself to his Ann Street location by this time, and even attempted
to turn it to his advantage. In a Lecture Room speech, he argued
that the Museum's status as the last place of amusement below
Canal Street made it attractive to patrons from Brooklyn and
New Jersey, as well as "the guests of the numerous down-town
hotels."[176] Conspicuously absent was any reference to the Museum's other, lower-class neighbors. Over the following years, the
showman never entirely gave up the idea of leaving the city's
crammed lower wards.[177] On the day after the fire that destroyed
the Ann Street Museum, he revealed his plan for building a larger
museum near Union Square.[178] Nevertheless, he wound up set-
tling for location further south: his second American Museum

opened at 539 and 541 Broadway in a building formerly occupied by Buckley's Minstrels and Van Amburgh and Company's menagerie (which would return to it as Barnum's partner). At this address, the Museum was closer to more New Yorkers than it would have been at Union Square, but Barnum still dreamed of escaping the plebeian wards. *Leslie's* described 539 and 541 Broadway as a temporary stop for Barnum, "preparatory to founding a grander empire higher up town, which shall represent more the national character."[179]

Barnum was able to offset some of the effects of the uptown migration by reaching out to "the guests of the numerous downtown hotels" and other strangers to the city's fractured social landscape.[180] From the first, the showman successfully cultivated a patronage among itinerant businessmen and tourists, especially rural ones. Looking back on his early years at the Museum in *Struggles*, he recalled, "[M]ost of my visitors were from the country" (143).[181] It is impossible to know whether most of Barnum's patrons remained rural over the following decades, but many of them clearly were. Matthew Hale Smith remembered the "country visitors with valise in hand" who stopped by Barnum's hall before taking breakfast or checking into a hotel (603).[182] Those visitors drew the *Tribune's* pity (and condescension) after the fire at the second Museum: "What in the world will our country friends do now? What inducement will they have to visit the great Metropolis, which heretofore they have regarded simply as the big town whereof Barnum's Museum was the center and the charm?"[183] The Museum's popularity among country people was no accident. Many of its ads and attractions were specifically aimed at the rural districts.[184] Barnum encouraged country patrons to spread the word by supplying them with "placards and show bills, to carry home and place in conspicuous places." He also timed Lecture Room performances to fit the schedules of rural visitors taking day trips into the city.[185]

Despite the American Museum's popularity in the rural districts, there was no ignoring its urban context. By the 1860s, Barnum was finding it difficult to shield his respectables from crime and class strife. He resorted to increasingly elaborate strategies for keeping the city at bay, from placards on the walls listing rules of behavior and warning of pickpockets, to newspaper attacks on the "parties who lounge about the doors and stairways of the Museum," to plainclothes detectives who ejected people "whose actions indicated loose habits."[186] Perhaps the best evidence of the losing battle Barnum was fighting came during the fires that destroyed the Museums. The spectacular blazes at midday 13 July 1865 and midnight 2–3 March 1868 gathered huge crowds that proceeded to mock much of what Barnum and his Museums stood for. In its account of the "FIERY CARNIVAL" at the Ann Street Museum, the *Herald* depicted rowdies who shouted witticisms about the destruction of Barnum's animals and helped themselves to his property:

> There was a steady current of men down the street, as if in procession, with spoils. One had an eagle without wings; another, an indescribable monster of the reptile race; several had bright plumaged birds and rare curiosities. There was an unheard of antiquarian taste made manifest, and men bore away the burden of Barnum's glories with delight.[187]

Although the police attempted to prevent the looting during the fire (by temporarily locking up "suspicious persons"), the following day they allowed a crowd to comb the smoldering ruins for the remnants of Barnum's collection.[188] When the scavengers were done, the *Herald* observed, "[M]any a relic of Barnum's Museum is now carefully secreted in various tenement houses of this city."[189] The process was repeated three years later during the fire at Barnum's second Museum, when "thieves...swarmed from their nests in the neighborhood at the first alarm, and almost defied authority in their eager efforts to secure plunder."[190] After listening to Barnum's incessant appeals to the city's "BEST FAMILIES," the Museum's lower-class neighbors were coming to have their say.[191]

Barnum would remain a major player in the museum business after his 1868 fire. Over the next decade, as Saxon points out, the showman was a consultant and partner, respectively, in the museums of his New York successors, George Wood and George Bunnell (*PTB* 109). Barnum's interest in the form persisted into the 1880s, when he toyed with various schemes for proprietary museums in New York and other U.S. cities. In 1880, the showman joined other wealthy businessmen in founding the Barnum Museum Company, which proposed to build a vast structure in

New York that would have included shops, concert and lecture halls, gardens, museum collections, a theater, and a "Colosseum" (*PTB* 109–10). Barnum's abandonment of this and later museum schemes is at least partly attributable to the bifurcation that had taken place in U.S. museum culture. In the years after the showman's 1868 fire, the middle and upper classes increasingly congregated in the newly formed public art and natural history museums, while the lower classes turned to those other innovative cultural institutions, the dime museums. Barnum's dream of a middlebrow amusement hall survived at some of the more family-oriented dime museums, but it looked increasingly anachronistic in an age when natural history and art had finally succeeded in segregating themselves from commercial amusements. Barnum and his circus partners responded by staking out their own cultural space between the nation's highbrow and lowbrow museums. They collaborated with the Smithsonian Institution and the American Museum of Natural History in the quest for ethnological and zoological exhibits, but they also shared performers with the dime museums.[192] Many of the stars of the Greatest Show on Earth spent their off-seasons in the curio halls of places like Harris' Mammoth Museums in Cincinnati and Pittsburgh and Drew's Museum in Providence. To grasp the American Museum's legacy fully, however, one had to take a seat in the theaters attached to the dime museums, where late-nineteenth-century audiences encountered plays that Barnum had popularized fifty years before.

# 4

## Barnum's Lecture Room: Excavating the Politics of the Moral Drama

[T]he theatres have become Barnumized.
— *New York Herald* (1866)

And the moral drama! The impossible heroes, the improbable heroines, the villains of unprecedented villainy, the clowns of unapproachable clumsiness, the inimitable plots, the apparently inextricable plots, the plots seemingly beyond the power of mortal man to understand or to work out to a solution; they are all things of the past, which can please no more except in dreams.
— *New York Tribune* on the fire at the Barnum and Van Amburgh Museum (1868)

For many of Barnum's most loyal patrons, as well as his most hostile critics, the combined delights of the American Museum's exhibition halls paled in comparison to what happened on the Lecture Room stage.[1] When he began producing plays at his Museum in the 1840s, Barnum joined Moses Kimball in igniting a theatrical phenomenon that would quickly sweep across the United States; by 1855, opera manager Max Maretzek was complaining that almost every U.S. city had its "theatrical traps," which "cloak themselves under the name of Museums" (200–201).[2] Despite such attacks from highbrows, museum theater would remain an enormously generative and popular form for the rest of the century. By the 1880s, dime museums were still drawing on the lessons of Barnum and Kimball as they shaped the newest U.S. culture industry: vaudeville.[3] Twentieth-century scholars, however, have tended to pay less attention to the masses who embraced museum theater than the elitists who reviled it; it is only recently that critics have begun to take the form seriously.[4]

We still do not fully understand the effect of the proprietary museum's collections and performers on the playgoing experience. How, for instance, was an individual's perception of a play colored by an approach to the playhouse through halls of curiosities? Or by the freaks and variety performers who took the stage between the acts? This chapter explores such questions by focusing on some of the American Museum's most popular and controversial productions: its temperance and slavery dramas. In isolating a group of Lecture Room plays for close analysis, I risk giving a distorted picture of its repertory. Indeed, most of the hundreds of melodramas, comedies, tragedies, pantomimes, fairy spectacles, and farces that appeared on Barnum's stage had little or nothing to say about either alcohol or slaves. And yet, whether one measures by box-office receipts, column inches of press commentary, or rhetorical force, slavery and temperance wielded a clout in the Lecture Room unrivaled by any other themes. It was not by chance that Barnum dedicated his Lecture Room to moral drama in 1850 with *The Drunkard*, or that the 1868 fire that destroyed the Barnum and Van Amburgh Museum also cut off a run of *Uncle Tom's Cabin* in the Lecture Room. After the Museum's destruction, temperance and slavery dramas would remain workhorses on the U.S. stage. But it is the period leading up to the Civil War that primarily concerns me here — the years when the nation was divided first by conflicts over temperance and antislavery, and again by disputes within the reform movements over the roles of women, workers, and radicals. In the Lecture Room, Barnum worked to suture the splits in his audience by aligning patrons with temperance philanthropists and liberal slaveholders and against feminists and radical abolitionists. His strategy can be gathered from the plays he chose to stage as well as the way he staged them. Barnum's Museum often deployed its collections and nontheatrical performers to limit, or even alter, a play's meaning. The success of its efforts attests to the power of proprietary museums to refashion drama in a day when, for many Americans, the museum play was the thing.

Barnum publicly committed his Lecture Room to moral drama at a gala Museum reopening on 17 June 1850, following nine weeks of remodeling. The celebration marked the culmination of a series of expansions to the Lecture Room from its origins in the early 1840s as a cramped hall where a few hundred patrons watched nightly variety acts. By 1850, the Lecture Room had grown into an ornately—and patriotically—decorated playhouse with a capacity nearing three thousand (five thousand by Barnum's count).[5] Its personnel had expanded as well. Although Barnum chiefly relied on itinerant entertainers for most of his first decade as proprietor, in 1849 he had begun assembling a permanent stock company under the management of Francis Courtney Wemyss. When the showman unveiled his refurbished theater the following June, he could boast a company numbering twenty-seven, which would soon include such notables as comedians Thomas Hadaway and Corson W. Clarke. (Clarke would serve as stage manager from 1850 to 1857.) And yet the most obvious change in the Lecture Room in 1850 was not its size or personnel, but its rhetoric. At the reopening, one of the actresses outlined the Lecture Room's mission in verse:

> Here vice shall be portrayed, with such a mein
> That all shall hate it when it once is seen—
> And virtue, with its rich rewards and fun
> Nightly before this altar you shall see.[6]

With this, the Lecture Room dedicated itself not to drama, but to "moral drama." It was a distinction that Barnum had learned from Moses Kimball, who had begun commissioning and staging moral reform melodramas at his Boston Museum in the 1840s. Among Kimball's productions were Charles H. Saunders's *The Gambler* (1844), F. S. Hill's *Six Degrees of Crime; or, Wine, Women, Gambling, Theft, and the Scaffold* (1846), and the play that reopened Barnum's Lecture Room, William H. Smith's *The Drunkard* (1844).[7] Many of Kimball's and Barnum's detractors dismissed the moral drama as a cynical gimmick—akin to calling their theaters "lecture rooms"—aimed at pious dupes and hypocrites.[8] For Thomas Ford, Kimball's plays were "sugar-coated pills" (27), greedily gobbled down by Christians who shunned the regular playhouses. Ford had ample reason to scoff at the museums' moral pretensions, as Kimball and Barnum shared both plays and players with the ordinary theaters. Such was the case during the Lecture Room's 1850 reopening, when two East Side theaters, the National and Bowery, mounted their own productions of *The Drunkard*.[9] Despite the efforts of the museums to lay claim to the moral drama, the regular theaters had a perfect right to the genre: didactic plays attacking gambling and seduction were common on the U.S. stage long before Kimball and Barnum arrived on the scene, and the museum theaters drew on this tradition when they revived such classics as George Lillo's *The London Merchant* (1731) and Edward Moore's *The Gamester* (1756).[10]

What made the museum theaters distinctive was not so much their plays as their framing of them. At a time when the defenders of the stage were absolving it of any responsibility to teach, the museum owners continued the time-honored practice of offering their plays as moral lessons. Barnum put it baldly at his 1850 reopening: his Lecture Room would present "specimens of Comedy or Drama, upholding virtue, portraying its beautiful and certainly happy consequences, and as vividly painting the positive and inevitable evil consequences of vice."[11] Over the next eighteen years, the Lecture Room rarely missed an opportunity to underline a moral. In 1863, for example, it identified the "lessons" of Tom Taylor's *The Ticket-of-Leave Man* as "CHARITY TO THE OUTCAST" and the "BEAUTY OF HONESTY AND HONOR."[12] Such moralizing was common among early-nineteenth-century theater managers and critics (Levine 39–40), but by midcentury it had fallen out of favor among the friends of the theater. In 1851 author/playwright William K. Northall ridiculed Barnum for presuming to teach:

> Theatres and museums were never intended to be schools of ethics. It is a mistaken notion of the purposes of the stage. The stage, to be respected, must be careful not to offend good manners or violate the moral principles which govern every well regulated community; but they have no more to do with the promulgation of ethical doctrines than they have with the teaching of astronomy. (166)

As Neil Harris points out, Northall spoke for other supporters of the nineteenth-century stage who sensed the threat to artistic freedom implied in the moral drama (107–8). The threat loomed larger in the mid-1850s, as theaters across the nation devoted themselves to the genre (McConachie *Melodramatic* 176). By 1857

the movement was widespread enough for Henry Bellows to inter-
rupt his defense of the theater for an attack on stage didacticism
(16–19). Even a reformer who wanted the "moral and religious
portion of the community" to take control of the stage perceived
the danger in what the museums were doing (38).[13]

Barnum's critics had ample reason to finger him as an opponent of the theater, because this was how he often presented
himself. The showman did not hesitate to denigrate the regular
playhouses in order to promote museum drama. One 1850 Bar-
num-sponsored pamphlet juxtaposed praise for the Lecture Room
in his Philadelphia museum with a sweeping dismissal of the
U.S. stage: "[T]he theatre has undertaken, not to *lead* the public
taste, but to follow it in its most pernicious obliquities, minister-
ing to a depraved appetite and a morbid imagination" (*Ten* 202).
With such attacks Barnum was obviously trying to capitalize on
the antitheater prejudice common among midcentury Christians.[14]
The showman had many collaborators, as clergymen never wea-
ried of painting the theater as a cesspool of drunkenness, obscen-
ity, and sexual license. And many antebellum playhouses invited
censure by supporting themselves with prostitution and in-house
bars. Claudia Johnson has documented the widespread presence
in Jacksonian playhouses of the "third tier"—the gallery set aside
for prostitutes and their clients (576–81). By midcentury, reformist managers such as Noah Ludlow and William Niblo had banished the third tier from many of the nation's theaters, but playhouse prostitution still thrived. In 1853 the *New York Clipper* went
so far as to cite the persistence of the tier in the city's plebeian
theaters as proof of their moral superiority to their Broadway
counterparts: in the latter, the paper contended, "disreputable
characters" mingled freely among the respectables.[15] Despite the
fact that prostitutes were also reported in Barnum's Museum, the
showman appears to have reassured many of his patrons with
his pledge to keep out "FEMALES OF KNOWN BAD CHARAC-
TER."[16] The wisdom of Barnum's strategy was demonstrated by
the prudish authors of guidebooks and travelogues who attacked
New York's theaters while praising the American Museum. Joel
Ross, for one, claimed he had never set foot inside a theater, but
lauded the "rational entertainment" of Barnum's "splendid lecture
room" (184–85).[17] The Lecture Room's repertory was also calcu-

lated to confirm patrons' faith in its propriety. Barnum's productions of antiseduction moral dramas such as Charles Saunders's *Rosina Meadows* (1843) would have further underlined his stand against sexual license.[18]

## "On the Temperance Plan"

Both on and off the stage, the chief reform of Barnum's Lecture Room was not sexual purity, but temperance. At a time when bars were standard at most theaters and other places of amusement, Barnum and Kimball not only served refreshments "on the Temperance plan," they also dedicated their collections and theaters to the battle against the bottle.[19] Both men entered the museum business at a time when the control of elite evangelicals over the temperance movement was being challenged by the Washingtonians, the nation's first national temperance organization drawn primarily from the lower and middle classes.[20] As that was also whence Barnum drew his patronage, it is not surprising that he committed his Museum to temperance under the banner of Washingtonianism. During the showman's first year at the Museum, he set aside a day for "three splendid performances for the Benefit of the Parent Washington Temperance Benevolent Society."[21] With this benefit, Barnum backed the Washingtonians in one of their most innovative reforms: the creation of an alternative, alcohol-free popular culture in an age when drinking was an integral part of many workers' labor and leisure hours (Tyrrell 176–79). The American Museum took its place as a site of regenerative amusement alongside the Washingtonians' temperance concerts, picnics, and bazaars (Wilentz 309–10). Moreover, the ties would persist into the mid-1840s, as the Museum shared variety acts (e.g., Charles White's Kentucky Minstrels) with Teetotaler's Hall, the Washingtonian headquarters (Tyrrell 195).

By the time of the Lecture Room's 1850 reopening, Washingtonianism was largely dead, though its artisanal mantle had been taken up by temperance groups such as the Rechabites and the Good Samaritans.[22] Those organizations, however, were poorly suited to the middle-class aspirations of Barnum's refurbished Museum. The Lecture Room found a more congenial temperance vehicle in William H. Smith's *The Drunkard; or, The Fallen Saved,* the play whose stunning success, in the words of William Clapp, "established permanently the popularity of [the] Boston Museum" (471).[23] Smith appears to have drawn upon the plebeian temperance groups in constructing his play, especially in his famous delirium tremens scene, which boasts all the horror and melodrama of a Washingtonian experience meeting.[24] But Barnum's Lecture Room ignored the play's debt to the lower classes, stressing instead its ties to the bourgeoisie. One ad claimed that *The Drunkard* carried the imprimatur of "all the first families" of Philadelphia, where it had appeared at Barnum's Museum.[25] Further assurances as to the gentility of the play—and by extension the Lecture Room—came from Barnum, who aligned his public image with those first families. After the curtain fell on opening night, he took the stage in the philanthropic guise that he had tried on four months earlier in announcing his signing of Jenny Lind. This new Barnum claimed to have renovated the Lecture Room not primarily for money, but for the moral elevation of his patrons:

> I conceive it possible...to distil for the great Public every species of the popular drama, and present them all so completely divested of mental impurity, so perfectly racked off the lees of verbal pollution, that the most inexperienced may imbibe them without apprehension, and the most cautious prescribe them with a confident hope of intellectual advantage.[26]

With its vinous metaphors, Barnum's speech could hardly have failed to provoke comparison with the play that had preceded it. In particular, the showman's philanthropic pose seems a deliberate echo of *The Drunkard*'s temperance advocate, Arden Rencelaw, who is lauded by the play's hero as "[t]he princely merchant! the noble philanthropist! the poor man's friend! the orphan's benefactor!" (3.1). The Lecture Room went to some lengths to link the real and fictitious philanthropists. The stage directions of one scene place Rencelaw on Broadway, walking in front of the American Museum (4.3). Any doubts about the point of that juxtaposition would apparently have been dispelled by Rencelaw's appearance. According to Harry Birdoff, the actor playing the philanthropist was made up and dressed to look like Barnum (85).

Rencelaw was not the only character in *The Drunkard* who called to mind a Barnum persona. By uniting the philanthropist with the Yankee William Dowton, *The Drunkard* conjured up shades of past and present Barnums.[27] But rather than playing up the Yankee egalitarianism that shows up in the likes of Barnaby Diddleum, Smith makes Dowton the obedient servant of the play's upper-class characters, including his foster brother, Edward Middleton, whom he addresses as "sir." Despite the fact that the Yankee rescues most of the virtuous characters over the course of the play, he remains irrelevant to the central moral crisis: Middleton's battle with alcohol. Marked by the play's social hierarchy as a figure of low comedy, "honest William" is helpless to stop Edward's drinking—that is left to Rencelaw, who rescues the hero from the bottle as well as from the machinations of the villain, Cribbs.

In the social landscape of *The Drunkard,* the respectable classes are not only uniquely capable of saving drunkards, they are also uniquely worthy of being saved. Such are the implications of the scene in which Rencelaw stops Middleton from committing suicide. Immediately recognizing Middleton as an alcoholic, the philanthropist queries him about his origins. After learning that the drunkard has slipped down the social ladder, Rencelaw proclaims:

> There you have the greater claim upon my compassion, my attention, my utmost endeavors to raise you once more, to the station in society from which you have fallen, "for he that lifts a fallen fellow-creature from the dust, is greater than the hero who conquers a world." (4.1)

Here Rencelaw indicates that we are to read the play's subtitle, *The Fallen Saved,* in social as well as moral terms. Middleton has clearly been saved from a fall, but Smith strategically blurs the full extent of his financial salvation. Although the hero has regained his fortune by the end of the play, he is last pictured in domestic bliss with his wife and child in a cottage, rather than the mansion of his ancestral estate. Smith's decision to conclude the play in the humbler setting would have allowed lower- and middle-class audiences to identify with the again-wealthy hero without being reminded of their social distance from him. By passing for middle-class, Middleton helped Barnum sell an elite-led temperance movement to a popular audience.

The Museum's choice of *The Drunkard* as the inaugural drama of its refurbished Lecture Room suggests the ideological distance it had traveled since its early ties with the Washingtonians. Whereas the Washingtonians promoted artisanal self-help, *The Drunkard* presents temperance as a reform for the middle and upper classes. By 1850, it was not just the Museum but the temperance movement as a whole that had been co-opted by the bourgeoisie. This shift is registered in the class politics of *The Drunkard*. First performed in 1844 during the takeover of the Washingtonians by an evangelical middle-class minority, the play valorizes Rencelaw's Christianity and demonizes the sellers of alcohol.[28] Both stances flew in the face of the secular, moral suasionist Washingtonians and the plebeian temperance organizations that followed them. With their sensitivity to the financial needs of small-scale liquor sellers (some of whom were members), the Washingtonians would have protested Smith's attack on the traffic. As Ian Tyrrell notes, artisanal organizations like the Rechabites continued to resist the call for prohibition after the decline of Washingtonianism (209–11). They were eventually outnumbered, however, by a national alliance of prohibitionists led by the middle-class American Temperance Union and Sons of Temperance (of which Barnum was a member). In the early 1850s, those groups would rally in the North and West behind the prohibitionist Maine Law. The middle-class organizations spotted a fellow traveler in the American Museum: two months into *The Drunkard*'s record-breaking run in the Lecture Room, the Sons of Temperance staged a "GRAND PRESENTATION ... of a valuable Gold Watch and Chain" to Corson Clarke for his performance as Edward Middleton.[29] In Barnum's Lecture Room, as in the U.S. temperance movement, the middle class was now firmly in the saddle.

*The Drunkard* remained a favorite temperance vehicle in the Lecture Room into the 1860s, but by that time its preeminence was challenged by a host of temperance plays, including *The Bottle, The Curate's Daughter, The Last Nail; or, The Drunkard's Vision,* and *Workmen of New York; or, The Curse of Drink.* But *The Drunkard*'s chief rival was *Ten Nights in a Bar-Room,* William W. Pratt's 1858 dramatization of the 1854 Timothy Shay Arthur novel. It was perhaps inevitable that *Ten Nights* find its way onto the Lecture Room stage, as Arthur's involvement in temperance activism closely paralleled the Museum's: as a journalist in Baltimore in 1840, Arthur was the first to cover the newly formed Washingtonians (Koch lx-lxi); two years later he published his reworked stories in *Six Nights with the Washingtonians: A Series of Original Temperance Tales*. Over the following decades, however, Arthur would increasingly lend his pen to the middle-class prohibitionists. In 1854 he attempted to arrest the backlash against the Maine Law with *Ten Nights*, the first temperance novel to advocate prohibition openly (Koch lxxvi–lxxvii). As both a play and a novel, *Ten Nights* picks up where *The Drunkard* leaves off by presenting temperance as a movement of, and for, the middle and upper classes. Pratt streamlines Arthur's story to focus on a once-respectable hero (i.e., ex- and future miller Joe Morgan), who drags his family down the social ladder before rising to status and prosperity by the play's end. Like *The Drunkard*, Pratt's play spells out in the clearest terms the class consequences of the traffic in, and consumption of, alcohol. Liquor selling is an illegitimate means of social advancement for landlord (and ex-miller) Simon Slade, who argues:

> I don't see why a tavern-keeper is not just as respectable as a miller—in fact, more so. The very people who used to call me "Simon," or "Dusty Coat," now say "Mr. Slade," or "Landlord," and treat me in every way more as if I were an equal than ever they did before. (1.2)

But as Pratt and Arthur relentlessly demonstrate, Slade's respectability is illusory; it lasts only as long as it takes the bottle to destroy him and his family. Morgan, on the other hand, rises through temperance to prosperity; by the end of the play he fulfills his daughter's dream of a father who is "not old Joe Morgan, but Mr. Morgan now" (4.3). There to applaud Morgan's recovery is the temperance philanthropist Romaine. Pratt confirms Romaine's power by having him lead the cry for prohibition in Bolton County despite the fact that the local "temp'rance folks" have apparently been organizing in his absence (5.2). (In Arthur's novel, Morgan proposes the ban.) Like William H. Smith, Pratt employs his conclusion to identify audiences with the teetotaling philanthropist: after entering Cedarville at Romaine's elbow, we leave the play with his reminders of "the lessons taught" (5.4).

Romaine, however, is not allowed the final word in either the last scene or the rest of the play. That honor belongs to the Yankee Sample Swichel—a character Pratt fleshes out from the most skeletal of antecedents in Arthur's work. Swichel adds a disruptive comedy to the play that is entirely lacking in the novel. His prominence is suggested by the fact that the play was apparently written as a vehicle for G. E. "Yankee" Locke (Locke was still playing Swichel in American Museum productions of *Ten Nights* in the 1860s [Odell 8:180]). To create his Yankee, Pratt appears to have drawn upon Smith's William Dowton: both are servants of intemperate masters whose honor they are eager to defend with their fists and both are rewarded for their fidelity with new suits of clothes. But whereas Dowton never swerves in his devotion to his superiors, Swichel spends most of *Ten Nights* flouting Romaine's temperance sermons. His rebelliousness is made all the more attractive by the woodenness of those around him. In a typical exchange, Swichel replies to the philanthropist's preachment by reminiscing about "a drink that made me wish my throat was a yard long, it felt so good all the way going down" (2.1).

Since his class marks him as a figure of low comedy, Swichel's drinking is of a different moral order than that of his social superiors. In his intemperance, his social "decline" (in the final act, he announces, "Wal, I guess I've got down about as fur towards the foot of the ladder as I intend a-goin'" [5.1]), and his last minute taking of the pledge, Swichel's career parallels that of Morgan. But rather than emphasizing the moral of Morgan's story, Swichel threatens to undermine it. Liquor is a vicious interloper in the lives of the play's respectable characters; in contrast, Swichel enjoys what might be called in Emersonian terms an original relation to the bottle. He tells Romaine, "[T]hat's the reason they gave me the name of Sample, because I was weaned on gin and bitters" (1.1). The Yankee deflates the melodrama of Morgan's story through his ludicrous drunken behavior and his apparent immunity to the bottle's ill effects (only his clothing appears to suffer). His respectable counterpart finally overcomes his habit only after indirectly causing his daughter's death and sinking into the d.t.'s. Afterward, Morgan's wife confesses that she would have preferred his death to his continued intemperance. Swichel, in contrast, jests about his own decision to stop drinking, at one point bargaining with his sweetheart, Mehitable Cartwright: "Now, jest give up all your old novels, and I'll give up all the rum" (5.1). By implicitly equating the dangers of the bottle with those of a yellow novel, Swichel belittles the "direful pestilence" that stalks his respectable fellows (5.4).

The final act of *Ten Nights* suggests that Pratt recognized his Yankee's threat to both the dignity and the authority of his respectable characters. The last scenes are largely devoted to subordinating and domesticating Swichel: before the curtain falls, the Yankee has acquired a new fiancée, boss (Morgan), and suit of clothes. By drying out Swichel and submitting him to the power of the man whose career he parodied, Pratt is clearly working to steady the social hierarchy shaken by the rest of the play. But that does not explain why he added the destabilizing Yankee to Arthur's story in the first place. To account for Swichel, we must explore his embodiment of the bourgeois male's frustrations with the temperance movement.

*Ten Nights* followed a stream of plays, farces, and variety acts in the Lecture Room that generated comedy from the drinking of preindustrial characters, such as blacks, Indians, and traditionalist white workers. Typical of such works were Thomas Egerton Wilks's popular farce *State Secrets: or, The Tailor of Tamworth* and T. D. Rice's blackface minstrel playlet, *Oh, Hush! or, The Virginny Cupids*. Drunken comedy might appear counterproductive in a Lecture Room where the newly converted could take the teetotaler's pledge on the spot. Instead of subverting the Museum's temperance program, however, the tippling of the nonwhite and plebeian characters may have furthered it. As they identified with the middle-class white characters' struggle for sobriety, Barnum's audience may have taken a vicarious pleasure in the drunken antics of characters whose race or class kept them at a safe distance.[30] Those characters' drunken buffoonery would have enabled patrons to indulge their desires vicariously with little sense of guilt. After all, Sample Swichel seems to thrive on the same dissipation that destroys his superiors.

Middle-class male Lecture Room patrons may also have been drawn to Pratt's Yankee for his masculinist treatment of Mehitable Cartwright. Swichel's proprietary attitude toward Cartwright is egregious, even by Yankee standards. He calls our attention to Cartwright's virginity in their first exchange ("Your eyes sprung a leak—or have you broken something you can't mend?" [2.1]), and spends the rest of the play boasting of his entitlement to it. When he suspects the villain Green of pursuing Cartwright, he promises dire consequences "if he meddles with my pasture ag'in" (2.1) or, as he later puts it, "if he troubles my calico doings any more" (3.1). Having successfully warded off Green by the final act, Swichel celebrates his engagement to Cartwright with a song to the tune of "Yankee Doodle." In the final verse, he envisions himself as a Yankee patriarch surrounded by miniature versions of himself:

> When time rolls on, pray call around,
> And happen in to meet me;
> Some little Swichels will be found
> To straighten up to greet ye. (5.1)

Notably absent from Swichel's dream future is Cartwright; after having given birth to those erect little Swichels, she has presumably been relegated to the margins of Sample's idyll.

Swichel's plebeian masculinism would have spoken to the frustrations that many of Barnum's middle-class male patrons were feeling in the 1860s. By identifying downward with the patriarchal Yankee, those men could surreptitiously protest the power that women of their own class had seized through temperance activism. That power was considerable by midcentury, when middle-class women dominated many phases of the temperance movement (Ryan 135). In 1850, Barnum (who was a popular, and devoted, temperance lecturer) was already acknowledging the clout of the temperance women. At a New York temperance meeting, he argued:

> The ladies can win the victory. It is no sacrifice to them to identify themselves with the cause of temperance. We are not living in Arabia or Turkey, where they say women have no souls; but we are under petticoat government; and let that government only set about the work of reform, and it must be accomplished.[31]

Barnum could chuckle at the power of a women's movement that he supported, but many of his contemporaries saw nothing amusing in the rise of the temperance women. In the 1850s and 1860s, bourgeois men worked to shut off the opportunities that the temperance women had seized for campaigning, organizing, and lec-

turing (Epstein 93).[32] Pratt's Simon Slade speaks for those threatened males when he grouses to his wife, "[Y]ou might as well
turn temperance lecturer at once. . . . what's come over you all of
a sudden?" (1.2). Men resistant to the female temperance lecturers could point to the fact that most of this country's first generation of feminist leaders were schooled in the temperance movement. Susan B. Anthony put it bluntly at an 1853 New York
meeting: "[T]his Temperance demonstration is . . . another way of
seeking Women's Rights" (quoted in Spann 246). Bourgeois male
Lecture Room patrons bothered by the political gains of the temperance women would have found reassurance in *Ten Nights*. After sending Mrs. Slade off to a lunatic asylum, Pratt leaves temperance advocacy squarely in the hands of the play's respectable
male characters.

## Uncle Tom in the Lecture Room

The Lecture Room not only staged the class and gender conflicts
within the temperance movement, it also dramatized the vexed
politics of antislavery. In the 1850s, Barnum's Museum established itself as one of the most popular, and controversial, repre-
senters of slavery to a public whose views on the institution were
rapidly evolving. Like the rest of the North, Barnum's audience
was divided over slavery, and those divisions would deepen as
the 1850s produced a series of escalating crises—the fugitive
slave cases, Bleeding Kansas, the beating of Charles Sumner, the
Dred Scott decision, Harper's Ferry. By middecade, many northerners felt sufficiently threatened by the Slave Power to rally behind the openly sectionalist Republican Party. But in New York
City, whites were more likely to respond to the latest news from
Kansas or Harper's Ferry by blaming the Republicans, rather than
joining them. The city continued to support the Democratic Party
as the party of Union long after most of the North had rejected
it as the party of slavery. The split between the city and the country on the question of slavery was borne out in Barnum's patronage. In the mid-1850s Barnum found himself with two very
different audiences for his slavery plays: a rural patronage that
was heavily antislavery and a city patronage that supported compromise with the South at all cost. The split in Barnum's patron-

age showed up in the Lecture Room's repertory, which combined the antiabolitionist blackface minstrelsy of Charles White, the antislavery dramas of George Aiken and J. T. Trowbridge, and the fence-sitting works of H. J. Conway and Dion Boucicault. But the dominant note at the Museum right up until the Civil War was captured by the fireworks display that commemorated its 1860 renovation. The *Herald* described it as "a 'Union' piece. In the centre was displayed an American eagle, with the hand of friendship underneath, on either sides were the words, 'North and South,' the whole being encircled in an arc, on which was emblazoned the word 'Union.'"[33] By 1860 the Museum had been extending the hand of friendship to the South for the better part of seven years, especially in its Lecture Room. As abolitionists defied the South in northern courthouses and Kansas towns, the American Museum countered by subordinating the fight against slavery to the bond between slavocrats and Yankees.

In 1853 Barnum foisted his transsectional ideal onto the antislavery movement's chief cultural weapon when he staged H. J. Conway's dramatization of *Uncle Tom's Cabin*. Conway's *Uncle Tom* was the first of a series of plays in which the Museum countered sectional conflict with a celebration of white patriarchy. By the time *Uncle Tom* appeared on Barnum's stage, that conflict had been enormously intensified by the aftermath of the Compromise of 1850. Although it was promoted as the final solution to the problem of slavery in the nation and its territories, the Compromise merely sharpened the battle lines. Its most notorious feature, the Fugitive Slave Law, provoked a series of court and street fights pitting fugitive slaves and their antislavery allies against slaveholders and the U.S. government. These battles found their ultimate cultural expression in 1851–52, when Harriet Beecher Stowe published her response to the Fugitive Slave Law, *Uncle Tom's Cabin*. It is almost impossible to overstate the impact of Stowe's novel on discourses about slavery. Within a year of its publication, *Uncle Tom's Cabin* had so pervaded U.S. culture that it was difficult for anyone, whether pro- or antislavery, to talk about the institution without resorting to Stowe. The novel would remain *the* literary signifier of slavery well into the twentieth century. Thus, when Barnum decided to capitalize on the slavery crisis in 1853, it was inevitable that he turn to *Uncle Tom*. But, as his critics charged, the play that Barnum staged bore little resemblance to Stowe's book.[34] The Lecture Room took up *Uncle Tom* at a time when it had already begun to mutate into forms that Stowe would hardly recognize, much less claim. Undaunted, Barnum's Museum co-opted Stowe's celebrity while using attacks on a rival production to distance itself from her politics.[35] Through its opposition to the National Theatre's *Uncle Tom*, the Lecture Room tried to convince patrons that they could simultaneously support Stowe and Compromise, slaveholders and slaves, North and South.

Despite his claims to the contrary, when Barnum brought *Uncle Tom* to the Lecture Room he was following not Stowe but Moses Kimball. Kimball had commissioned Conway's play in 1852, and had staged it for thirteen weeks at his Boston Museum.[36] Barnum's interest in the play would also have been piqued by the stunning success of George Aiken's dramatization of *Uncle Tom* at New York's National Theatre. By the time the American Museum opened its production of Conway's play, the National's production had racked up one hundred performances, with no end in sight.[37] Barnum implicitly attacked Aiken's play in ads detailing what his *Uncle Tom* was not. His play did "not foolishly and unjustly elevate the negro above the white man in intellect or morals," nor did it represent "the ignorant slave as possessed of all the polish of the drawing-room, and the refinement of the educated whites."[38] But if these were the crimes of Aiken's drama, they were also the crimes of Stowe's novel, which supplied the playwright with the vast majority of his speeches and scenes. To charge Aiken with upending racial hierarchy seems ludicrous today: his play advances Stowe's twofold project of attacking slavery while reassuring panicky whites with its nonresistant black hero. And yet many of Stowe's readers were outraged at the thought of a black character who is morally superior to whites. Edward Pollard spoke for southerners offended by Stowe's black Christ when he insisted, "There are no Uncle Toms in the South" (quoted in Gossett *Uncle* 202). Pollard would also have scoffed at Aiken's play, which climaxes with Tom's determination to be crucified by Legree rather than betray his fellow slaves. Barnum, however, cut Aiken's hero down to size with his play's most notorious feature — an ending in which Uncle Tom walks away from the South a free man. Museum ads proclaimed: "[I]nstead of turning away the audience in tears, the author has wisely consulted dramatic taste by having Virtue triumphant at last, and after all its unjust sufferings, miseries and deprivations, conducted to happiness by the hand of Him who watches over all."[39]

This ad reveals the way the Lecture Room's Christian morality underwrote its racial and gender politics, given that the phrase "Him who watches over all" could refer to either God or the white man. Indeed, it is the latter who conducts Conway's slaves to happiness for most of the play.[40] The playwright painstakingly reduces the moral stature of Stowe's black characters by placing them in the hands of white male benefactors. He omits or revises Stowe's unforgettable scenes of black heroism — Eliza Harris crossing the Ohio on the ice and George Harris defying his white pursuers with word and bullet. Aiken entranced theater audiences by staging these episodes, but Conway not only omits Tom's martyrdom, he also places Eliza and George Harris under the protection of the rifle-toting Drover John. It is John, not George, who fires the last word and the first shot at the slave catchers. Conway's subjugation of his black characters also extends to less pivotal scenes, including the one where Tom takes leave of George Shelby in Kentucky. In Stowe, Tom gently but firmly controls this scene, quelling George's anger and reminding him of his duties as a son, a Christian, and a future slaveholder. Conway, however, gives young George the upper hand: commanding Tom to kneel before him, the boy vows to free him if he grows up to be a man, which promise he fulfills in the final act. As Tom gushes his thanks, Conway's audience could rest easy in the assurance that the slave would wind up under the white male's protection.[41]

Conway's emphasis on George Shelby's pledge typifies his valorization of white male supremacy. As Bruce McConachie has argued, Conway masculinizes Stowe's story by cutting and revising her strongest female characters ("Out" 10–11). His strategy is most obvious in his reduction of Stowe's Ophelia St. Clare to the low-comedy spinster he rechristens Aunty Vermont. Over the course of the play, Aunty Vermont marries, gets pregnant, and trails after a spouse who calls her "Duck." Conway cannibalizes most of Ophelia's forthrightness and many of her lines to create

Aunty Vermont's husband, the Yankee Penetrate Partyside. Partyside's marriage, however, pales in comparison to his relations with the play's male characters. Conway uses the Yankee's friendships and rivalries with the slaveholders to advance what Eric Lott has identified as the play's Compromise politics (214). Partyside enters the play as outraged and baffled by slavery as any white character in Stowe, but is taught to take another view of the institution by his southern friends. By educating his hero about slavery, Conway obviously intended to school his northern audience in the virtues of Compromise.

To speak of the education of a character as flat as Partyside may appear farfetched, as he often threatens to collapse into a mindless assemblage of Yankee mannerisms: always on the lookout for a "spec," he drinks and fights like the best of his literary forbears. The Yankee's name, however, is clearly meant to suggest an inquisitive, open mind. Penetrating party rhetoric, he claims to "look at two *sides* of a question ginerally" (my emphasis; 3.1). Conway wastes no time clarifying the question his hero is to look at: Partyside stumbles into the play over a coffle of slaves, whom he mistakes for chained criminals. His disgust upon discovering the truth is compounded when his new friend, Augustine St. Clare, decides to buy Uncle Tom. By this point Partyside has seen enough to damn all white southerners: "They're all alike by thunder! I did think the Squire's heart was in the right place, but 'taint" (2.4). It is here that Partyside's education begins in earnest. Recasting a conversation that in the novel takes place between St. Clare and Ophelia, Conway has his slaveholder argue for the superiority of slavery to English capitalism in its treatment of the worker. As we have seen, the comparison between white workers and slaves was a favorite one on all of the many sides of the slavery debate.[42] St. Clare's real-world counterparts, the proslavery ideologists John C. Calhoun and George Fitzhugh, favorably compared the condition of slaves to that of white workers in the North. Like other middle-class abolitionists, Stowe responded by shifting the grounds of the argument: she has St. Clare compare the slaves not to northern workers, but to English ones. This allows her to maintain her portrait of the North as a free-labor paradise where workers have less in common with either slaves or European proletarians than with their own employers. Ignoring U.S.

workers' cries of class oppression, middle-class abolitionists believed they could offer emancipated slaves a system of sure rewards and social mobility. In an America rid of slavery, they argued, the George Harrises of the world would rise to the top.

For many of Stowe's contemporaries, however, free labor meant free *white* labor. When confronted with a comparison between English workers and black slaves, those white "egalitarians" pitied the former and resented the latter. It is this brand of white "egalitarianism" that Partyside apparently gleans from St. Clare's speech.[43] After his conversation with the slaveholder, the Yankee treats blacks less as victims of racial oppression than as foils to white male power. Partyside's newfound allegiances are most obvious in his section- and class-bonding friendship with St. Clare. He follows the slaveholder to New Orleans, marries his cousin, and (after St. Clare's death) devotes himself to fulfilling his pledge of liberating Uncle Tom. Conway strengthens the ties between Yankee and slaveholder by masculinizing Stowe's "womanish" St. Clare (Stowe *Uncle* 232). Conway's St. Clare drinks without remorse, and his idea of breaking up a fight is to punch one of the participants, who turns out to be Legree.[44] St. Clare's bare-knuckled, champagne-fueled masculinity would have tested the American Museum's temperate, self-restrained ideal, but this was the price Barnum paid to secure the bond between St. Clare and his Yankee friend, who also takes the opportunity to knock down Legree later in the play. It is perhaps inevitable that both knockdowns occur in the defense of slaves, given that Conway's white male "egalitarianism" is built in opposition to black male submissiveness. Conway heightens the vulnerability and humility of Stowe's Uncle Tom to sharpen the contrast with his white heroes. So opposed are the concepts of manhood and blackness for Partyside that he rarely invokes one without the other. At the slave auction where he has gone to purchase Tom, the Yankee challenges his white fellows to prove their manhood by standing up to Legree (who has rigged the bidding): "Look a here! among the hull lot of you ain't there no white *men* here, no men *free* enough to express their own opinions fair and open to a bully with a knife in his hand" (4.3). The racist subtext of Partyside's speech derives from its being delivered in a room filled with unfree people about to be sold. Partyside calls on his white male listeners to differentiate themselves from the slaves surrounding them through a manly show of resistance.

Conway also uses his black characters to absorb class tensions springing up between Yankee and slaveholder. Partyside articulates his class identity largely through his relations with the black characters. As Alexander Saxton has demonstrated, there was nothing new about this: antebellum playwrights regularly used the stage Yankee's racism to reveal his views on white social hierarchy (chap. 5). But as the two major dramatizations of *Uncle Tom* would suggest, Yankee racism could carry vastly different implications for a play's class politics. Whereas Conway valorizes the white "egalitarian" possibilities of Partyside's bigotry, George Aiken offers the racism of his Yankee, Gumption Cute, as proof of his dangerous social ambition. The difference has everything to do with the Yankees' contrasting class affiliations. Unlike the well-connected Partyside, Cute is obviously plebeian. After drifting through jobs as a schoolteacher, spirit rapper, and overseer, Aiken's Yankee turns beggar and attempts to sponge off Ophelia (his distant relative through marriage). Also unlike Partyside, Cute's effort to cultivate ties to the Vermont St. Clare is presented not as amusing, but menacing. Aiken registers his disapproval of the Yankee's aspirations in a scene where Cute tries to get Topsy to introduce him to Ophelia. Showing up on Ophelia's doorstep in Vermont after having walked all the way from New Orleans, Cute resorts to racist condescension in an attempt to leap the class divide separating him from his "rich relation" (4.1). He greets Topsy with a stream of racist taunts ("Charcoal," "Stove Polish," "Day & Martin")—all by way of asserting a class status that his tattered clothes belie (5.2). Aiken's audience probably laughed at Cute's insults, but after watching Ophelia disavow her own racism and (in a revision of Stowe) adopt Topsy, they would have perceived Cute's bigotry as another sign of his difference from the play's paternalistic elites. They would not have needed Topsy's assessment: "Does you call yourself a gentleman? By golly! you look more like a scar'-crow" (5.2).

Aiken's portrait of the disreputable Cute would have helped manager A. H. Purdy cultivate a new class of patrons for his National Theatre. Purdy's production of Aiken's *Uncle Tom* amazed New Yorkers by luring middle-class Christians to a theater known primarily for plebeian melodrama and comedy.[45] Remarking on the pilgrimage of respectables to unfashionable Chatham Square, the *New York Evening Post* observed, "Mr. Purdy has entirely changed the audiences in his place of amusement by the production of this piece, and it is suggested that, by converting the upper part of the building into a museum, and playing moral dramas, he would receive the support of the religious community."[46] Purdy never went so far as to install a collection, but he eagerly embraced the techniques of the museum managers to gentrify his audience: restyling his theater the "Temple of the Moral Drama," he banished the third tier, replaced his pit with a parquette, and added the matinees and explicit appeals to Christians and mothers that Kimball and Barnum had pioneered.[47] He also mimicked Barnum in encouraging his cross-class audience to identify with his play's bourgeois characters—to side with the elite Ophelia against the impoverished Cute. That Purdy saw Barnum as a rival as well as a model was evident in his use of Cute to puncture Barnum's social pretensions. In a passage apparently added to the National's *Uncle Tom* after the opening of Conway's play at the American Museum, Cute asks Topsy: "Did you ever hear of Barnum?" (5.2).[48] Learning that she hasn't, the Yankee proceeds to describe his Barnumesque "idee" for an exhibition: "Barnum made his money by exhibiting a *woolly* horse; now wouldn't it be an all-fired speculation to show you as the woolly gal?" (5.2). Coming from the ragged Cute, these lines would have carried an attack on the Museum's claims to gentility, which were based in part on Barnum's pose as a philanthropic amusement reformer. As Purdy counted on audiences remembering, however, Barnum had gotten his start in the plebeian humbuggery that Cute represents. The Yankee's plan of exhibiting Topsy would have reminded New Yorkers both of Frémont's Woolly Horse, Barnum's infamous 1849 sham, and of his even more notorious exhibition of the slave woman Joice Heth. We have seen Barnum immortalize the Heth hoax in *Adventures of an Adventurer,* a work narrated by an antiabolitionist Yankee con man who bears more than a passing resemblance to Cute. By 1853, Barnum would have preferred that people forget that portion of his past, but the National was making sure they did not.

Whereas the Yankee's racism in Aiken marks him as a threat to the play's respectables, it serves a different function in Conway. Partyside's racism helps negotiate the social distance separating him from St. Clare. That distance is somewhat indeterminate. Like those of many stage Yankees before him, Partyside's class identifications are complex: his plebeian ties are legible in his Down East dialect, his open sympathies for northern workers, and his habit of addressing St. Clare as "Squire." On the other hand, his profession—he is a writer—qualifies him to marry Aunty Vermont and to serve as the onstage surrogate for Barnum's implied middle-class audience.[49] Rather than alienating those respectables, Partyside's racism may have vented their resentment of the upper class. Where one would expect such class antagonism to arise in the play (between Partyside and "Squire" St. Clare), Conway inserts the slave dandy Adolph. By having Partyside mistake Adolph for a white relative of St. Clare's, Conway encourages us to see the slave as a surrogate for the upper-class male. Such a displacement would help explain the unusual hostility the Yankee, usually a patronizing racist, bears Adolph. In the auction scene, for instance, Partyside's derision of the dandy is matched only by Legree's. Adolph's race would have permitted his function as a lightning rod for anti-elite sentiment to remain covert—crucial in a Lecture Room that had given itself up to the dominance of princely merchants and princely showmen.

With white male supremacy overriding class difference, Partyside can step effortlessly into St. Clare's shoes after the slaveholder's death. Conway's final two acts are largely taken up with Partyside's struggle to carry out his dead friend's pledge to free Uncle Tom. Opposing Partyside is Legree, who also values Tom chiefly for his attachment to St. Clare; in an important revision of Stowe, Conway has Legree buy Tom not as a worker, but as the object of his revenge.[50] In the struggle over Tom, Partyside and his allies have the law on their side. This, as McConachie points out, is another major revision of Stowe, who documents the state and federal laws ranged on the side of slaveholders like Legree (*Melodramatic* 188). In Conway, the white male heroes and their mulatto ally, George Harris, turn those laws to their own account in freeing Tom, Eliza, and Cassy.[51] Conway is so scrupulous in honoring the legal rights of the slaveholders that he requires George and Eliza Harris to pay for themselves after escaping from their owners. These revisions allow Conway to condemn slavery while upholding the legal structure—including the Fugitive Slave Law—that sustained it. Whereas Stowe forces characters like Senator Bird and Mrs. Shelby to side with slavery or against it, Conway lets his whites have it both ways.

Conway's revisions of Stowe earned him and the Lecture Room bitter attacks from antislavery critics.[52] Compromise proved quite lucrative for Barnum, however. The Lecture Room's *Uncle Tom* ran stiff competition to the National Theatre's production in the final months of 1853, and Conway's play returned to the Museum for a shorter run in 1855.[53] In the meantime, the Museum continued to celebrate Compromise in the form of a portrait of Henry Clay and a waxwork of Daniel Webster, the leading architect and advocate, respectively, of the 1850 measures. Given New York City's ties to the South, the Museum's stance on slavery made good business sense. The city was the leading supplier of merchandise and credit for the plantation market and the trading capital for cotton (P. Foner 1–8). After the Civil War, Barnum would recall that many northerners felt "[t]he Southern planters were good customers and were worth conciliating" (*ST* 631). In the early 1850s those with the greatest stake in conciliating the planters— New York's merchants, manufacturers, and bankers—had taken a position on the South that closely paralleled Conway's. Panicked by southern threats of disunion, the businessmen formed the Union Safety Committee to defend the Compromise against its antislavery opponents. When the enforcement of the Fugitive Slave Law produced a series of notorious court cases, the Committee upheld the slaveholders' rights to the fugitives.[54] As Philip Foner points out, however, the New York merchants also attempted to purchase the freedom of fugitives James Hamlet and Henry Long (35–36, 61). The effort of the city's merchants to side with both slaveholder and slave was the real-world analogue, and quite possibly an inspiration, for Conway's *Uncle Tom*. Dramatizing Stowe's novel while living in New York City in the summer of 1852, Conway could hardly have helped notice the exploits of New York's leading supporters of Compromise.[55] Whatever Conway's sources, his Lecture Room audience had been prepared for his scrupulous respect for the slaveholders' property rights by the Union Safety Committee.

## "Freedom and Happiness"

It is a testament to the rapid expansion of antislavery sentiment in the North that by 1856 Conway's play had been displaced from the Lecture Room stage by Aiken's *Uncle Tom*.[56] In that year Barnum formed his ties to the Howard family, whose performances in Aiken's drama at the National Theatre had established them as the nation's premier *Uncle Tom* players.[57] As part of his effort to recover his finances, Barnum managed the Howards' 1856–57 British tour. Over the next eleven years the Howards would also regularly perform Aiken's *Uncle Tom* in the Lecture Room.[58] By the mid-1850s, Aiken's un-Compromised play would have appealed to the large, predominantly rural segment of Barnum's patronage that had gravitated into the Republican Party.[59] The party was born in northern outrage against the Kansas-Nebraska Act of 1854, which overturned the Missouri Compromise ban on slavery in the northern territories; it gained converts with every word of conflict between pro- and antislavery forces in Kansas. Together with the related beating of antislavery Senator Charles Sumner, the Kansas violence had whipped tensions between North and South to new heights by the time of the presidential election of 1856—the first to feature the openly sectionalist Republicans. In New York, the months before the election saw voters divided among the Republican John Frémont, the Democrat James Buchanan, and the American (Know-Nothing) Millard Fillmore. The American Museum documented the three-way split in mid-September with a Test Vote in which Fillmore received 5,425 votes, Frémont 5,261, and Buchanan 2,814.[60] A Museum puff indicated that its city patrons were voting for Fillmore, whereas "the country folks" supported Frémont.[61] This was only half right as a forecast of Election Day, when rural voters would give Frémont the victory in New York State, while the city would go for Buchanan. Yet Fillmore's strength and Buchanan's weakness at the Museum should not prompt us to dismiss its Test Vote. The poll proved misleading only because of subsequent shifts among voters: as the election neared, numerous city conservatives turned from Fillmore to Buchanan as the strongest anti-Republican candidate (P. Foner 132–34). Nevertheless, Fillmore's second-place finish in the city in November suggests that many conservatives continued to see the signer of the Compromise of 1850 as the country's best hope for sectional peace.

Three weeks after Fillmore and Frémont split the bulk of the Test Vote, Barnum's Lecture Room offered an equally divided representation of slavery in *Dred; A Tale of the Great Dismal Swamp.* The play was H. J. Conway's dramatization of the latest novel by Harriet Beecher Stowe.[62] In *Dred* Conway tackled a novel even less suited to his Compromise politics than *Uncle Tom's Cabin.* Writing in the months of 1856 that saw the sack of Lawrence, Kansas, and the beating of Sumner, Stowe lost her faith in southern reform.[63] In *Uncle Tom* she had held out hope for a peaceful end to slavery by concluding with George Shelby's freeing of his slaves. *Dred*'s final chapters, however, portray the liberal slaveholder Edward Clayton being beaten with a cane (à la Sumner) and driven from his North Carolina plantation by proslavery vigilantes. Clayton eventually flees with his slaves to Canada, symbolically surrendering the South to the slavocrats. His flight is the culmination of Stowe's attack on the South as undemocratic, uneducated, and economically and socially stagnant. It is a critique that would have sounded familiar to anyone exposed to Republican Party rhetoric.[64] Stowe's husband, Calvin, acknowledged the novel's party leanings in summarizing its reception: "The Fremonters [*sic*] eulogize it, the Buchaners curse and damn it, and the Fillmorites moan and whine and deprecate its injurious tendencies" (quoted in Hedrick 263). Thus, in *Dred* Conway faced the daunting task of turning an openly sectionalist novel into a Barnumesque celebration of Union. He responded with a play that had something for both the Museum's Frémonters and its Fillmorites.

As with *Uncle Tom,* Conway's most obvious revision of Stowe's *Dred* is found in his ending, described by the *New York Daily Express* as a "striking development, which is rather deduced than embodied from the text of the novel."[65] But Conway's conclusion is less a deduction from the novel than a refutation of it. Whereas Stowe leaves us with no hope for southern reform, Conway confidently predicts both peace and freedom for the slaves. He contrives his sunny finish by ridding his play of the proslavery vigilantism that crushes Stowe's liberal. He packs all of his play's disruptive forces into a mutually destructive confrontation between the fugitive slave leader, Dred, and the chief proslavery vigilante, Tom Gordon. By altering Stowe's plot to kill off Gordon, Conway seems to believe he has exorcised the pressing injustices of slavery. Only this could explain Dred's dying words to his would-be lieutenant:

> Harry, I meant to use you in deeds of blood, to set the black man
> free; but 'tis not so decreed—other means must work out
> Heaven's will. Blood has been shed enough—shed no more—
> your greatest enemy is removed. Be patient, if made to suffer;
> Heaven will, in its own good time, set all free. (3.8)

Conway justifies Dred's reversal (which does not occur in Stowe) by blaming slavery entirely on the wickedness of men like Gordon. In contrast, Stowe is at pains to show the array of institutions (including the courts, the church, the press, and the state and federal governments) conspiring to keep blacks in bondage.[66] This proslavery phalanx drives Clayton from the South in the novel. Conway, on the other hand, presents the death of Tom Gordon as the dawn of a new South.

Conway's Clayton stays on his plantation to preside over a rosy future that is foreshadowed in the play's concluding tableau. The stage directions read, *"Morning breaks—freedom and happiness,"* as Clayton prepares to marry fellow liberal Nina Gordon (4.1).[67] Conway seizes the occasion to spell out literally the moral of his story. He unites the white lovers with their friends, including two groups of black schoolchildren, who frame a figure of the "Goddess of Liberty."[68] Over this tableau stretches a transparency that reads:

EDUCATION
LEADS TO PRESENT AMELIORATION
AND ULTIMATE
LIBERTY. (4.1)

Although Conway refuses to specify *when* Clayton's slaves will be freed, he leaves no doubt as to the success of the liberals' plan of educating, and then emancipating, their slaves. The playwright provides his liberals with the endorsement of the mulatto slave Harry, who is the half brother of Nina. In both Conway and Stowe, Harry is the embodiment of the virtues sacred to the Republicans' free-labor male ideal: industry, intelligence, self-discipline, honesty, and economy. As she had in *Uncle Tom* with George Harris, Stowe indicts the South for wasting the talents, and crushing the dreams, of men like Harry. In both novels, Stowe's mulatto hero ultimately finds the independence and prosperity he deserves in Canada. Conway, in contrast, has Harry stay South to bless Clayton's philanthropy and lay Dred permanently to rest: "When education is fully carried into effect, we shall need no more Dreds to protect fugitive slaves, nor read more tales of the *great Dismal Swamp*" (4.1).

It was perhaps inevitable that Conway conclude with Harry's requiem for Dred, given that, for most of the play, the rebel functions less as a character in his own right than as the embodiment of Harry's rage. Whenever the mulatto slave is goaded to the point of throwing off his chains, the black insurgent magically appears to urge him on. It is Harry who largely determines the nature and scope of Dred's resistance: at one point, the rebel explains to his comrades that his insurrection will begin when the mulatto joins them. Thus, the slave uprising ultimately dies not with Dred's murder in the third act, but with Harry's alliance with the slave-holders in the fourth. In case any of Barnum's patrons missed the point about the dwindling of black heroism, Tom Thumb was there to emphasize it for them. The General blacked up to head-line the play's cast in the comic role of the slave boy Tom Tit (see Figure 7). In the scene following the death of Dred, however, Tom Thumb dropped his role—and his trousers—to perform his famous Grecian Statues routine. Wearing only a body stocking, he struck poses borrowed from ancient statues of Ajax and Hercules that mocked Dred's embodiment of black male power.[69]

Conway's ending was complex enough to appease both of Barnum's main constituencies. On the one hand, his trivialization of proslavery violence echoes Fillmore, who angled for southern votes in 1856 by refusing to condemn the attacks of the Missouri border ruffians in Kansas. Both playwright and politician were ignoring the fact that the lynching and torture of whites accused of abolitionism were well-established means of suppressing dissent among southerners.[70] But the Lecture Room's Fillmorites

Figure 7. General Tom Thumb as Tom Tit on an American Museum bill for
*Dred*. (Harvard Theatre Collection, the Houghton Library)

would have squirmed at Conway's vague, but unmistakable, call
for an end to slavery.[71] Indeed, Conway's final tableau was better
suited to the Museum's Republicans in placing slavery in what
Lincoln would call the "course of ultimate extinction." Some of
the Museum's Frémonters were doubtless pleased by Conway's
promise of a permanent southern home for the freed slaves. By

the mid-1850s substantial numbers of free-soil racists had migrated into a party whose hostility to slavery was sometimes underwritten by a hostility to blacks (E. Foner *Free* 265–67). Republican racists in the Lecture Room would have taken solace in Harry's assurance that the freed slaves would remain on the plantation, rather than follow Conway's Uncle Tom north.

Yet, in a notable departure from his *Uncle Tom*, Conway refuses to allow northern racism to go unchallenged. The contrast in his plays' racial politics is most obvious in their Yankees. In *Dred*, Conway supplements Stowe's cast with the Yankee Cipher Cute, who both echoes and critiques his racist predecessors. Like Penetrate Partyside, Cipher Cute is a newcomer to the South, ignorant of what one slavocrat calls "our Southern institutions" (1.5). But whereas Partyside's southern experiences moderate his revulsion for slavery, Cute's stay in North Carolina turns him against the institution. By the middle of the play he has concluded that "niggers shouldn't be any body's property, any how; if they be, they're a dreadful skeany property. Now you have 'em, and now you don't have 'em" (2.5). Here as elsewhere, Cute's nascent abolitionism is "balanced" with racist wisecracks, but he never engages in the bigoted bullying of earlier Yankees. To the contrary, he several times indicates that his "egalitarianism" is racially inclusive. Upon entering the play, he immediately establishes himself as both a "working-class" egalitarian and an antiracist. Told that blacks are denied education in the South, he explodes: "Don't the stars and stripes float over this part of the country and over all 'The land of the free and the home of the brave?'" (1.5). Conway further identifies Cute with blacks in one scene where he shares his flask with a slave (but insists that his white owner drink from a horn) and another where he is mistaken for a fugitive after donning a slave's coat. The Yankee underlines the point of these episodes by singing:

> Yankee doodle, he's the chap
> Cries freedom in every station,
> But all the freedom for the whites
> The blacks — may see tarnation. (2.2)

In this remarkable (but probably unwitting) moment of self-critique, Conway attacks the hypocrisy of the stage Yankee's "egalitarianism." Cute's "nigger" jokes may make him a dubious mouth-piece for this sort of sentiment, but Conway clearly intends him as an advocate of racial equality. Moreover, the playwright endorses Cute's utterances through his characterization of the slaves. Whereas in Conway's *Uncle Tom* the slaves were thoroughly subordinated to the white characters, in *Dred* they act with considerable autonomy. This is obvious when Cute mimics Partyside by stepping between the slave Harry and his nemesis, Tom Gordon. But this time Conway refuses to allow his Yankee to patronize the slave: it is Harry, not Cute, who fights Tom, just as later it will be Dred, not Cute, who kills the slavocrat. The enhanced autonomy of Conway's black characters is as hard to account for as Cute's antiracism, but it may speak to a shift in northern racial feeling in the four years since Conway's *Uncle Tom*. Most whites remained deeply hostile to political or social equality for blacks, but by 1856 a number of prominent Republicans had begun to fight Democratic encroachments on the civil rights of African Americans (E. Foner *Free* 284–95).

Conway invited Lecture Room patrons to adopt Cute's racial views by rewarding him with a trip up the class ladder. Cute's rise over the course of the play from worker to lawyer is directly attributable to his antislavery turn. Despite the Yankee's pose of sacrificing money for morality, his hostility to slavery (and its champion Tom Gordon) ultimately wins him a job as Nina's legal adviser. Cute embraces the chance to remain South and thereby renews the transsectional bonds that Conway had created in *Uncle Tom*. But in *Dred* the Yankee's rise from northern worker to southern professional also highlights the differences between the sections. Cute succeeds, Conway makes clear, because he has the education most southerners lack. Amplifying a theme in Stowe, Conway has his slavocrats blame education for everything from slave insurgents like "the educated nigger" Dred to uppity workers like Cute. Confronted with the latter, one planter sputters: "What do working-men want with education? Education ruins 'em, sir, ruins 'em. . . . It raises them above their station" (1.5). The social consequences of this view are embodied in the poor white drunkard, John Cripps, who saddles his family with ignorance and poverty. But Conway holds out hope for Cripps's children in the final tableau's vision of an educated, dynamic South.

Conway leaves us with the vision of a South that is educated and (eventually) emancipated, but still male supremacist. Over the course of the play, he subordinates all his female characters, including the financially and emotionally independent Nina Gordon, to male domination.[72] Nina finally gives in and agrees to wed Clayton after deciding that she needs protection from her brother Tom. Clayton's response ("Then have I a husband's right!" [3.3]) typifies a play in which women function primarily as objects of struggle between men. Harry, Clayton, Dred, and Cute fight to protect the play's helpless females from the depredations of the evil Tom.[73] As in *Uncle Tom*, Conway masculinizes Stowe's plot by cutting her female characters: Anne Clayton collaborates in her brother's plan to educate the slaves in the novel but is eliminated from the play. Her place is filled by Cute, who sets a masculine tone by drinking, fighting, and boasting about his manhood.[74] Cute's contribution to the gender politics of *Dred* strongly foreshadows Sample Swichel in *Ten Nights in a Bar-Room*. In both cases, male playwrights used Yankees to masculinize political causes being advanced, to a considerable degree, by women. Like temperance, the antislavery movement enlisted women as organizers, petitioners, editors, and lecturers. By the mid-1850s many of the antislavery women were also agitating for women's rights. Aileen Kraditor has pointed out that *all* of the founders of the U.S. women's rights movement were abolitionists (Swerdlow 31). The radical women drew attacks from both outside and inside the antislavery movement. Capitalizing on the taboo against political, public women, antiabolitionists (including the early Barnum) attacked the antislavery women as libidinous negrophiles. The radical women were also resisted by antislavery conservatives—most notably in 1840, when Lewis Tappan led a revolt of evangelicals in the American Antislavery Society to protest, among other things, its inclusion of women in its leadership.[75]

The conflict over the antislavery feminists was also waged across U.S. culture, especially in drama and fiction. Antislavery short stories and novels boast several positive portraits of antislavery feminists (Yellin 69–70), but those radical women did not make it into the patriarchal confines of the antebellum theater. The conservatism of the stage was evident at Barnum's Museum, which trumpeted the participation of women in its 1856 Test Vote before putting them back in their place with Conway's *Dred*.[76] The resistance to the antislavery feminists was mounted by play-wrights who agreed in little else: it was no coincidence that both Conway and Aiken felt it necessary to marry off Stowe's Ophelia St. Clare. Her outspoken independence had no place in a genre where the chief female roles are divided between low-comedy spinsters and passive True Woman heroines.

A sure sign of the theater's opposition to the antislavery femi-nists is the popularity of the slave version of the True Woman: the tragic mulatta.[77] The stage mulatta is a complex amalgama-tion of radical and reactionary impulses. Her racial ambiguity, as we shall see, made her a threat to white supremacy, but her passive femininity made her valuable to the exponents of male power. Played by white actresses without the theatrical markers of blackness (blackface makeup and dialect), the stage mulatta served the male playwrights as a cross-racial icon of female sub-missiveness. In an age when many northerners viewed the South as a land of sexual license, antislavery writers created a pornog-raphy of sexual domination around the mulatta.[78] The most pop-ular antislavery plays all feature plots or subplots in which chaste mulattas are pursued, but never raped, by lustful slaveholders. Significantly, the stage mulatta's black and white female counter-parts are rarely the victims of white male sexual exploitation — a fact that suggests the worthlessness of the antislavery dramas as representations of the female experience. The plays, however, have much to tell us about the racial and gender ideologies of their white male creators.

## The Octoroon

On 6 February 1860, Barnum's Lecture Room introduced its patrons to one of the century's most famous mulattas when it opened its production of Dion Boucicault's *The Octoroon; or, Life in Louisiana*. By the time she arrived on Barnum's stage, Bouci-cault's octoroon was among the most contested features of a play whose two-month production history was rich in controversy. *The Octoroon*'s first performances the previous December had sparked a series of debates over its representation of race, gender, and slavery — controversies fueled largely by the contemporane-

ous furor over abolitionist raider John Brown. Although Boucicault craftily blurred his play's politics, his veiled gestures to
Brown and antislavery were enough to outrage southern-sympathizing critics. Barnum, however, set the antiabolitionists at ease
by juxtaposing *The Octoroon* with some of his most reactionary
attractions. With the aid of the Museum's permanent collection
and nontheatrical performers, the Lecture Room rescripted the
politics of Boucicault's play—thereby extending the "hand of
friendship" to the South long after many northerners had with-
drawn it.[79]

To understand the scope of Barnum's revision of *The Octoroon*,
we must return to its news-making opening run up Broadway
from the American Museum at the Winter Garden Theatre. Under
ordinary circumstances, no drama as cautious as this one would
have sparked so much debate. *The Octoroon* was far more conservative than either Aiken's *Uncle Tom* or Conway's *Dred*. What
made Boucicault's play controversial was not so much its content as its timing. It opened on 6 December 1859, four days after
John Brown's execution by the state of Virginia for crimes committed in his 16 October takeover of the federal armory and arsenal at Harper's Ferry. The execution sent a stunning wave of
sympathy rolling across the North for a man whose name had
spent the past six weeks on the front page of every newspaper and
in the mouth of every politician. Looking back on those weeks,
Henry David Thoreau insisted, "I know of nothing so miraculous
in our history" ("Last" 145). By the time of his death, John Brown
was bigger than William Lloyd Garrison, bigger than Harriet
Beecher Stowe, bigger even than P. T. Barnum. Six days after his
execution, a *New York Evening Post* story titled "A Fortune for
Barnum" described a freak as rare as any in the Museum: "A man
has been found who has never heard of John Brown!"[80] But some
New Yorkers were not amused. Panicked by the pro-Brown editorials, sermons, and public rallies, the antiabolitionist *New York
Herald* called for the suppression of Boucicault's play: "[W]e wage
war against the 'Octoroon,' and declare, in the name of the good
citizens of the metropolis, that neither that nor any other play
of the same character should be performed."[81] When this call for
a theater riot failed to take effect, the *Herald* renewed its attack,
charging Boucicault with disguising his abolitionism: "[T]he spec-

tator is drawn on by degrees, without perceiving it, till at the end he finds himself a sympathizer with John Brown."[82] The Republican *Evening Post* reviled the *Herald*'s politics, but agreed with its reading of the play. In an editorial titled "John Brown on the Stage," the paper used Boucicault's success to taunt the Union Savers, the group of New York City merchants who were rushing to appease the South in the wake of Harper's Ferry.[83] The *Evening Post* painted the Union Savers as a band of cowards isolated in a city where "crowds nightly throng, and will continue to throng, the display of the chain-gang and the slave auction."[84] Caught up in its polemic, the paper exaggerated the radicalism of Boucicault's play, which depicts a slave auction, but no chain gang. Indeed, many critics argued that *The Octoroon* was actually noncommittal or even southern in its sympathies.[85] The *Times* seemed genuinely baffled at the heat generated by what it termed an "impartial" drama; the paper would eventually dismiss the *Herald*'s attacks as a publicity stunt masterminded by none other than Boucicault himself.[86] Boucicault was certainly capable of such Barnumesque intrigue, and there is tantalizing evidence to suggest that he wanted antiabolitionists to protest his play.[87] But if that was his strategy, it seems to have worked a bit too well. As the attacks multiplied, Boucicault bent over backward to conciliate his southern-sympathizing critics. In a reply to the *Herald,* he claimed that his goal was "sketches of slave life, truthful I know, and I hope gentle and kind."[88] The following month the playwright even identified himself as a "Southern Democrat" in an open letter that solicited responses from his play's Louisiana readers.[89]

Just how far Boucicault was willing to go to appease the South is clear when one compares his play with its primary source, Mayne Reid's 1856 novel, *The Quadroon.*[90] From Reid, Boucicault took his plot of a white outsider who comes to Louisiana and promptly falls in love with a beautiful mulatta whom he meets on a plantation. Both Reid and Boucicault pit the lovers against an evil slaveholder who schemes to purchase the mulatta to satisfy his lust. The villain is ultimately foiled by the surprise exposure of documents that reveal his crimes against the mulatta and her liberal slaveholding defenders. This sensational plot afforded Reid and Boucicault plenty of opportunities to attack slavery, though neither was eager to seize them. Reid disavows any abolitionist intentions in an author's note and at one point favorably compares the condition of U.S. slaves to that of British citizens (37–39). Nevertheless, his novel depicts enough of slavery's brutality to stand as a clear indictment of the system. The critique is predictably sharpest where his heroine is concerned. The quadroon is threatened by a long line of slaveholders who attempt to purchase and exploit her. Boucicault, on the other hand, concentrates all of slavery's evil in his villain M'Closky, whose greed, dishonesty, and lust make him unique among the play's slaveholders. The writers' contrasting depictions of the slaveholders are complemented by contrasting responses from the slaves. In Boucicault, not even M'Closky's atrocities are enough to inspire the slaves to flee or rebel. Reid, however, depicts slaves escaping and physically resisting their oppressors. And whereas Reid's quadroon challenges the South's antimiscegenation laws by marrying a white man, Boucicault's octoroon dies while blessing the union of her lover and a white woman. In short, the *New York Tribune* was right to blame Boucicault for "a placatory tendency to the slave-owner."[91] His revisions of Reid's mildly antislavery novel leave a portrait of slavery that is, for the most part, as "gentle and kind" as he had promised.

Despite Boucicault's respect for the slaveholders and their laws, the New York papers were not seeing things when they glimpsed the ghost of John Brown in *The Octoroon*. Whether intentionally or not, Boucicault seems to have drawn on the mixture of fact and fantasy swirling around Brown to create his hero, the Yankee overseer Salem Scudder.[92] Of course, one could argue that John Brown had already turned himself into the hero of a play before Boucicault got to him. Brown's last weeks passed in a series of charged theatrical moments, as he addressed the nation from his jail cell and the courtroom. Thoreau found Brown's heroism more comprehensible as theater than as real life: "No theatrical manager could have arranged things so wisely to give effect to his behavior and words. And who, think you, *was* the manager? Who placed the slave woman and her child, whom he stooped to kiss for a symbol, between his prison and the gallows?" ("Last" 151–52).

That Boucicault might offer himself as Brown's stage manager should not surprise us. When the playwright began work on *The Octoroon* in the weeks after Harper's Ferry, he was already well aware of the theatrical potential of hot news stories.[93] He had recently cashed in on the real-life exploits of two contemporary celebrities in his plays *Jessie Brown* and *Brigham Young.* Nor should we be surprised by Brown's surfacing in, of all things, an overseer. Boucicault was far too cautious to include an abolitionist in his play, much less a revolutionary. If Brown was to be exploited, it would have to be obliquely—so obliquely, in fact, that Scudder scarcely resembles the raider in his attitude toward slavery. Scudder devotes himself to saving the fortunes of his slaveholding employers, rather than to freeing their slaves. In the course of his efforts, however, Scudder echoes the combination of moral vigilantism, racial paternalism, and insurrection with which Brown was synonymous. Like the raider praised by Wendell Phillips as "a regular Cromwellian dug up from two centuries" ("Harper's" 276), Salem Scudder possesses a moral authority directly linked to the Puritans who provide his first name.[94] Also like the financially destitute Brown, Scudder is far less adept at the affairs of this world than the next: in contrast to his hated predecessor M'Closky, Scudder has managed to bankrupt his employers without enriching himself.

It is Scudder's confident elevation of morality above institutional law, however, that most closely links him to Brown. Scudder endorses a moral vigilantism that at times threatens to turn Boucicault's *Life in Louisiana* into other dramas about other parts of the United States. This is especially obvious when Scudder places his vigilantism "here, in the wilds of the West, where our hatred of crime is measured by the speed of our executions— where necessity is law!" (4). The disorienting geographic referent here—Louisiana as the West—may come from Reid, who subtitled his novel *Adventures in the Far West*; in the wake of Harper's Ferry, however, Boucicault's audience may also have heard an allusion to John Brown's western exploits. Brown was notorious for having taken the law into his own hands at Pottawatomie Creek, Kansas, where in 1856 he orchestrated the murders of five proslavery settlers. Two years later he helped free eleven slaves in a spectacular raid on two Missouri planters. Scudder likewise anoints himself an agent of justice against the slaveholder in what is easily the most complex scene in *The Octoroon*: the one depicting the consecutive lynch trials of the Indian chief Wahnotee and M'Closky for the murder of the slave boy Paul. When the murder is discovered, M'Closky accuses Wahnotee before a hastily assembled lynch jury of white men. Scudder alone steps forward to defend the Indian. He condemns the lynch jury as "a wild and lawless proceeding" (4). Moments later, however, new evidence emerges that reveals Wahnotee's innocence and M'Closky's guilt, whereupon Scudder changes his mind about lynch trials and swears in the men he has just finished censuring. It is, to say the least, a reversal bordering on the absurd. To justify himself, Scudder distinguishes between the lynch juries that "try" Wahnotee and M'Closky: whereas the former is dedicated to racial revenge, the latter serves "a higher power than the law" (4). Scudder's notion of a moral law above human law surely would have resonated with the "higher law" that abolitionists frequently called upon to justify their beliefs—so frequently, in fact, that male abolitionists were sometimes known as "higher law men." For Boucicault's audience, the most memorable invocation of the higher law had come during John Brown's sentencing speech, when he defended his violation of the slaveholders' "wicked, cruel, and unjust enactments" in the name of justice (Oates 327). Boucicault, as we have seen, is not willing to go this far. His hero can transcend the law to punish a murderer, but not to free a slave. Although Scudder is revolted at the thought of M'Closky buying the octoroon Zoe, he joins the other characters—both slave and slaveholder alike—in scrupulously adhering to the laws that enslave her. Boucicault repeatedly identifies the law as the chief instrument in Zoe's oppression, but he refuses to follow writers like Stowe in explicitly calling for its violation. The result is a play that feels more antislavery than it literally is. Through Scudder, Boucicault appropriates the moral righteousness of the era's most famous radical by detaching it from its specific abolitionist goal.

As Boucicault no doubt realized, much of the country was fascinated with John Brown less as an abolitionist than as an insurrectionist. Brown's raid was intended to provide the inspiration, and arms, for a massive slave uprising sweeping from Virginia into the Deep South. As the scope of Brown's plans became known in the days after his capture, white southerners persecuted slaves and whites falsely accused of plotting rebellion (Oates 321). The specter of racial insurgency also floated through the public response to Brown in the North. Antiabolitionists and antislavery moderates comforted themselves with the fact that the slaves had failed to rally to Brown; on the other hand, many abolitionists eulogized Brown by openly endorsing slave rebellion for the first time. In the days leading up to his execution, the object of those eulogies repeatedly disavowed any insurrectionary intentions. A master manipulator of his celebrity, Brown portrayed himself as the protector of slaves who were unable to defend themselves. At his execution, for example, he requested that his attendants be "poor *little, dirty, ragged, bare headed, & barefooted Slave Boys; & Girls;* led by some old *grey headed Slave* Mother" (quoted in Oates 346). By depicting the slaves as helpless victims, rather than armed rebels—as Zoe rather than Nat Turner— Brown rescripted his raid to fit the racial paternalism of antislavery moderates.

Although some northerners believed Brown's pronouncements, most understood that he had come South to rescue the slaves by arming them. Boucicault capitalizes on Brown's transparent fiction in *The Octoroon,* where Scudder voices a comparable paternalism toward the victims of white oppression. At one point the Yankee spells out the white man's burden regarding his alleged racial inferiors:

> Nature has said that where the white man sets his foot, the red man and the black man shall up sticks and stand around. But what do we pay for that possession? In cash? No—in kind—that is, in protection, forbearance, gentleness, in all them goods that show the critters the difference between the Christian and the savage. (5.3)

For most of the play Boucicault endorses Scudder's sentiments by surrounding him with red and black victims who seem to need his paternalism. In the end, however, Scudder's rhetoric proves just as hollow as Brown's. The final act portrays Scudder as less a protector of the slaves than a facilitator of their revenge. He enacts the slaveholder's worst nightmare when he turns M'Closky over to the play's personification of racial vengeance: the Indian chief Wahnotee (see Figure 8). The consequences of Scudder's decision are spelled out in a haunting final tableau that depicts M'Closky lying dead on Paul's grave with "WAHNOTEE *standing triumphantly over him*" (5.4).

This tableau looks even more haunting when we realize that it is the single instance in which Boucicault is more radical than his source. In *The Quadroon*, Reid's slaveholding villain suffers imprisonment, not racial revenge. To be sure, Boucicault displays typical caution by opting for an Indian avenger rather than a black one: John Augustus Stone's *Metamora* is a more obvious antecedent here than Harper's Ferry. But Boucicault has already taken some pains to establish slave insurrection as a subtext to the tableau by linking Wahnotee to the play's slave characters, especially the victims Zoe and Paul; reviled by the slaveholders, who don't understand his language, Wahnotee can communicate only with the slaves. Scudder spells out the significance of these ties when, as we have seen, he couples "the red man and the black man" as victims of white oppression. This enables Wahnotee to stand as a symbol of both black and Indian revenge. But the precise motivation of Wahnotee's act remains unclear: Has he killed

Figure 8. Wahnotee on an American Museum bill for *The Octoroon*. (Harvard Theatre Collection, the Houghton Library)

M'Closky simply for his murder of Paul, or is he also exacting revenge for M'Closky's broader crimes as a slaveholder—the crimes
that John Brown had famously claimed would "never be purged
*away;* but with Blood"?[95] Boucicault prevents us from defini-
tively answering these questions. His tableau, like the rest of his
play, is ambiguous enough to support the most contradictory
interpretations.

The Indian's ambiguities made him less a threat for some members of Boucicault's audience than the self-annihilating octoroon.
New York's southern-sympathizing *Spirit of the Times* climaxed a
blistering attack on the play with a salvo for Boucicault's heroine:

> [I]f such a being as Zoe ever existed in person, her mind and the
> taint of her blood would create a gulf between her and the whites
> that would be wider than the poles asunder, and all the sympathy
> and sentiment the incendiary author of this piece creates is
> founded upon the false idea that there is an equality in the races,
> an idea that is preposterous, unnatural, and profane.[96]

This tirade amply demonstrates the threat some antiabolitionists
saw in the tragic mulatta—a literary type whose uses for male
supremacist playwrights have already been noted. According to
some critics, the mulatta's racial politics were equally reactionary.
They argue that the tragic mulattas who appear in the antislavery
fiction of Lydia Maria Child, Harriet Beecher Stowe, and William
Wells Brown were intended to appeal to middle-class white readers—a group that preferred their slave characters to talk, look,
and think like the fair heroines of sentimental fiction.[97] Boucicault may well have been stroking the racial prejudices of those
readers when he further whitened Reid's quadroon heroine. At
the same time, however, proslavery racial theorists would probably have found the whiter slave the more threatening. In the
years leading up to the Civil War, those theorists, the so-called
American school ethnologists, supplied intellectual ammunition
for the slavocrats with a new polygenetic model of racial origins. They rejected the eighteenth-century view that the world's
races were variations of a single species that shared a common
ancestry.[98] Instead, they claimed that races were separately created species, with contrasting physical and mental traits. Although the polygenesists' rejection of the Bible drew attacks from
Christian conservatives, their portrayal of blacks as an inferior

species proved popular among apologists for slavery in both North and South (Fredrickson 79–96). Indeed, the thorniest problem for the polygenesists was not the church, but the mulatto. Accepted notions of hybridity held that if blacks and whites were different species, any cross-breeding would produce sterile offspring. This forced the polygenesists to claim that mulattoes were either infertile themselves or became so in subsequent generations. The mulattoes were further doomed, the American school held, by the white race's repugnance for amalgamating with weakened stock (Fredrickson 80). That repugnance, however, is nowhere to be seen in Boucicault's play, where all of the leading white male characters are intensely attracted to Zoe. Even without her suitors, Zoe symbolically repudiates the polygenesists: as a third-generation mulatta she obviously challenges the American school's description of mulattoes as infertile hybrids.

Boucicault may have hoped to bring his mulatta in check by having her commit suicide in his final act, but her ghost lived on to haunt the friends of slavery. This was amply demonstrated the following spring by antiabolitionist humorist Artemus Ward. In a widely reprinted newspaper sketch, he narrated a fictional encounter with an "onprinsipuld Octoroon" who claimed to be a freed slave. She dazzles him with her beauty, which he describes as "rather more Roon than Octo" (Browne 45), and then she plays on his pity to swindle him out of his money. Ward's octoroon follows a long line of ex-slave con artists in antiabolitionist fiction that includes the Joice Heth character in *Adventures of an Adventurer*. The apologists for slavery used the ex-slave swindler to undermine their white readers' sympathies for blacks and, one assumes, to smother their own feelings of guilt toward the slave. That *something* is being repressed in Ward's story is clear enough when he responds to the swindle by falling under his seat, passing out, and dreaming of his hometown being captured by an army of octoroons. The swindle and the nightmare are striking in their reversal of the standard antislavery plot: Ward depicts the white male as the passive victim of an aggressive mulatta. His sketch embodied the threat that male antiabolitionists sensed in a figure who could play havoc with their feelings as well as their ideas. Ward's nightmare would have sounded especially familiar to the proslavery ethnologists who were struggling to defend their racial categories from the theoretical invasion of the mulatta.

By the time of Ward's sketch, the *Octoroon* army had taken much of the North by storm. In the winter of 1859–60, Boucicault's play appeared in four New York playhouses as well as in theaters in Boston and Philadelphia. The *New York Times* reflected on the phenomenon: "Everybody talks about the 'Octoroon,' wonders about the 'Octoroon,' goes to see the 'Octoroon;' and the 'Octoroon' thus becomes, in point of fact, the work of the public mind."[99] Any play this successful was bound to find its way into Barnum's Lecture Room, especially given that Boucicault and his ex-manager were racing each other to sell the script.[100] The Museum that raised the curtain on its *Octoroon* exactly two months after the Winter Garden production would seem perfectly suited to Boucicault's fence-sitting politics. As its divided critical reception would suggest, *The Octoroon* had something to offer both Barnum's antislavery country patrons and his antiabolitionist New Yorkers. In the wake of Harper's Ferry, however, the American Museum was not about to let patrons interpret Boucicault's ambiguities for themselves. It carefully closed off the play's most radical implications by displaying it alongside some of Barnum's most reactionary exhibits and performers. The Museum's strategy can be gathered from ads that couple *The Octoroon* with its waxwork exhibit of John Brown. The exhibit offers a far different Brown from the one who haunts Boucicault's play. It featured

AN AUTOGRAPH COMMISSION of JOHN BROWN, given to a lieutenancy in his army of revolution; A KNIFE from the hands of BROWN'S SON, accompanies these curiosities, as well as TWO OF THE FAMOUS PIKES OR SPEARS, captured from Harper's Ferry—one of which was taken from the hands of COPPIE [*sic*].[101]

Barnum's exhibit ignores the abolitionist champion of the higher law to portray the raider as a violent criminal. The Museum would eventually go so far as to group the Brown exhibit together with its waxworks of A. W. Hicks and Jackalow, "both on trial for piracy and murder."[102] Despite the contrary claims of southern fire-eaters, Barnum's waxwork reflected the view of the majority of white northerners in the wake of Harper's Ferry. Leading antislavery politicians such as Lincoln and William Seward called for Brown's execution, and the Republican Party's 1860 platform placed Harper's Ferry "among the gravest of crimes" (Potter 423). It was this view of Brown that Barnum stressed for patrons of Boucicault's play. As Lecture Room patrons heard Salem Scudder invoke a "higher power than the law," Barnum assured them that there was no law higher than the slaveholders'. That was just what the *New York Atlas* wanted to hear. The antiabolitionist paper instructed readers on the proper way to take in the Museum's latest production: "Go there, first in the lower saloon, take a look at John Brown; then in the upper saloon, and look in upon the 'Octoroon.' "[103]

To judge from the Museum's response, however, Scudder's vigilantism was less troubling than the racial unruliness of Wahnotee and Zoe. The Museum brought Boucicault's nonwhites in line by juxtaposing them against Barnum's latest star attraction, the "What Is It?" Beginning on 25 February, Boucicault's play and the John Brown waxwork shared Museum bills with the famous "CONNECTING LINK BETWEEN MAN AND MONKEY"—an attraction supposedly captured by adventurers hunting gorillas in the interior of Africa (see Figure 9).[104] As Saxon has argued, the enactor of this early "What Is It?" may well have been the black dwarf William Henry Johnson, who would later perform the role in Barnum's circuses (*PTB* 98–99).[105] This was not Barnum's first "What Is It?" nor was it the first time he had exhibited a sham connecting link between humans and animal.[106] It was, however, the first time Barnum had cast a black male in the role, and the press immediately seized the opportunity to make racist comparisons between the freak's physique and behavior and that of "the negro."[107] The Museum encouraged such commentary by displaying the "What Is It?" with a white "keeper" or "protector" who spun tall tales about his charge's capture in Africa, his shipment to the United States, and his recent efforts at walking on two legs and eating cooked food. During this spiel, the "What Is It?" typically grinned, made cheeping noises, and, when his "keeper" wasn't looking, indulged in what the *New York Clipper* called "many sly manoeuvers that lets in the light on the humbug terribly."[108] Those maneuvers were hardly necessary to tip off skeptical reporters, several of whom immediately exposed Barnum's

Figure 9. The "What Is It?" and American Museum patrons. (Collection of the New-York Historical Society)

latest fraud. The public, however, seems not to have cared: the "What Is It?" would remain a star attraction in Barnum's museums and circuses for the next three decades. One key to the act's popularity is clear enough: whether whites believed they were gawking at an African man-monkey or simply a black man, the "What Is It?" offered them a comforting image of white paternalism. Finding the freak "as lively and playful as a kitten," the *Tribune* praised the "brightness of its eye, and its intelligent responses to the words and motions of the person in charge."[109] The "What Is It?"'s obedience, like that of a well-trained pet, reflected the power and wisdom of his white "keeper." The freak was both helpless enough to need a master and intelligent enough to make the white man's mastery of him impressive.

The Museum brought this racist act to bear on the country's most pressing political question when it began displaying the "What Is It?" on the Lecture Room stage between first and second acts of *The Octoroon*. This juxtaposition seems calculated to encourage cross-readings between the freak and the play's characters of color. More specifically, by repeatedly asserting that the "What Is It?" "HAS NO FACULTY OF SPEECH!" the Museum would have called to mind Wahnotee, whom the *Tribune* labeled "the pantomimic Indian."[110] The connection was tightened when the Museum moved the appearance of the "What Is It?" to the break after the second act.[111] This brought the freak onstage just after the scene in which Wahnotee discovers Paul's body. The act closes with Wahnotee smashing a camera that he blames for killing Paul, and then sorrowfully taking the slave boy's body in his arms. Wahnotee's forceful display of compassion and rage would have been largely dissipated in the following moments by the sportive docility of the "What Is It?" The freak's eager responses to his keeper's commands would have set to rights the racial hierarchy shaken by Boucicault's play. Unlike Wahnotee, the "What Is It?" required the paternalism that Scudder identifies as the white man's debt to his supposed racial inferiors. Moreover, the freak's race would have laid to rest any phantoms of Harper's Ferry called up by Wahnotee: juxtaposed against the African man-monkey, the Indian would have appeared an unlikely standard-bearer for a black insurgency.

The "What Is It?" also contained Boucicault's other racial threat by bringing evolutionary rhetoric to bear on the mulatta. In 1859, American school theorists arguing for the status of race as species found an unlikely ally in Charles Darwin—unlikely because *On the Origin of Species* delivered a crushing blow to polygenesis. The American school and its slavocrat allies, however, cared far less about the origin of blacks than about their specific difference from whites. This was an issue that Darwin had carefully evaded in the *Origin*—a work with almost nothing explicit to say about human evolution. Undaunted, the American school immediately appropriated Darwin for its racial theory. As George Fredrickson points out, the polygenesists argued that "blacks and whites had diverged in their evolution to such an extent that their differences could now be considered specific" (232). Far from shaking the faith of white supremacists in their biological superiority to blacks, Darwinism supplied them with a powerful new model for proving it. This was evident in U.S. popular culture, where evolutionary rhetoric was quickly deployed against the intractable mulatta. In January 1860, Christy's Minstrels offered a vicious blackface assault on the nation's most famous mulatta titled *The Moctoroon*. While mocking all of Boucicault's characters, the sketch saved a special insult for its heroine Zoeasy, who was described as the "unhappy descendant of a Gorilla" (Odell 7:282). That the mulatta would draw this attack follows from what we have seen of her racial unruliness. That the attack took this pseudo-Darwinian form foreshadowed what would happen a month later when Barnum blindsided Zoe with his "CONNECTING LINK BETWEEN THE WILD NATIVE AFRICAN AND THE BRUTE CREATION."[112] In a culture obsessed with the line between blacks and whites, Barnum used the "What Is It?" to help fortify the racist tradition of a line between blacks and animals. The "What Is It?" was the first, and most popular, of a series of African exhibits at the American Museum in 1860 that depicted blacks as animalistic. Chief among them were the Earthwoman and the skin-clad representatives of five South African tribes. As the election of Lincoln made sectional war over slavery appear increasingly likely, the Museum was offering blacks as the scapegoat for the nation's problems. This Artemus Ward indicated when he used the "What

Is It?" to lay the crime of disunion at the feet of U.S. blacks. In a burlesque speech titled "The Crisis," Ward recalled his confrontation with the freak:

> I was into BARNIM'S Moozeum down to New York the other day
> & saw that exsentric Etheopian, the What Is It. Sez I, "Mister
> What Is It, you folks air raisin thunder with this grate country.
> You're gettin to be ruther more numeris than interestin. It is a
> pity you coodent go orf sumwhares by yourselves, & be a nation
> of What Is Its, tho' if you'll excoose me, I shooden't care about
> marryin among you." (Browne 52)

Ward's encounter with the "What Is It?" lays to rest the anxieties so palpable in his fictional run-in with the octoroon. Whereas her racially ambiguous beauty had threatened him with the specter of miscegenation, the "What Is It?" makes interracial marriage look revolting. And whereas she had aroused his pity for the slaves, the "What Is It?" allows him to read them as animalistic, unwanted intruders. Ward concludes his encounter with the freak shouting, "Go home, Sir, to Afriky's burnin shores & taik all the other What Is Its along with you" (Browne 53). It was a cry that was being joined by many supposed opponents of slavery, as the secession crisis won new Republican converts to black colonization (E. Foner *Free* 276).

Ward was not the only person comforted by the image of blackness on display at Barnum's Museum. The "What Is It?" proved widely popular in the New York papers, including the Republican *Evening Post* and *Tribune*. Meanwhile, the opposition used Barnum's star to ridicule the Republicans: in one satirical lithograph from 1860, president-elect Lincoln and *Tribune* editor Horace Greeley presented the "What Is It?" as their party's next "HEIR TO THE THRONE" (see Figure 10). But the most telling proof of the freak's powerful appeal came from the antiabolitionist *New York Herald*. As one would expect, that virulently racist paper eagerly reprinted the Museum's lies about the capture and exhibition of the "What Is It?" As few would expect, however, the *Herald* then proceeded to laud the Museum's production of *The Octoroon*: "It is very well put upon the stage, and the acting is highly creditable to the managers."[113] Modest as it may sound, this is startling praise from a paper that recently had spilled so much ink trying to suppress the play. The *Herald's* reversal at-

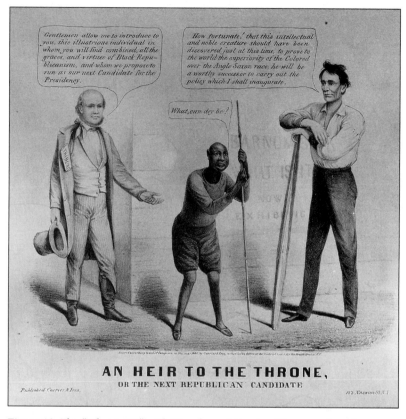

Figure 10. The "What Is It?" with Lincoln and Greeley. (Courtesy American Antiquarian Society)

tests to Barnum's success at making *The Octoroon* safe for even the most antiabolitionist of patrons. It also foreshadows the enormous popularity of the "What Is It?" and other racist exhibitions of people of color during and after the Civil War. In those years, the proprietary museums that followed in Barnum's wake extended his racial exotics into a full-blown celebration of U.S. imperialism. To be sure, *The Octoroon, Uncle Tom's Cabin,* and other antislavery dramas survived on the stages of late-nineteenth-century dime museums and theaters to offer a contrasting picture of U.S. race relations. But with the dearth of new antiracist challenges from the theater, a large segment of U.S. culture devoted itself to answering the loaded question, What is it?

# 5

## "A Stupendous Mirror of Departed Empires": The Barnum Hippodromes and Circuses

You are an old man, and the vim, vigor and sharp wit and cunning of your youth and manhood have left you. In the course of events you will soon join the famous celebrities that in years gone by adorned your "great moral show." Then your already written epitaph will, we suppose, be inscribed upon your circus wagons by your zealous partners,

> "The show is over, Barnum's gone?
> His earthly journey now is done;
> Ambition did his soul surround,
> The purchased votes could not be found.
> The Yankee people would not choose him,
> But sent him, stuffed, into his Museum.
> Preserved in wax, his eyes all glass...."

—from an ad for the Adam Forepaugh Circus titled "To P. T. Barnum," *Philadelphia Evening Bulletin* (1884)

When Barnum turned his attention to circuses and hippodromes in the wake of the fire at the Barnum and Van Amburgh Museum and Menagerie Combination, so did some of his star racial exotics. Museum favorites like the "What Is It?" and the Madagascar albino family showed up in the traveling shows that Barnum fielded with Dan Castello and William C. Coup in the early 1870s. But when it came to the exhibition of non-Western people, Barnum's museums and circuses shared more than a few key performers: in the last decades of the century the Barnum circuses framed their racial exotics in imperialist narratives that strongly echoed the American Museum at midcentury. The importance of those narratives to Barnum's circuses, and those of his rivals, has not been adequately explored. This chapter examines Barnum's exhibitions of non-Westerners for what they can tell us about the evolution of U.S. ideologies of race and nation in the post-Civil War era. All of Barnum's circuses and hippodromes celebrated white, bourgeois manhood under the banners of Christianity and Civilization, but the shows differed in their use of non-Westerners to articulate their social allegiances. I explore this transformation by focusing primarily on the international racial exhibitions of Barnum's Great Roman Hippodrome of 1874–75 and the Barnum & London Circus of the following decade. The former show brought its white patrons in contact with the East through cross-racial desire and identification. The latter, in contrast, emphasized the racial barrier between white patron and non-Western performer. Whereas the Hippodrome framed its Orientals in empowering political categories such as nationality and monarchy, the Barnum & London Circus reduced non-Westerners to the status of "specimens" in an ethnological schema. Barnum's reconstruction of the Oriental demonstrated both the expansiveness and the inadequacy of race as a marker of difference in late-nineteenth-century popular cultural and intellectual discourses; moreover, the shows' racial reconstructions carried contradictory implications for U.S. domestic politics in an age when the circus was often received as a model of industrial discipline. The Orientals offered white patrons a safely mediated access to the passion, poetry, and violence they had supposedly sacrificed to Western progress. But by Othering their non-Western performers in this manner, the Barnum shows betrayed the chinks in the armor of late-nineteenth-century white manhood.

Barnum first incorporated a non-Western performer in one of his traveling shows in 1851, when he joined Seth Howes and Sherwood Stratton (the father of Tom Thumb) as partners in P. T. Barnum's Asiatic Caravan, Museum, and Menagerie. Among that show's main Asiatic features was a herd of elephants captured by Barnum's intrepid agents in the wilds of Ceylon.[1] The elephants were impressive, but not more so than the Cingalese native — billed as a chief — who was imported and displayed with them; indeed, the show's ads devoted as much space to "chief" as to the herd.[2] Although the Cingalese was the first non-Westerner on a Barnum road show, he had several predecessors at the American

Museum, whose attractions in the 1840s included a "New Zealand Canibal [*sic*] chief" and a troupe of Bedouins.[3] Unlike those performers, however, the Cingalese was presented less as a curiosity in himself than as a representative of a larger ethnic group. One bill described him as a member of the "wild and wandering tribe of Kaffirs, whose ferocious habits are vividly described by Euguene [*sic*] Sue in the Wandering Jew."[4] Barnum's new ethnological rhetoric signaled his growing interest in international racial displays. Less than two years before the importation of the Cingalese, he had temporarily suspended plans for his most ambitious such exhibition, one that would occupy him off and on for the next three and a half decades. In *Struggles,* he recalls how the Lind concerts sidetracked his scheme for

> a "Congress of Nations" — an assemblage of representatives of all the nations that could be reached by land or sea. I meant to secure a man and woman, as perfect as could be procured, from every accessible people, civilized and barbarous, on the face of the globe. I had actually contracted with an agent to go to Europe to make arrangements to secure "specimens" for such a show. Even now, I can conceive of no exhibition which would be more interesting and which would appeal more generally to all classes of patrons. (271)[5]

In the 1850s and 1860s, Barnum made various unsuccessful attempts to bring off this exhibition at the American Museum. The showman and his partners sought Circassian women, South African tribesmen, and other exotic people for displays that Barnum planned to call either a "Congress of Nations" or "Human Menagerie."[6] Barnum's uncertainty over the title reflects a larger uncertainty over the conception of the exhibit: Would he organize it around the historical category of nation or the biological category of race? Or, to borrow the terminology of *Struggles,* was he planning a congress of national "representatives" or a menagerie of racial "specimens"? As Barnum's contradictory vocabulary suggests, by 1869 he still had not answered these questions.

### The Congress of Nations

It was only after the destruction of his Museum and his reemergence as a proprietor of traveling shows that Barnum finally suc-

ceeded in staging his international congress. In 1872 the circus
that Barnum had founded with Coup and Castello — P. T. Barnum's Great Traveling Museum, Menagerie and World's Fair —
boasted "Fiji cannibals, Modoc and Digger Indians, and representative types of Chinese, Japanese, Aztecs, and Eskimos" (Betts
360). But two more years would pass before Barnum unveiled
his first official "Congress of Nations." This took place in the
second traveling show that he formed with Coup: P. T. Barnum's
Great Roman Hippodrome. After opening in the spring of 1874
in a newly constructed building in New York City, this show spent
much of its two-year existence touring the United States. As its
name would suggest, the Great Roman Hippodrome featured primarily equestrian events, but its most famous attraction was a
pageant titled the "Congress of Nations" that opened its early performances. This spectacle only partly fulfilled the plan for a Congress that Barnum had outlined in *Struggles*. Whereas that scheme
called for the exhibition of the world's "civilized and barbarous"
peoples, the Hippodrome's Congress restricted itself to the "CIV-
ILIZED NATIONS." And whereas *Struggles* proposed a display
of contemporary countries, the Hippodrome's Congress re-created
both "ANCIENT AND MODERN MONARCHS."[7] The pageant's
national chariots bore performers who reenacted famous rulers
and notables ranging from Confucius to Queen Victoria. It took
its history from the Congress of Monarchs, a pageant created by
British showmen John and George Sanger. Barnum purchased
duplicates of the chariots, costumes, and other paraphernalia of
the Sangers' show for the Hippodrome's April 1874 opening. His
effort to adapt their historical pageant to fit his earlier plans produced some complicated results. In *Struggles* he recalled the Hippodrome's "allegorical representation of a 'Congress of Nations,'
in a grand procession of gilded chariots and triumphal cars, con-
veying the Kings, Queens, Emperors, and other potentates of the
civilized world, costumed with historical correctness" (*ST* 1875,
849). As Barnum's vocabulary suggests, in its voyage across the
Atlantic, the Sangers' "historical" Congress of Monarchs had been
partly transformed into the "allegorical" Congress of Nations —
in fact, it exhibited under both titles during the 1874 season. The
pageant's mingling of history and transhistorical allegory can be
seen in the Congress's U.S. and Irish entries. In those chariots, al-

legorical figures such as Hibernia and the American Goddess of Liberty shared a ride with political and military heroes, including George Washington and Daniel O'Connell. The pageant further complicated things by mocking its own concepts of "historical correctness" and nationhood in the miniature chariot filled with "beauteous little children" who represented Lilliput (Haines 80).

The pageant's hybrid, fragmentary, and self-parodying nature sparked conflicting readings from the Hippodrome's class-segmented audience. Patrons felt free to grant or dismiss as it served their purposes the Congress's premise of assembling the world's nations East and West. Whereas some took at face value the pageant's claim to depict "with historic truthfulness the Sovereigns of all Nations, and the manners and customs of nine centuries," others read through the pageant's international, multiracial representations to the white working-class performers beneath.[8] The Congress of Nations thus occasioned a conflict in styles of reading, pitting the allegorical interpretations of the pageant's working-class and female patrons and performers against the literalized dissections of the middle-class male reporters.

Those who looked no further than the Congress's surfaces would have found them controversial enough. Among the thirteen chariots that synecdochically represented "ALL CIVILIZED NATIONS" were ones bearing Muhammad Ali, Tippoo Sahib, and the rulers of Turkey and China.[9] In a decade that saw a rising tide of European imperialism, the display of these figures in the same pageant as Queen Victoria and the pope was remarkable in itself. The Indian chariot alone bore Tippoo Sahib, Aurangzeb, and Dalhousie, the British governor general. The Congress also equated Eastern and Western symbols of power: all the rulers entered the Hippodrome in ornate gilded chariots accompanied by armed cavalrymen, attendants, and national flags. That display forces us to rethink our notion of Orientalism, which is commonly understood as the West's construction of a unified identity for itself in opposition to the myth of a passive, decadent East.[10] Instead, the Congress of Nations was built on a more ambiguous relationship between East and West. The pageant invited white males to identify with the power of Oriental monarchs, but in the process of such cross-racial transactions, the East's Otherness threatened to disappear entirely.

In a pageant that boasted of its fidelity to historical detail, the representation of nonwhite rulers by white performers called into question the supposedly unbridgeable gulf of race. The Hippodrome's 1875 courier noted, "The persons chosen to represent the royal and celebrated individuals in this vivid pageant are selected with great care, so that each shall closely resemble in face and physique the originals [sic]."[11] White male Hippodrome patrons thus could identify with the emperor of China through the mediation of a white look-alike. The Congress of Nations encouraged cross-racial identification among heterosexual male patrons when it distinguished the Eastern rulers from Western ones by displaying the former with eroticized female companions. The result was a scopophilic gaze that can be discussed through the model developed by Laura Mulvey, who argues that the (implicitly heterosexual) male film viewer identifies with his potent on-screen counterpart through their shared female erotic object (59–67). Contemporary responses to the Hippodrome hint at similar fantasies of identification that took place between male patrons and Eastern rulers over the bodies of the women representing seraglios, houris, and harems. But given that all three terms in this equation were white, such identifications were as likely to obliterate racial categories as to transgress them. The *New York Herald* recorded this response to the exhibit's racial masquerade: "The Sultan of Turkey and his harem suggested a remark from some one that 'Barnum ought to represent Brigham Young and his wives in the next chariot.[']"[12] The comparison between Turks and Mormons suggests the contradictory responses called up by the Congress: Brigham Young can be read as supplying a mediating term between the phallic sultan and the Caucasian leer of the reporter and his fellow. But since it was widely recognized that the sultan was being played by a white man, the comparison can also be read as abandoning the fiction of a non-Western presence. Watching a white man playing a Turk, the anonymous spectator is reminded only of another white man.

Other commentators also found white meanings beneath the Congress's racial masquerade. When the Hippodrome returned to New York in November 1874 after a five-city tour, the *Tribune* read through the Oriental costumes of the Congress to suggest that its stakes were domestic, rather than international, power relations.

In reviewing the Hippodrome's parade, the paper estimated that "the largest proportion" of the Congress's Oriental potentates and their attendants were being played by Irish Americans:

> Many of these seemed oppressed with their burden of responsibility as representatives of distant countries, and their downcast eyes and uncertain gait might have been attributed to sad memories of native lands far away, but that their occasional ejaculations evinced a surprising familiarity with the vernacular albeit tinged somewhat by a brogue.

With their downcast eyes, these "Eastern rulers" are the ridiculed objects, rather than the identificatory subjects, of the male audience's gaze. Spectators heckled the Congress's "monarchs" as they passed in procession (mocking a "solemn Turk" for his big blue beard). Although the *Tribune*'s reporter shares their derision of the performers, he also patronizes the parade's audience. The spectacle, he notes, was "well calculated to excite the Bowery, to drive the East side frantic with delight, and to astound the casual countryman."[13] The Congress's real meaning, he suggests, lies in its affirmation of U.S. hierarchies of class and ethnicity. Moreover, he marks his (and his reader's) place in those hierarchies through his ability to read beneath the Congress's allegory. Unlike the pageant's naive immigrant, rural, and working-class audience, the *Tribune*'s middle-class reader knows better than to believe what he or she sees on the surfaces.

In reading beneath the Congress of Nations to mock its Irish American performers and their audience, the *Tribune* tacitly recognized the pageant's, and indeed the entire Hippodrome's, tribute to Irish nationalism and culture. If the Congress's depths revealed Irish humility, its surfaces celebrated, in the words of one reporter, "Hibernia riding in triumph."[14] The Hippodrome played to its Irish American patrons with a grand finale titled "DONNYBROOK FAIR and the LANCASHIRE RACES." Billed as "a medley of entertainment characteristic of the national sports of Ireland," this segment included sack, wheelbarrow, and donkey races; also featured, according to the *Spirit of the Times*, was the "fighting Celt, who hits a head whenever he sees it."[15] Irish American patrons who winced at such scenes of peasant fun could take solace in their homeland's dignified entry in the Congress of Nations. Reporters in New York and Boston agreed that one of the most heavily applauded chariots in the pageant carried an allegorical female "genius of Ireland" who smiled to the band's rendition of "Wearing of the Green."[16] The patrons' cheers for the Irish chariot accord with Michael Denning's discussion of allegory as a mode of reading characteristic of oppressed groups (73–74). It was in opposition to the Congress's Irish allegory that the metropolitan press dissected the show in terms of the social variables of class and ethnicity.

Irish Americans were also prominent among the workers in the Hippodrome's crew and supporting cast. With its roster of nearly one thousand performers, the Congress of Nations required substantial temporary, low-wage labor of the sort that was in ample supply in the wake of the 1873 depression.[17] That pool of unemployed workers enabled Barnum and his partners to take the Hippodrome on the road in 1874 and 1875. They hired local labor to build the huge wood and canvas structures in which the Hippodrome exhibited outside New York.[18] A reporter who visited the show's grounds before its 1874 Boston opening noted, "The locality of the show has been the centre of attraction for all the unemployed and unwashed of the city for many days, and when the actual labors of preparing for the assembling of the initial audience began, the crowds about the tents could be numbered by hundreds."[19] At a time when the unprecedented phenomena of massive industrial unemployment and nationwide working-class radicalism were beginning to panic the middle class, this reporter was comforted by the Hippodrome's ability to discipline its temporary help. He marveled at the "prevailing system" that dominated all the show's employees, including "the human animals, hired for the assistant parts." As the opening act and the sole opportunity of the temporary employees to come out from behind the scenes, the Congress of Nations stood as the epitome of "well-directed labor." The reporter was especially impressed by the work of the show's permanent employees, "busied in the arrangement of the thousand auxiliaries to the public exhibition, and preparing their human and other animals for the 'Grand Entree' called 'The Congress of Nations.'"[20] He thus manages to find what amount to racialized differences in the Congress, even while ignoring its ostensible display of the world's races: he denigrates the pageant's white, working-class "human animals" in the same bestial terms his contemporaries applied to people of color. This racialization of class differences indicates the mutually reinforcing character of imperialist and domestic oppression in bourgeois discourses of the period, a mutuality that Richard Slotkin has discussed in terms of "the reversible analogy" between white workers and Native Americans that pervaded contemporary journalism (311).[21] Racist, classist accounts of "urban savages" and "tramp armies" proliferated throughout the decade as a series of railroad strikes culminated in the Great Strike of 1877.[22]

Against such menacing images, Barnum offered armies of a different sort. His show's 1875 courier quoted General Sherman's testimony that "the whole of the Hippodrome scenes are marvelous for their excellence, and the perfect training, discipline, and system which pervades it."[23] Military imagery would recur in the Barnum circuses' advertising for the next two decades, but only rarely were the coercive class implications of such ads so explicit as during the Hippodrome's 1874 Boston appearances. One local reporter recast the show's temporary laborers as "recruits" in a military campaign being waged by commander Barnum: "The supernumerary wing of the army is composed largely of Bostonians. When the commander proceeds to the capture of Philadelphia, he will muster out these recruits, and enlist, in their places, Philadelphians."[24] In a decade that would see militias (including the one from Philadelphia) firing on crowds of unemployed and striking workers, the Hippodrome's military metaphors suggested that everybody was on the same side.

The Congress's disciplining of its plebeian male auxiliaries was crucial to the Hippodrome's image as a respectable, feminized, "moral show," an alternative to male-oriented, working-class amusements. Like the American Museum, the Great Roman Hippodrome marketed its supervised, alcohol-free environment as ideal for "ladies" and their children. One ad for the show quoted the praises of New York's religious press, which were typified by the *Christian at Work*: "Never was there such a show, as to the matter of decency and good morals. In this respect Barnum is entitled to the heartiest thanks of all good Christian people."[25] The Hippodrome cultivated such reviews by distancing itself from the disreputable connotations that clung to the nineteenth-century circus. Despite the fact that it boasted all the standard features of a circus except the clowns, its ads insisted: "NOTHING CONNECTED WITH THIS ESTABLISHMENT RESEMBLES A CIRCUS."[26] Even reviewers who ignored such claims agreed that the Hippodrome was a haven for respectable mothers and their children. The *New York Times* acknowledged: "The establishment has already become the resort of ladies and little ones, who seem especially delighted with what they see."[27]

Activities taking place both outside and inside the Hippodrome's walls compromised its respectable, feminized public image. Adjacent to the 1874 Hippodrome in Philadelphia, Barnum and lesser entrepreneurs cashed in on the market for masculinist, plebeian amusements with "Barnumville," a ragtag collection of sideshows (one of them belonging to Barnum), bars, and quack medicine displays.[28] A reporter who toured Barnumville noted the frankly sexual behavior of many of its patrons, as well as the scantily clad females advertised by Barnum's own sideshow.[29] The conventions of bourgeois womanhood were also being contested inside the Hippodrome. As equestriennes, chariot drivers, and high-wire walkers, the Hippodrome's female performers took risks, suffered injuries, and won praises usually reserved for men. The show acknowledged the fine line it was treading by gendering its performers' acts whenever possible, as in the case of the high-wire performer Mlle Victoria: "No such exhibition of feminine intrepidity and daring nonchalance has ever been known in the profession."[30] But in a show that featured four-horse chariot races between male and female drivers, feminine intrepidity was often difficult to distinguish from the masculine variety. Ignoring the careful distinctions of the show's ads, reviewers praised the female performers in language usually coded masculine. One commentator remarked on the riders' "skill and courage," and another found the women's races "exciting and gallant."[31] Underlying such comments was genuine surprise at the women's competitiveness. A Boston reporter noted the "peculiar and, as may b[e] believed, unlooked-for difficulty" that arose when the "ladies" began competing among themselves during Hippodrome rehearsals.[32]

To gauge fully the transgressive force of the Hippodrome's equestriennes, one must turn from the racetrack to the Congress

of Nations, where they also performed, inspiring both condem-
nation and arousal in male commentators. A *New York Herald*
reporter demonstrated the inseparability of the two responses:

> The ladies of the seraglio of the Pasha of Egypt, mounted on
> camels, were not improved in beauty or gracefulness by their
> wiggle-waggle riding on the backs of the animals. But that may
> be the custom of the country. Those who "saw the elephant" in
> the line of the cortége [*sic*] of the representative of India had
> their impressions improved in regard to the creature by the
> beautiful houris who were in the same company.[33]

The reporter oscillates between blaming the women for their
cross-racial performance and submerging them in it. He initially
chastises them for betraying the traditional virtues of American
womanhood (i.e., "beauty...gracefulness") by posing as sensual
Orientals, but his moralizing tone evaporates in the final sentence.
There he accepts the pageant's Orientalist fiction in order to sa-
vor the "houris" as an ornamental, inseparable part of the elephant they accompany.

The *Herald* reviewer's selective unmasking of the Congress's
brown-face performers can be read as an attempt to reassert the
gender hierarchy challenged by the Hippodrome's women. When
he unveils the white women enacting the seraglio but not the
white man playing the pasha, he raises the specter of miscegenation, thereby linking the gender transgressions of the Hippodrome's women to the infinitely more terrifying "crime" of interracial sex. To forestall such readings, the Hippodrome went to
some lengths to paint its numerous unmarried female performers as both intrepid and respectable. The most spectacular instance of this was the world's first wedding aboard a balloon,
which took place above the Hippodrome's Cincinnati grounds on
19 October 1874. Equestrienne Mary Walsh married ticket seller
Charles Colton in a balloon decorated with "[f]our flags, two American, and two of Ireland's green."[34] The presence of Barnum's partner Coup in the basket and some thirty thousand spectators on
the ground speaks to the Hippodrome's desire to domesticate
the image of its female performers.[35] The following year, a Wisconsin reporter indicated the success of that strategy when he
observed, "The class of women in the employ of the Hippodrome
is...much superior to any we ever remember having seen."[36] Al-

though they handled their chariots like men, Barnum's "Amazonian Drivers" were as respectable as the ladies who watched them.

## The Ethnological Congress

The subordination of white women to white men remained a primary symbolic goal in 1884, when Barnum unveiled his next major racial exhibit, the Ethnological Congress of the Barnum & London Circus (the show that Barnum then owned with James A. Bailey and James L. Hutchinson). But whereas white male spectators and white female performers had skirmished across the Congress of Nations's racial masquerade, this new Congress positioned white men and women on the same side of the color line. With the Ethnological Congress, the Barnum & London Circus began privileging race as a marker of the radical difference between its predominantly white audiences and its nonwhite performers. The new Congress can be seen as the second half of Barnum's midcentury vision of "representatives ... from every accessible people, civilized and barbarous, on the face of the globe" (*ST* 271). With its thirteen chariots, the Congress of Nations had synecdochically exhibited "ALL CIVILIZED NATIONS," whereas the Ethnological Congress boasted "100 UNCIVILIZED, SUPERSTITIOUS AND SAVAGE PEOPLE" (see Figure 11).[37] The Congress of Nations and the Ethnological Congress, however, also stood as competing descriptions for the same people, as both represented Egypt, China, and India. The reconception of the Oriental as the savage "specimen" rather than the potent, civilized monarch reveals the sharper, institutionally policed racial lines that characterized the Barnum circuses after 1880.

The Ethnological Congress amounted to a thoroughgoing rebuttal of the Congress of Nations. Whereas the latter offered allegory, self-parody, and dazzle, its successor stood for empiricism, scientific detachment, and discipline. With its Lilliputian chariot and cross-racial performances, the Congress of Nations mocked and undermined the categories of nationhood and civilization upon which it was based. In contrast, the Ethnological Congress was largely concerned with proving the clarity and permanence of its racial categories. The Congress of Nations put a blue beard on an Irishman and called him a Turk; ten years later, the Ethno-

Figure 11. The Ethnological Congress. (*Frank Leslie's Illustrated Newspaper*)

logical Congress insisted on the authenticity of its rare, nonwhite human "specimens," taken from their native habitats. It boasted "THE ONLY GENUINE ZULUS EVER EXHIBITED IN AMER-ICA" and attacked other circuses' Zulus as costumed "Southern negroes" (*History* 3).[38] At a time when African American circus laborers routinely doubled as racial exotics, the Congress's critics inevitably questioned the authenticity of its "specimens."[39] Rival showman Adam Forepaugh taunted Barnum: "YOU advertise '100 superstitious and idolatrous people.' If you include your agents and partners in this enumeration it may approach the truth!" (*Too White*). Barnum & London responded by depicting its Congress as the product of three years' labor in places "where a white man never trod before."[40] This was only a slight exaggeration: Saxon has documented the agents and letters that Barnum sent "to *every* part of our little ball of earth" on behalf of his exhibit (*SL* 228).[41]

The difference between the Congress of Nations and the Ethnological Congress is evident in the contrasting audience responses they implied. In *Struggles*, Barnum recalled that the Congress of Nations was intended to overpower the beholder with "an effect at once brilliant and bewildering" (*ST* 1889, 291), a phrase that hints at the scopophilic identification between male spectators and the pageant's phallic "Orientals." In contrast, Barnum imagined a coolly detached, professional male viewer of the Ethnological Congress: "The ethnologist finds gathered together for his leisurely inspection representatives of notable and peculiar tribes...types which otherwise he would never see, as they can only be sought in their native countries" (*ST* 1889, 349).[42] Barnum's ideal spectator views the representatives not as people with whom he might identify but as specimens who fit the racial categories in his head. The showman's memory accurately reflects the exhibit's construction of the male response. The Ethnological Congress's publicity materials posited a different reaction from women, however. Newspaper ads proclaimed that the exhibit would be "of incalculable benefit to scientists, naturalists, and students, and a never-ceasing source of wonderment to ladies and children and the entire community of the country."[43] Lacking the education that allowed their male counterparts to analyze the exhibit dispassionately, women would be struck spellbound in passive wonderment. By gendering the responses in this fashion, the Ethnological Congress worked to reinstate the white male atop the social hierarchy that had been shaken in the Hippodrome.

The Ethnological Congress worked to elevate white men above not only white female patrons, but also nonwhite performers. Indeed, an 1884 courier presents the Congress's representatives reacting to their display with an emotionalism that rivals that of the hypothetical female spectator: "[T]heir suspicious natures are the more aroused and irritated from being surrounded by hated strangers, in a strange land, where everything is at variance with their customs and superstitions."[44] As the victims of their emotions, the Congress's representatives could be the objects, but never the subjects, of knowledge—a view that marked a break with earlier Barnum & London non-Westerners. This transformation is evident in the presentation of two Chinese stars of the early-1880s Barnum & London show, Chang Yu Sing and Che Mah the Rebel Chinese Dwarf. Chang's presentation exemplified what Robert Bogdan has called the aggrandized mode, which emphasized a freak's cultural or intellectual attainments rather than his or her physical oddity (108–9). An 1881 ad described Chang as "the Chinese Giant, not the ogre of Fairy Tales, but [a] Gentleman, Scholar and Linguist—the tallest man in the world."[45] The epitome of the civilized Oriental, Chang combined erudition, cosmopolitan sophistication, and paternalism; one engraving from the period features him towering over a crowd of white people as he carefully supports a tiny white girl in the palm of his hand (see Figure 12).[46]

But in 1882 Chang's image of benevolent wisdom was countered by the sinister intelligence of Che Mah, which was portrayed in a Barnum & London courier:

> [H]e is cunning, crafty and a diplomat, whose tact and ingenuity
> have been a source of great annoyance and bloodshed to his
> government. In Western China, on account of his diminutive
> physique and superior erudition, he became an oracle and was
> WORSHIPED AND SET UP AS A GOD! whose commands
> became law among his fellow men.[47]

Recognizing the threat represented by Che Mah's power, the emperor declared him a rebel and sent an army against him. Che

Figure 12. Chang Yu Sing. (Circus World Museum, Baraboo, Wisconsin)

Mah courageously led his forces in the ensuing battle, and then fled to Siberia. It was not his gallantry, however, but his terrible power over his fellow Chinese that dominated his presentation in the Barnum & London show. Ads depict the dwarf impassively enthroned above a group of energetically genuflecting Chinese. In the year of the Exclusion Act, knowledge in the hands of an Asian was clearly a dangerous thing.

Although Che Mah was no longer with the show at the debut of the Ethnological Congress, Barnum & London used Chang to reconstruct the Oriental as the raw material, rather than the repository, of knowledge. By 1884 the circus's advertising still stressed Chang's benign mental attainments, but at the official unveiling of the Ethnological Congress he was rescripted as "THE GOLIA[T]H OF HIS RACE AND THE TALLEST GIANT ALIVE."[48] Reduced to bits of information about his body and race, Chang was assigned the duty of leading the Ethnological Congress into the big top.[49]

Like so many enterprises carried out before and since in the name of science, the Ethnological Congress couched its white male supremacy in the vocabulary of objectivity and empiricism. The circus boasted of its agents' tireless pursuit of their human "specimens" in a globe-embracing quest undertaken with no concern for cost. A Louisville reporter demonstrated the success of the circus's rhetoric: "There are enough of these people from all over the world to afford material for [a] very serious and important scientific investigation."[50] But even the show's claims to objectivity suggest its contrived nature: "EVERY RUDE BARBARIAN PRESENTED EXACTLY AS DESCRIBED IN HISTORY" (*History* 2). Since the "history" the "barbarians" were said to fulfill was written by white imperialists, the Ethnological Congress neatly demonstrates the closed loop that is Orientalism.

The Congress's particular brand of scientific rigor was the culmination of Barnum's four decades of planning. Whereas at midcentury he had envisioned a collection of sample humans "as perfect as could be procured" (*ST* 271), he soon changed his notion of what he was looking for in a specimen. In an 1860 speech, he announced his intention of displaying at the American Museum a "'Congress of Nations,' composed of *outré* specimens of humanity, male and female, from all nations on the globe."[51] This paradoxical collection would have represented each nation with its particular human oddity. Reversing the metonymic function that Susan Stewart attributes to museums—that of creating an illusion of completeness and autonomy by wrenching objects out of their original contexts (161–62)—Barnum's collection would have underlined rather than disguised the partial and unrepresentative nature of its sampling. It would have called attention to what was *not* represented rather than what was.

By the time he began assembling the Ethnological Congress, Barnum had reconceived his categories of perfect and outré humans along racial lines. Now, the Congress would gather only "uncivilized races." In an 1882 circular, Barnum requested the aid of overseas U.S. government officials in

> forming a collection, in pairs or otherwise, of all the uncivilized races in existence.... My aim is to exhibit to the American public not only human beings of different races, but also, when practicable, those who possess extraordinary peculiarities, such as giants, dwarfs, singular disfigurements of the person, dexterity in the use of weapons, dancing, singing, juggling, unusual feats of strength or agility, &c. (*SL* 226)

Here Barnum seeks people distinguished not only from "the American public" but also from their own societies on the basis of "extraordinary peculiarities" ranging from the physical to the cultural. Yet what binds these people to their native societies, while doubly isolating them from U.S. whites, is their race. While Barnum's final plan plays up the differences between spectator and performer, it elides the differences *among* performers by grouping them under the single heading "uncivilized." Barnum's circular thus exhibits the classic tendency of Orientalism to treat non-Westerners as "almost everywhere nearly the same" (Said 38).

Commentators followed Barnum's lead in reifying the common nonwhiteness of the representatives into a single racialized category. The *New York Herald*, for example, spoke of the Barnum & London Circus's "representatives from the four continents" as "a cavalcade of Orientals," and it described the Congress as

> comprising all kinds of black and tan personages, from the bearded woman to the latest importations from Burmah and

Hindostan, and including the remarkable females who do not
shrink from the barbarous custom of marrying a whole family,
no matter how many brothers said family may contain.[52]

In a statement that suggests the Congress's multiple, contradictory interpretations of race, this reporter first establishes nonwhite skin as the common denominator of the "personages" and
then proceeds to describe the representatives in terms of physical
oddity, native lands, and customs — potentially overlapping subcategories that he makes no attempt to relate to one another: the
bearded woman's homeland and marital status go unmentioned.
In these subcategories, the Ethnological Congress demonstrates
both the expansiveness and the inadequacy of race as a signifier
of difference in the late-nineteenth-century United States.

As the Congress began coming together during the 1883 season, its billing tapped into long-standing notions about the breadth
and permanence of racial categories. Barnum & London promised
to "place upon exhibition the various types of humanity from all
sections of the earth," thereby demonstrating to youths "the
marvelous work of our Creator that can never be effaced."[53] Such
ads invoked the ethnological concept of the racial type, the biological norm to which any person could be traced (Odom 6–9).
For a century in the West, the categories of *race* and *type* had been
steadily broadened to include an array of nonphysical characteristics, including intellect, morality, and psychology (Odom 7–8).
The Barnum & London Circus demonstrated the inclusiveness
of its own racial categories in listing the Congress's highlights:
"Cannibals, Nubians, Zulus, Mohammedans, Pagans, Indians,
Wild Men."[54] Although this list mixes what are, in current usage,
terms for tribe, religion, and race, in the Ethnological Congress
they all signified racial types "that can never be effaced." The
broad conception of race was at times incorporated into the exhibit's titles, which included the "Ethnological Congress of Hea-
thens and Barbarians" and the "Ethnological Congress of Strange
and Heathen Types of Human Beings."

When Barnum & London followed contemporary ethnologists
by reading into racial categories characteristic personalities, beliefs, and states of consciousness, it risked diluting the signifying
power of its performers' nonwhite skin. Because cultural terms

such as *heathen* could be employed cross-racially (for example, to attack non-Christian white Americans), the Ethnological Congress had to anchor cultural markers of difference with physical ones. The *Chicago Tribune* indicated the relative power of the two levels of signifiers in its story on those "genuine ethnological curiosities," the circus's Australian aborigines (see Figure 13). It describes their culture in sensational detail, noting their diet, clothing, dwellings, and treatment of the dead. But bracketing its references to the Australians' bizarre cultural practices are views of their bodies; the story opens with references to their small stature, "almost jet black skin," and "gorillaish features," and closes with descriptions of their scarification and the quills they wear in their nostrils.[55] Although the paper's anthropological evidence allows it to quantify the Australians' Otherness in lurid detail, their marked bodies prove it with an irrefutable finality.

The circus's search for the anatomical markers that would signify racial difference came amid an unprecedented effort on the part of Darwinian ethnologists to measure and systematize the physical differences among the races. As Thomas Gossett writes, Social Darwinists sought physical confirmation of their belief that the Anglo-Saxon had evolved from darker, more primitive races that supposedly still inhabited Africa and Asia. By the final decades of the century they had measured various races' skin color, skulls, foreheads, brains, body lice, and hair—all in a vain search for the physical proof of the superiority of Euro-Americans to the rest of the world's peoples. Some ethnologists openly despaired of finding physical criteria with which to distinguish (and thereby rank) the world's races (Gossett *Race* 69–83). But where ethnology failed, the Ethnological Congress succeeded. If there was no infallible means—not even skin color—of separating white people from everybody else, the bodily Otherness of the Congress's freaks was beyond dispute.

In a show that already boasted a separate, well-advertised collection of human curiosities, the presence of tattooed Hindu dwarves, giants, bearded women, and "big lipped people" in the Ethnological Congress testified to Barnum & London's efforts to mark its racial types with bodily difference.[56] Granted, some of the people in the Congress were billed as "well-proportioned."[57] More typical of the representatives, however, were the "short-headed,

A TRIBE OF MALE AND FEMALE

# AUSTRALIAN CANNIBALS

Also known as Bushmen, Black Trackers, and Boomerang throwers. These are the only ones of their monstrous, self-disfigured and hopelessly embruited race, ever lured from the remote, unexplored and dreadful interior wilds, where they wage an endless war of extermination, that they may gratify their hellish appetite, and

## GORGE THEMSELVES UPON EACH OTHER'S FLESH

Their chief weapon, in the use of which they display deadly skill, is

# THE BOOMERANG

A crescent-shaped club of hardest wood, which is made to reverse the accepted laws of projection and gravitation. It is not thrown at, but from the object it is destined to return and strike, with unerring skill and crushing force. No other people have ever been able to master this extraordinary weapon.

## UNDERSIZED AND DISTORTED IN FORM

With bestiality, ferocity and treachery stamped upon their faces; their cruel eyes reflecting but a glimmering of reason; having no gift of speech beyond an ape-like gibberish, utterly unintelligible to any one else; they are but one step removed from brutes in human form, and

### BEYOND CONCEPTION MOST CURIOUS TO LOOK UPON.

Figure 13. Australian cannibals in the Ethnological Congress. Circus World Museum, Baraboo, Wisconsin.

broad-skulled and flat-faced" Buddhist priests and Arada the
Guatemalan dwarf, "The most astonishing specimen of BE-LIT-
TLED, MIS-SHAPEN, SAVAGE HUMANITY ever discovered."[58]
Arada and his fellows were not to be seen alongside Barnum &
London's white fat women, living skeletons, and armless men.
While the latter appeared in the museum tent, members of the
Ethnological Congress took up their positions around the cages
of the menagerie tent.[59] The appearance of the non-Westerners
alongside the animals would have supported the show's depic-
tion of them as "BESTIAL" and "Embruited [sic]."[60]

The Ethnological Congress's strategy of marking race with "sin-
gular disfigurements of the person" reshaped the construction of
later Barnum & London curiosities. This was most spectacularly
demonstrated in 1887, when the show unveiled its latest prize, the
Hairy Family of Burmah. Mah-Phoon and Moung-Phoset were
distinguished from earlier Barnum & London curiosities (including the hirsute Jo-Jo the "Dog-Faced Russian Boy") who were celebrated for their physical uniqueness. The circus's courier insisted
that the Burmese "do not come heralded as either freaks or mon-
strosities, but as pure, long-established types of the most weirdly,
peculiar, distinct race of mankind of whom there is any trace or
record."[61] Ads traced the pair's lineage back four generations to
some earlier representatives of their "race" who belonged to a
late-eighteenth-century Burmese king. The implications of this
genealogy were corroborated by Lady Dufferin, the wife of the
governor general of India, who allegedly exclaimed upon seeing
the Burmese: "OH! WHAT A WONDERFUL RACE."[62] If the Ethnological Congress sought to produce race through bodily "dis-
figurement," the Hairy Family represented the elevation of "dis-
figurement" to the status of race.

## White Manhood and Departed Empires

To understand more fully why the Barnum & London Circus
marked race with physical "peculiarities," one must turn from
its non-Western bodies to the white male body that was their un-
spoken subtext. Though not a physical presence in the Ethnological Congress, the white male body, and the ideology of manhood it
symbolized, showed up in the exhibit's contradictory construction

of the Oriental. It is only by looking to the anxieties of middle-class white men that one can explain the apparent conflicts in the show's representation of nonwhites. Barnum & London depicted its non-Westerners as brutal and gentle, innocent and wise, animalistic and etherial. Equally ambiguous was the circus's attitude toward the destruction of its non-Westerners by white "civilization"; although it inevitably heralded this "progress," it sometimes lamented what was being lost. By constructing their Orientals as contradictory and even self-contradictory, the Barnum & London Circus and its successor, the Barnum & Bailey Show, generated in white audiences the play of identification and Othering that Stuart Hall has analyzed as the internal dynamic of racism (28).[63] The circuses exploited the non-Westerner not simply as the decadent Other of their images of potent white manhood, but also as the vehicle of an implicit critique of Western rationality, science, and capitalism.

When they supplied white male patrons with Orientalized Others, the Barnum shows were intervening in a crisis of middle-class manhood that has been traced by historians and cultural critics to an array of intellectual and social sources. In the last decades of the nineteenth century, unprecedented psychological and philosophical critiques of the self combined with economic transformations to undermine the middle-class male's sense of his own autonomy.[64] In the workplace, men participated in the emergence of an industrial economy where, as Anthony Rotundo has written, even the top executives had to submit to the new structures of authority (248–49). The growth of a permanent bureaucracy of male clerks, accountants, and middle managers signaled for some commentators the decline of white manhood into dependency and timidity. The promise of steady upward mobility—extended to white youths by Barnum and other advocates of self-made manhood—was beginning to sound increasingly anachronistic: in 1885 William Dean Howells invited readers to chuckle at Silas Lapham's naive faith in the old success ethos. Late-nineteenth-century reformers and commentators responded to the crisis in middle-class manhood by calling for a strenuous, even "primitive," style of white masculinity based on athletics and militarism. By the turn of the century, advocates of American strenuosity such as Theodore Roosevelt were tapping the alleged primitivism of the dark-skinned victims of U.S. imperialism. But as early as the 1880s, the Barnum circus had already demonstrated the importance of non-Westerners to the formation of the new masculine ideal.

The circus had obvious uses for a cult of masculinity obsessed with the power and beauty of the white male body. After preaching bodily self-control to earlier generations of American youths, middle-class ideologists ended the century calling for a more muscular and aggressive style of white manhood. Reverend Josiah Strong, one of the era's most influential social commentators, suggested the racial importance of embodying strenuous masculinity when he proclaimed: "We now know that the [white] race cannot be perfected without perfecting the body" (quoted in Takaki 263). Throughout the 1880s the Barnum show helped embody the new white masculinity by featuring individual sports (including boxing, gymnastics, and wrestling) calculated to display its male performers' strength and beauty. At times, the circus dropped all pretense of competition to feature the white male body as a spectacle in itself; the Silbon Troupe, for example, offered "Classic Posturing and Display, reproductions of Ancient Gladiatorial Combats and celebrated groups of Statuary."[65] Fueling the demand for such acts was the suspicion of many Anglo-Americans that they belonged to a decadent, emasculated race (Gossett *Race* 303–9). With white manhood on the defensive as never before, even rivalries between circus owners could become cruelly embodied. In 1884, Adam Forepaugh attacked Barnum's show by drawing attention to Barnum's seventy-four-year-old body: "You are an old man, and the vim, vigor and sharp wit and cunning of your youth and manhood have left you."[66]

The anxieties of white males over their youth and manhood frequently found expression in the Barnum show's depictions of racial conflict. From the menacing Native Americans of the Great Roman Hippodrome to the Afghans and Zulus of the Greatest Show on Earth, Barnum regularly titillated audiences with images of their destruction at the hands of darker, more masculine races. The Barnum & Bailey Real Wild Moorish Caravan, for example, was pictured in ads with their phallic rifles upraised, charging off the page at newspaper readers.[67] But for every menacing Moor or Afghan, the later Barnum circuses offered two images of decadent nonwhites who were no threat to anyone but themselves. So dominant was this emphasis on dying peoples and cultures that by 1889 the Barnum & Bailey Circus could refer to itself as "A STUPENDOUS MIRROR OF DEPARTED EMPIRES."[68] The departed and departing races in the Ethnological Congress ranged from the Australian "cannibals," who waged "an endless war of extermination" upon themselves, to the polyandrous Todars and last Aztecs — all of them vestiges of older, obsolete peoples.[69] The decadence of the races manifested itself in the fragility of their individual members: "Many of the rarest savage representatives have reached these shores but to die, and fresh expeditions had to be again started to replace them."[70]

This emphasis on the moribundity of the non-Westerners brought the circus in line with Social Darwinist anthropologists and social critics who were convinced that nonwhite races, including Native Americans and African Americans, would soon be extinct by "natural" causes.[71] The familiarity of U.S. audiences with such discourses would have allowed them to read domestic meanings into the decadence of Barnum's exotic nonwhites. The Barnum show encouraged such readings by comparing its non-Westerners to U.S. minorities: the color of the Ethnological Congress's Nubians, for example, was said to be "not unlike [that of] the ebony negroes" (*History* 6).[72] Such comparisons were supported by the dearth of nonprimitive roles for people of color in the nineteenth-century circus. Barnum's patrons were far more likely to see nonwhites performing as skin-clad "savages" than as equestrians, acrobats, and musicians.[73]

Barnum's decadent non-Westerners were clearly intended as a foil to his circus's images of potent white manhood, but that was not their only function. As they were killed off, the Barnum racial exotics took with them cultures and societies that were sometimes depicted as preferable to those of their white conquerors.[74] Such eulogies obviously countered the Barnum show's usual celebration of Western capitalism and science, but the contradiction allowed the decadent races to stand as a seductive, safely distant alternative to the circus's regime of military-style discipline. A Barnum & London courier sounded the characteristically elegiac note: "[L]ike most of the ancient people of the world, the GLORY OF THE ANCIENT HINDOO HAS DEPARTED And is now a dream of the past before the aggressive stride of civilization" (*History* 4). Edward Said has argued that at stake in such nostalgia for a lost, mystical Orient is actually a longing for a lost romantic West (113–23). In Orientalism, the West constructs an idealized, anachronistic East to embody the impulses it has supposedly sacrificed to the "aggressive stride of civilization." This dynamic ran through the Barnum Circus's presentation of its non-Westerners as the embodiments of everything that had been trained out of its white performers, crew, and audience. Given the level of discipline at which the show operated, its need for an Orientalist safety valve was at times great.

The Barnum & London Circus could be surprisingly explicit in preferring its non-Westerners to the white imperialists who had overrun them. The Ethnological Congress sometimes even raised doubts about its own colonizing intentions, as in its portrait of the Aztecs, "that once invincible race ... whose half-obliterated history, the key to which science has never been able to discover, is written upon the monuments of their gigantic genius, which were as old as the ages ere Cortez came, in the name of christianity and civilization, to plunder, murder and enslave."[75] Science here stands as the latter-day Cortez, the European discoverer who cynically exploited Aztec culture under false pretenses. Whereas this juxtaposition is the Ethnological Congress's most explicit acknowledgment of the imperialist politics behind its own scientific rhetoric, the construction of many Barnum non-Westerners displays a similar ambivalence about ethnology. Indeed, some of their value as exhibits seems to depend upon their defiance of the explanatory powers of Western science. The Hairy Family, for example, was described as "the most difficult problem with which ingenious speculative ethnological science has had to contend. ... solitary, u[n]paralleled, inexplicable" (*In Grand*).

The Barnum Orientals were the one unknowable, uncontrollable, unassimilable feature of a circus that by the 1880s was offering itself as a model of capitalist rationality and discipline. The Barnum show sold reporters on its management by inviting them behind the scenes to witness its intensively disciplined crew:

> It is a perfect system, maintained by the most rigid discipline, that does the work. The 600 or more employes are assigned to the several departments. Every man has his particular piece of

work to do, just the same as in a great factory....Each gang of
men is in charge of a boss, and, depend upon it, these bosses
keep their eyes wide open.[76]

Barnum's working-class patrons must have found such puffery
especially ironic. For them, Circus Day meant a holiday from the
factory—one worth struggling over if necessary: when an Easton,
Pennsylvania, cotton mill refused to close during an 1883 stand
of the Adam Forepaugh Circus, four hundred female operatives
walked out "in defiance of an order threatening a discharge."[77]
Like Mark Twain's Connecticut Yankee (who attributes his revolutionary impulses to "the circus side of my nature" [*Connecticut*
129]), the Easton operatives still found something liberatory in
one of the nation's most heavily capitalized culture industries.
One wonders, however, if they would have walked out over Barnum's show, which was far less interested in a working-class patronage than Forepaugh's. Barnum would later observe of his rival: "He don't cater for the genteel & refined class & *he don't get
them*, but he pleases the masses" (*SL* 294).

Barnum not only catered to the "genteel & refined class," he
got them. He sought his patrons among those who valued not
an escape from discipline, but a heightening of it. Barnum &
London promised patrons that inside the tents, "SYSTEM, That
wonderful disciplinarian, rises in its power and might on every
hand."[78] Such order attracted audiences whose gentility frequently
surprised reporters.[79] Recalling the "howling mobs" that had once
gathered under the big top, a St. Louis journalist marveled at
the carriages outside the Barnum & London show: those vehicles
"suggested that there might be grand opera going on within."[80]
Barnum had clearly "elevated" the circus, but in the process he
had bored some of his patrons. By the end of the decade, his show
had incorporated audience participation, surprise appearances
by celebrities, and other "spontaneous" touches, all apparently in
an attempt to counter charges that the circus had become too
routinized, safe, and stale.[81]

The ultimate safety valve for the discipline of the Barnum circus was to be found in the racial exotics, whose status as outsiders
to Western systems of morals, knowledge, and economics enabled
them to embody a whole range of white fantasy and fear. Patrons

could lose themselves in the sensual beauty of the Nautch dancers or "the extraordinary concatenation of sound produced by [the] half-a-dozen turbaned desperadoes" accompanying Barnum's white elephant.[82] Typical of such cross-racial transactions is the *Chicago Tribune*'s description of the Australian "cannibals," which was followed by a story titled "Barnum's Perfect System — How It Got Away with a Hurricane." The piece's Wheeling author marvels at the "wonderful system upon which the show is run." He is particularly struck by the silent, lightning-quick response of the canvasmen and animal trainers to their supervisors' whistles. Searching for the secret to such an impressive display of discipline, the reporter turns to showman James A. Bailey, who intones: *We know our men.*" But in the next column readers would discover that the coercive power of Bailey's knowledge did not apply equally to all his men. The Australians not only tested the boundaries of ethnological "knowing," but they also lay outside the boundaries of capitalist discipline, given that, as the Chicago reporter notes, they "do no work."[83] The contrast points to a final interpretation of the "disfigured" bodies of the Barnum non-Westerners: whereas the "perfect," white bodies of the circus laborers disappear into their function (i.e., if the circus is a "great factory," these operatives have become part of their machines), the "disfigured," scarified bodies of the Australians stubbornly resist appropriation. Even as it celebrated the disciplining of its white workers and audiences, the Barnum & London Circus thus offered a glimpse of a world where labor was not alienated.

Given the transparency of the circus's Orientalism, it was perhaps inevitable that commentators begin reading the Barnum non-Westerners as thinly disguised versions of their white audiences. By the mid-1880s, the circus's Orientalized performances were already accepted by some writers as performances instead of objective ethnological demonstrations. One reporter noted how a trip to the Barnum & London dressing room could transform an "unassuming and quiet-appearing citizen" into a "wild warrior of the desert plains ... or perhaps a dark-hued Nubian."[84] Another told how the Barnum & Bailey Moors and Algerians "gave exhaustive illustration of Arab life in fierce fights and unique dances, and then silently folded their tents and stole away into the dressing rooms."[85] After establishing its Ethnological Congress as an authentic scientific sampling of the Orient, the circus saw its Orientals being read through like their brown-face counterparts a decade earlier in the Congress of Nations. The Barnum & Bailey Circus of the late 1880s and early 1890s ultimately encouraged such interpretations by staging the meeting of East and West primarily in terms of Hippodromesque pageantry and fantasy rather than science.[86] It was a trend that would culminate with the show's giant productions of Imre Kiralfy's spectacles, *Nero; or, The Destruction of Rome* and *Columbus and the Discovery of America*. As in the Hippodrome, these spectacles filled arenas with thousands of performers who enacted allegories of imperial power.

In a country that would continue to nourish racist anthropological theory for at least another half century, Barnum & Bailey's turn to spectacle in the showman's last years may tell us more about the form's patrons than about its contents. This was the period in which, once and for all, children emerged as the circus's implied audience. In 1884 the Ethnological Congress could still imagine male professionals as a primary audience of its exotic nonwhites, but by the end of the decade the East was more likely to be represented for juvenile patrons in the shape of a pony float of Bluebeard or Sinbad. Barnum & Bailey's new Orientalist narratives and images preserved the racial ideologies of the earlier Barnum shows, but in a form so mediated by legend and fantasy as to cut down dramatically on the possibility of oppositional interpretation. U.S. social hierarchies might have become a bone of contention in the Hippodrome, and the Ethnological Congress may have implicitly questioned the West's fetishism of science and capitalism, but by the time of Barnum's death, his show was more interested in turning politics into spectacle than in acknowledging the politics of its spectacles.

# Conclusion
## "A Transient Disease": Barnumism at the World's Columbian Exposition

Although he had been dead for two years when it opened in May 1893, P. T. Barnum was very much a presence at the Chicago World's Columbian Exposition. The culminating U.S. cultural event of the nineteenth century, the fair drew more than ten million visitors to its temporary White City of exhibition halls erected on marshlands south of Chicago. U.S. visitors responded to the fair in wildly divergent ways, some hailing it as a symbol of their nation's cultural and industrial preeminence, others attacking it as an exercise in racism and elitism. One thing shared by friends and foes of the exposition, however, was a tendency to invoke the name of the nation's greatest showman. Barnum's prominence in discourses about the fair amply suggests his legacy for U.S. culture. It was perhaps inevitable that the showman haunt an event so intent on containing, and even denying, the lessons of his career.

The obvious place to look for Barnum at the World's Columbian Exposition was in the commercial amusements, most of which were crowded onto the Midway Plaisance—the mile-long street of theaters, shops, restaurants, and rides adjacent to the White City. Aside from the giant Ferris wheel, the midway's main attraction was its collection of ethnological villages, which featured natives of various lands, including Ireland, Algeria, Dahomey, Germany, Java, and Egypt. Fairgoers could ogle Algerian dancers, dine on Berlin cuisine to the accompaniment of a German army band, and ride camels and donkeys through the "Streets of Cairo." The direct inspiration of the midway's villages was the colonial city of Africans and Asians at the 1889 Paris Exposition (Rydell 55–56), but the *New York Times* acknowledged another antecedent when it dubbed the midway the "Greatest Show on Earth."[1] The midway's blend of anthropology and popular culture owed an obvious debt to Barnum's circuses. The fierce Dahomeyans, the sensual Egyptians, and the athletic Moors all had forebears in his shows. One reporter acknowledged the connection when he concluded his tour of the villages with the observation: "The late P. T. Barnum should have lived to see this day."[2]

Ironically, when the midway echoed Barnum's Orientalism, it was defying his advice. Three years before the exposition opened, Barnum had responded to a request from the *North American Review* with an article titled "What the Fair Should Be."[3] It lauded the antiracist potential of world's fairs, crediting the 1850 London Exposition with overcoming Europeans' prejudices against Turks and Chinese, and predicting an even greater "broadening effect upon the popular mind" from the Chicago exposition.[4] But the midway concessionaires opted instead for the lucrative narrowing effect of Barnumesque racial primitives. It was a choice that would be repeated over the following decades throughout the nation's popular culture. As the United States took its place among the major imperial powers, dark-skinned "savages" from hot spots like China and the Philippines would show up in jingoistic spectacles at amusement parks, world's fair midways, and circuses.[5] Fairgoers could glimpse the future of U.S. popular culture a few blocks away from the exposition at Buffalo Bill's Wild West Show. For its 1893 season, the Wild West Show had added a new attraction clearly inspired by Barnum: the Congress of Rough Riders of the World, also billed as "A Kindergarten of Anthropology." Buffalo Bill Cody's vaqueros, gauchos, Cossacks, and Indians were targeted to connoisseurs of horsemanship as well as students "of human progress, of racial peculiarities, of national characteristics" (*Buffalo* 33). In the decades after the World's Columbian Exposition, cultural entrepreneurs would increasingly follow Barnum in measuring American "progress" against the "racial peculiarities" of subject peoples.

Few fairgoers would have been surprised to spot Barnum's ghost at the Wild West Show or on the midway, but when it drifted into the fair's most rarefied cultural spaces, many of them were appalled. During the first three months of the exposition, Bar-numesque amusements were banned from the high-culture fan-tasyland that was the White City. The collaboration of the nation's most prominent artists and architects produced an exposition of unprecedented scale, order, and, to some eyes at least, beauty. For U.S. highbrows, the fair was a cultural collaboration that ri-valled the Renaissance (Burg 79). The White City proved a bit too elitist for many Americans, however. In July, the directors of the World's Fair corporation claimed liabilities of more than a mil-lion dollars, which they largely attributed to poor attendance and costly, unpopular classical music. They responded by adapting the exposition to a middlebrow audience: after canceling orches-tral and choral concerts, they instituted a series of outdoor amuse-ments, which brought midway performers into the White City for international concerts, multiracial swimming matches in the Great Basin, and an Indian "torture dance," in which perform-ers submitted to mutilation.[6] These controversial changes were commonly known—among proponents and opponents alike—as "barnumising the Fair."[7] The strategy swelled attendance, but incensed critics.[8] The *Chicago Tribune* complained that the di-rectors had "dispensed with the highest form of the highest art upon the theory that the people must be amused."[9] Such attacks did not forestall the barnumization of subsequent U.S. world's fairs. From Atlanta (1895), to Nashville (1897), to Omaha (1898), to Buffalo (1901), to St. Louis (1904), midway amusements ab-sorbed a steadily increasing share of the money and patronage flowing into U.S. expositions (Nasaw 68–71). Many Americans clearly valued the fairs not for their artistic and scientific exhibi-tions, but for their pop cultural innovations: it was on the mid-way that an enormous cross-class public got its first taste of such amusements as the nickelodeon and the roller coaster (Nasaw 72).

According to Charles Dudley Warner, it was not just the nation's expositions that were being barnumized. The famous novelist/critic delivered a sweeping indictment of U.S. culture during a session of the Literature Congress held in conjunction with the Chicago fair.[10] Decrying the absence of a tradition of literary crit-icism in the United States, Warner traced the roots of the prob-lem to a uniquely American combination of cultural and social ills, among them superficiality, boastfulness, and "a disregard of

moral as well as of artistic values and standards."[11] Having identified the plague, Warner attempted to classify it in terms popularized by Matthew Arnold: "[T]his is not Philistinism. I am sure,
also, that it is not the final expression of the American spirit, that
which will represent its life or its literature. I trust it is a transient disease, which we may perhaps call by a transient name, —
Barnumism."[12] Warner should have known better than to call
Barnumism "transient." By 1893, four decades of U.S. highbrows
had employed the name of P. T. Barnum to attack what they saw
as dishonest, immoral, and crass in U.S. culture. Nor would the
"disease" fade. At the end of the twentieth century, the showman's
name remains a powerful epithet among critics who use it much
the same as did Warner.[13] Their invocation of Barnum is perhaps
the best indication of the breadth and duration of the showman's
cultural impact. Though not perhaps the final expression of the
American spirit, Barnumism is surely a lasting one.

# Notes

The following abbreviations are used throughout the notes as well as in citations in the text:

CWM    Robert L. Parkinson Library and Research Center at the Circus World Museum
*HJ*     *Home Journal* [New York]
HTC    Harvard Theatre Collection
*Life*     *The Life of P. T. Barnum*
*NYAtlas*  *New York Atlas*
*NYClip*  *New York Clipper*
*NYH*    *New York Herald*
*NYSun*   *New York Sun*
*NYT*    *New York Times*
*NYTrib*   *New York Tribune*
PTB     *P. T. Barnum: The Legend and the Man*, by A. H. Saxon
SL      *Selected Letters of P. T. Barnum*, edited by A. H. Saxon
ST      *Struggles and Triumphs*

## Introduction: "E Pluribus Barnum"

1. Barnum's career on New York's working-class Bowery is explored in Buckley chap. 6 and Lott 72, 76, 112, 228. On Barnum's ties to the middle class, see Allen *Horrible* 64–71 and McConachie *Melodramatic* chap. 6.

2. *HJ* 26 Oct. 1850.

## 1. "All Things to All People": P. T. Barnum in American Culture

1. *Washington Post* 8 Apr. 1891, 4.

2. Barnum *Struggles and Triumphs* (1882) 328. Henceforth, the 1869 edition of *Struggles and Triumphs* will be cited in the text as *ST*, and later editions will be identified by date, for example, *ST* 1882, 328.

3. Biographer A. H. Saxon deserves credit for identifying and analyzing Barnum's *Atlas* publications (*PTB* chaps. 5–7). It is important to note that my own sense of *Adventures* remains fragmentary, as I have been unable to locate copies

of the *Atlas* from June to September 1841, which presumably contain Diddleum's final chapters.

4. Diddleum spells Heth's first name "Joyce."

5. For the articles, see *NYH* 8, 13, 17, 24 Sept. 1836.

6. For Barnum's account of the *Herald* articles, see *Life* 175. Saxon details the aftermath of the Heth hoax in *PTB* 69–73.

7. *NYH* 24 Sept. 1836.

8. The shift in emphasis is particularly obvious in the several chapters where Diddleum ignores the Heth tour while discussing his other ventures.

9. It may attest to Barnum's doubts about the enterprise that none of the ads or press accounts of the Heth exhibitions that I have seen mentions him by name. This is particularly ironic in view of the way Heth's name dogged Barnum for the rest of his career.

10. *NYAtlas* 25 Apr. 1841.

11. See, for example, the tale of the turkey-eating "gourmand" in *Adventures* (*NYAtlas* 23 May 1841) and *Life* 294.

12. In the year following the publication of *Adventures*, Herrick and Ropes would hire Democrat Walt Whitman to edit their New York *Aurora*.

13. *NYAtlas* 11 Apr. 1841.

14. As Allen Read has shown, Arnold created Joe Strickland in 1825 to advertise his New York lottery parlor in the local press. Barnum was one of many writers and merchants to appropriate Arnold's persona (Read 277–85). As he recalls in *Life*, Barnum popularized his lottery business by developing a persona, Dr. Peter Strickland, with obvious debts to Arnold's creation: "In my bills and advertisements I rung [*sic*] all possible changes upon the renowned name" (129).

15. *NYAtlas* 2 May 1841.

16. Levi Lyman may have inspired Barnum's transsectional protagonist with his tall tale about the Yankee and Virginian who exhibited Heth.

17. Significantly, it is the antiabolitionist editor Anne Royall who mistakes Diddleum for "Clapham" of Mississippi (*NYAtlas* 11 Apr. 1841).

18. *NYAtlas* 25 Apr. 1841.

19. The struggle between the pro- and antislavery movements for the legacy of the Founding Fathers is discussed in E. Foner *Free* 75–86 and Baker 166–76.

20. *Boston Morning Post* 7 Sept. 1835. The *Albion* had introduced the piece as "an interesting article, with which a gentleman has favoured us in relation to *Joice Heth*, the nurse of Washington" (29 Aug. 1835, 279).

21. *NYAtlas* 23 May 1841.

22. *NYAtlas* 30 May 1841. During the real Heth tour, this fraudulent promise was reported in the *Providence Journal* (31 Aug. 1835) and the *Lowell Courier* (12 Sept. 1835); it is further elaborated in the anonymous pamphlet *The Life of Joice Heth*. In that work, apparently the one that Barnum attributed to Lyman, the profits from Heth's exhibition are pledged to the purchase of her five "great grandchildren, who are now held by a highly respectable gentleman of Kentucky, who has generously offered to set them free on being paid two-thirds [*sic*] they cost him" (9).

23. *NYAtlas* 23 May 1841. The *Boston Courier* saw Heth as "a breathing skeleton, subjected to the same sort of discipline that is sometimes exercised in a menagerie to induce the inferior animals to play unnatural pranks for the amusement of barren spectators" (8 Sept. 1835).

24. *NYAtlas* 9 May 1841.

25. See Gossett *Uncle* chap. 12 on the plays and novels intended to rebut Stowe's novel.

26. *NYH* 5 Dec. 1859, 6.

27. On the Democratic Party's reliance on populist rhetoric, see Ashworth chaps. 1, 3; on the party's substantial wealthy constituency, see Pessen chap. 11.

28. *NYAtlas* 18 Apr. 1841.

29. On the lower-class affiliations of the Yankee, see Saxton 186.

30. *NYAtlas* 23 May 1841.

31. *NYAtlas* 30 May 1841.

32. Barnum gives Proler & Company's recipes for their phony goods in *Life* 209–10. One ad for their waterproof leather paste began, "As I was walking up the Bowery, / The weather being very showery, / Although my boots were nearly new, / I found the MOISTURE soaking through" (*NYAtlas* 11 Nov. 1838).

33. Halttunen analyzes three major types of confidence men in the advice books (chap. 1).

34. For one such reading of the confidence man, see Lindberg 4–9.

35. *NYAtlas* 16 May 1841.

36. On the feminization of the U.S. middle class, see Blumin 179–91 and Ryan chap. 5.

37. *NYAtlas* 23 May 1841.

38. For Barnum's boast to Albert Smith of having originated the Heth hoax, see Saxon *PTB* 73. For his denial of having ever preached, see *NYAtlas* 24 Nov. 1844.

39. As late as 1854, Barnum would be depicted as a former "preacher of the gospel" in the anonymous book *The True Lamplighter, and Aunt Mary's Cabin* 29.

40. *John-Donkey* 1 Jan. 1848, 13.

41. *NYAtlas* 17 Mar. 1844. The Correspondent was just as sentimental ten months later in taking leave of the United States after a brief trip home (*NYAtlas* 12 Jan. 1845).

42. *NYAtlas* 25 Jan. 1846.

43. *NYAtlas* 1 Mar. 1846.

44. *NYAtlas* 26 Apr. 1846.

45. *NYAtlas* 5 Jan. 1845. Although he remained a fervent Democrat into the 1850s, Barnum demonstrated some real interest in the nativist National Republican Party in the mid-1840s. See Barnum to Moses Kimball, 30 Jan. 1845, in Moses Kimball, Letters received, 1840–78, Library of the Boston Athenaeum.

46. On the British travelogues, see Cunliffe chap. 2 and Berger.

47. *NYAtlas* 12 Oct. 1845.

48. Barnum's first European tour coincided with that of Frederick Douglass, though the two never seem to have crossed paths. On the cooperation of British and U.S. abolitionists, see Sklar.

49. *NYAtlas* 21 July 1844.

50. The Native American was probably part of the group of Iowas Barnum had brought over for an exhibition (partly managed by George Catlin) in a room adjacent to Tom Thumb at Egyptian Hall (Dippie 102). On the female abolitionist petitioners, see Lerner chap. 8.

51. Stowe has Augustine St. Clare resort to this argument in his debate with Ophelia in *Uncle Tom's Cabin* 230–33. For widespread references to European class oppression in U.S. antiabolitionist discourses, see Cunliffe.

52. *NYAtlas* 16 Feb. 1845.

53. For an acute discussion of white slavery and wage slavery, see Roediger chap. 4.

54. See Cunliffe chap. 1.

55. *NYAtlas* 20 Apr. 1845.

56. *NYAtlas* 16 Feb. 1845.

57. *NYAtlas* 23 Feb. 1845.

58. For a detailed comparison of the circumstances of the U.S. and European lower classes, see Stott chap. 6.

59. *NYAtlas* 10 Nov. 1844.

60. *NYAtlas* 10 Nov., 6 Oct. 1844.

61. On the Lowell operatives' participation in the Ten Hour Movement, see Dublin chap. 7.

62. *NYAtlas* 19 Jan. 1845.

63. *NYAtlas* 5 Jan. 1845.

64. Ibid.

65. *NYAtlas* 28 Apr. 1844.

66. *NYAtlas* 23 Mar. 1845.

67. *NYAtlas* 10 Aug. 1845.

68. *NYAtlas* 25 Aug. 1844.

69. *NYAtlas* 16 June 1844.

70. This anecdote was in circulation by 1851, when William K. Northall included it in his *Before and Behind the Curtain* (158). Author Edward P. Hingston, who visited Barnum at the American Museum in 1864, claimed that the showman intentionally put himself on display by leaving the door to his office open: "He knew that half his patrons regarded him as the greatest curiosity of the show" (339).

71. For a valuable discussion of Barnum's importance to the New York humor sheets, see Reynolds *Beneath* 466–83.

72. On the formation of literary Young America, see Miller 71, 76–87 and Bender 141–42. On the distinction between literary and political Young America, see Rogin 71–73.

73. *Yankee Doodle* 7 Aug. 1847, 174.

74. The "Authentic Anecdotes of 'Old Zack'" are reprinted with annotation in Melville 212–29.

75. *Yankee Doodle* 14 Aug. 1847, 189.

76. He presents Tom Thumb as the foremost of the "universal Yankee nation" of American performers who "will be able to pocket and carry back a few of the pounds which their brethren lavished upon foreign talent in America" (*NYAtlas* 26 Apr. 1846).

77. *Yankee Doodle* 28 Aug. 1847, 201. For Barnum's account of his efforts to move Shakespeare's birthplace and Madame Tussaud's wax museum to the United States during his first European tour with Tom Thumb, see *ST* 365. On that same tour, Barnum also apparently tried to buy a tree in Newstead upon which the poet Byron had carved the names of himself and his sister (*NYT* 16 Dec. 1854, 2).

78. On Mathews's early portrayals of urban life, see Miller 80, 82, 93.

79. Except for a few minor changes, this is the biography that Mathews had published in his short-lived journal *The Prompter* 15 June 1850, 34–38.

80. *NYTrib* 19 June 1850.

81. Grimsted *Melodrama* 22–23; Buckley 598–601.

82. *NYAtlas* 16 May 1841.

83. Barnum compiled his "Rules" in 1852 at the request of Edwin Freedley, who published them in *A Practical Treatise on Business* 307–12. In that advice book, Freedley compliments Barnum as "the ablest tactician, and one of the most successful business men of the age" (306).

84. *Littell's Living Age* 10 Mar. 1855, 665. See Neil Harris's discussion of this review (213).

85. The biographical sketch that appeared in the Jenny Lind concert programs also fictionalized Barnum's life story by declaring him fourteen at the time of Philo's death. That these distortions were intentional can be surmised from an 1852 autobiographical sketch in which Barnum got the facts straight (Freedley 309–10).

86. *NYT* 16 Dec. 1854, 4. Barnum was still embellishing the myth of his impoverished childhood as late as 1884 (*PTB* 34).

87. On the myth of the self-made man at midcentury, see Cawelti chap. 2. For a discussion of *Life*'s debt to Franklin, see Buell 58–60.

88. For samples of hostile reviews, see N. Harris 225–29.

89. *NYT* 16 Dec. 1854, 4.

90. Barnum omits any mention of the gunfire that punctuated the first Cincinnati concert and refers only briefly to the "thousands of persons, who . . . disturbed the [Pittsburgh] concert" (*Life* 338–39).

91. This passage occurs in Barnum's account of his experiences as a clerk at a store in Grassy Plain (a mile from Bethel).

92. For Barnum's reflections on the moral consequences of his clerking experiences, see *Life* 99.

93. Barnum's nostalgia can be compared to that of midcentury advice book writers, who, according to Halttunen, also rooted their social critiques in the preindustrial past of the United States (18–19).

94. For a discussion of Walt Whitman's nostalgia, see Reynolds *Walt* 7–8.

95. *Knickerbocker* Mar. 1855, 236. For a discussion of this review, see Lindberg 167–68.

96. The *New York Picayune*, for example, referred to "[t]he art of puffing" as "the etherialization of Barnumism" (3 July 1852).

97. In an obvious reference to Lind, Emerson notes: "We have seen a woman who by pure song could melt the souls of whole populations" ("Success" 286).

98. Emerson insists "the mob uniformly cheers the publisher, and not the inventor. It is the dulness of the multitude that they cannot see the house in the ground-plan" ("Success" 293).

99. See Neil Harris's discussion of this review (226).

100. For evidence of Barnum's experiences as a bearer of theatrical bills, see the brief Barnaby Diddleum anecdote in *NYAtlas* 26 Sept. 1841.

101. For Barnum's symbolic importance to New York highbrows, see Bender 174.

102. See Strong (86); for E. L. Godkin's comparison of Bonner to Barnum, see Denning 218 n. 3; Wallis's comparison came in a joint review of Barnum's *Life* and Stowe's *Sunny Memories of Foreign Lands* (1854). Originally published in the *Metropolitan Magazine*, this review is reprinted in Wallis 69–84.

103. *Boston Daily Advertiser* 15 Sept. 1855.

104. Wallis, for example, feared Stowe for her power over "the large and most impressible class, who insist upon thinking, without knowing exactly how" (80).

105. In 1864, Barnum's American Museum held a benefit for the U.S. Sanitary Commission (*NYH* 9 Apr. 1864, 7).

106. On the gentry's alignment with Arnold, see Bernstein 153 and Bender 172.

107. For attacks on Arnold's elitism during his 1883–84 U.S. tour, see Raleigh 58–67.

108. *NYTrib* 21 Mar. 1886, 7.

109. *P. T. Barnum's Roman Hippodrome Advance Courier* 4 (CWM).

110. Saxon summarizes the complex publication history of *Struggles* in *PTB* 19–23, 417–18.

111. When Barnum spoke, suffrage in Connecticut was limited to literate white males (E. Foner *Reconstruction* 447).

112. He depicts blacks as uniquely unvengeful among the world's races (*ST* 623).

113. *NYT* 16 Dec. 1854, 4.

114. Barnum affirms the potential for social mobility in the United States at the beginning of his reprinted speech "The Art of Money Getting" (*ST* 457).

115. See my discussion of the anecdote featuring Barnum and a boisterous Independence Day crowd outside the American Museum in chapter 3.

116. In a later article titled "The First Jenny Lind Ticket," Barnum notes that this episode occurred in Dubuque, Iowa (*The Cosmopolitan* Oct. 1887, 109).

117. *Cincinnati Gazette* 9 Sept. 1879; reprinted in Presbrey 223. Buffalo Bill Cody similarly advertised his Wild West Show with lithographs featuring his famous visage and the legend, "I Am Coming."

118. For a speech in which Barnum promises to stand behind his name, see *ST* 1875, 772.

119. Lawrence Buell discusses a different sort of decentering in Barnum's *Life* (59).

120. For the anecdotes, see *Life* 374–76 and *ST* 374–76.

## 2. The Jenny Lind Tour: "Where's Barnum?"

1. *HJ* 21 Sept. 1850.

2. For the most recent accounts of Lind's U.S. tour, see *PTB* chap. 8; Buckley chap. 6; N. Harris chap. 5; Ware and Lockard.

3. In addition to the for-profit concerts, Lind performed in at least ten charity and benefit concerts during her tour with Barnum.

4. *NYH* 6 Sept. 1850.

5. On the importance of the ideology of separate spheres to middle-class formation, see Ryan chap. 5.

6. See Ryan's discussion of the substantial number of middle-class Utica women who worked for pay outside the home (172, 203–10).

7. On True Womanhood, see Welter; Ryan 189–91; Halttunen 57–59. Lind is described as a "true woman," in *Cummings' Evening Bulletin* [Philadelphia] 19 Oct. 1850 and *Holden's Dollar Magazine* Nov. 1850, 699.

8. *New York Evening Post* 2 Jan. 1849.

9. *Brooklyn Daily Eagle* 27 Aug. 1850.

10. *NYH* 12 Sept. 1850.

11. *NYH* 2 Oct. 1850; *Cummings' Evening Bulletin* [Philadelphia] 18 Oct. 1850.

12. *NYH* 12 Sept. 1850. In *Life,* Barnum would imply that one of his primary motives in signing Lind was to clear his "name," which had "long been associated with 'humbug'" (297).

13. *NYH* 20 Feb. 1850.

14. The *New York Herald* led the attack on Barnum for his alleged stinginess. See *NYH* 14, 15 Oct. 1850 for editorials with the refrain: "Where's Barnum?" The *New York Morning Express* came to Barnum's defense by suggesting that the showman had silently paid the expenses of Lind's charity concert in Boston: "This fact he has kept from the world, notwithstanding the hypocritical cry in a certain quarter for him to 'give'" (1 Nov. 1850).

15. For contemporary commentary on Lind's humble beginnings, see *Godey's Lady's Book* Dec. 1850, 353 and *HJ* 14 Sept. 1850. On the actual straitened conditions of Lind's childhood, see Bulman chap. 1 and Holland and Rockstro chap. 2.

16. *HJ* 14 Sept. 1850. The *National Police Gazette* concluded a summary of Lind's U.S. charities by praising "the lone girl who unassisted has done all this" (9 Nov. 1850).

17. On Lind's plans for a children's hospital and schools in Sweden, see Holland and Rockstro 408–9.

18. See Rosenberg for the recipients of the $53,210 that Lind dispersed to U.S. charities (*Jenny Lind in America*). The rest of her earnings ended up in a fund that the singer willed to Swedish universities and the Children's Hospital of Stockholm (Holland and Rockstro 408–9).

19. *HJ* 7 Dec. 1850.

20. Edward Everett to Benjamin Seaver, 8 Oct. 1850, Edward Everett Papers, Massachusetts Historical Society.

21. For Lind's involvement in the distribution of the receipts from a Boston charity concert, see the letters from Edward Everett to Benjamin Seaver for 8, 11 Oct. 1850 in the Edward Everett Papers, Massachusetts Historical Society.

22. On the middle-class charities' notion of the worthy poor, see Stansell 72–73.

23. *Godey's Lady's Book* Nov. 1850, 312. For this magazine's support for separate spheres, in an issue that also includes "A Reminiscence of Jenny Lind," see Dec. 1850, 380.

24. *Godey's Lady's Book* Nov. 1850, 312.

25. The *Daily Globe* [Washington] likewise observed that the singer was "adorned with every virtue that crowns the female character—piety, charity, modesty, gentleness, humbleness, kindness" (19 Dec. 1850).

26. One reviewer observed that Lind's "white and simple costume...well became the beautiful sincerity of her face and the angelic purity of her character" (*Boston Herald* 28 Sept. 1850).

27. On middle-class sincerity, see Halttunen 34. See also her discussion of the "sentimental typology of conduct" (40–42, 60, 159).

28. See, for example, *Cummings' Evening Bulletin* [Philadelphia] 19 Oct. 1850 and *Boston Courier* 28 Sept. 1850.

29. *New York Morning Express* 11 Sept. 1850.

30. *Godey's* is quoted in Halttunen 80; *NYH* 12 Sept. 1850. A critic at Lind's second Cincinnati concert complained that she "appeared in a much more brilliant gay dress than on Monday, and in that respect appeared to less advantage—for nothing could be more unpretending than her simple, unaffected dress, in her first appearance" (*Pittsburgh Gazette* 22 Apr. 1851).

31. According to Lois Banner, coiffeur William Dibbee built his career on his reputation as Lind's hairstylist (37).

32. *Richmond Enquirer* (20 Dec. 1850). On the sentimentalists' critique of corsets, see Halttunen 82–83.

33. *Brooklyn Daily Eagle* 10 Sept. 1850. For a story on the New York women who imitated Lind's hairstyle, see *Cincinnati Daily Enquirer* 1 May 1851.

34. On Lind as a former peasant, see *Godey's Lady's Book* Dec. 1850, 353 and *NYSun* 9 Apr. 1891, 5.

35. *HJ* 21 Sept. 1850.

36. On Lind's Norma, see Bulman 30, 82–84.

37. *HJ* 21 Sept. 1850.

38. *NYTrib* 14 Sept. 1850, 1.

39. Willis lamented the prejudice against female opera singers among the religious classes in "Are Operas Moral, and Are Prima-Donnas Ladies?" (*Hurry* 351–55).

40. *Boston Courier* 14 Oct. 1850. For an argument against separating Lind's performance and persona, see *Albion* [New York] 2 Nov. 1850, 523.

41. Foster *Memoir of Jenny Lind*; Rosenberg *Jenny Lind: Her Life*.

42. *HJ* 14 Sept. 1850. Bremer's sketch also appeared in the antislavery *National Era* 26 Sept. 1850, 1.

43. *HJ* 13 Apr. 1850.

44. *HJ* 16 Nov. 1850.

45. *HJ* 9 Nov. 1850.

46. For one such occasion, see *Republican and Daily Argus* [Baltimore] 29 Apr. 1851. Willis undermined Barnum's claim with an anecdote in which the singer "wept bitterly" while reading press speculation about the motives behind her philanthropy (*HJ* 28 Sept. 1850).

47. *Cincinnati Gazette*; reprinted in *Pittsburgh Gazette* 19 Apr. 1851. A Charleston reviewer similarly remarked of Lind's "Home, Sweet Home," "[S]he seemed the impersonation of all that was requisite to make Home a paradise" (*Charleston Mercury* 28 Dec. 1850).

48. My sense of the relation between Lind's fame and that of the female novelists is based on the acute discussion in Brodhead chap. 2.

49. Fanny Fern was the pseudonym of Sara Parton, who was N. P. Willis's sister; Grace Greenwood was the pseudonym of Sara Jane Lippincott.

50. Kelley 29–31, 315; Brodhead 52–57.

51. *Daily Union* [Washington] 19 Dec. 1850.

52. For speculation on Lind's marital prospects, see *Daily Republic* [Washington] 21 Dec. 1850 and *HJ* 28 Sept. 1850.

53. *Boston Herald* 14 Oct. 1850.

54. *Pittsburgh Gazette* 11 Apr. 1851.

55. *HJ* 14 Feb. 1852; quoted in Ware and Lockard 124.

56. *Boston Daily Evening Transcript* 6 Feb. 1852; quoted in Ware and Lockard 122.

57. *HJ* 28 Sept. 1850. Lind publicly wept upon glimpsing the Swedish flag in Alexandria, Virginia (*Richmond Enquirer* 20 Dec. 1850), after making a sentimental speech at a New Year's celebration (*ST* 316–17), and while being presented with a special railroad car (*Boston Courier* 15 Oct. 1850).

58. *Mobile Advertiser*; quoted in *Boston Daily Advertiser* 27 Sept. 1850.

59. *London Atheneum* 28 Sept. 1850; quoted in *NYH* 22 Oct. 1850.

60. *Richmond Enquirer* 20 Dec. 1850.

61. At her most Barnumesque, Lind was reported to have wished that the Swedish people "might have the same energy of character and enterprizing [*sic*] spirit as Americans, who have the courage to expend money in order to make money" (*NYH* 17 Oct. 1850).

62. Lind's refusal to cede to Claudius Harris control over her earnings was largely responsible for ending her 1849 engagement to him (Holland and Rockstro 391; Bulman 215). Despite Barnum's frequent claims to the contrary, Lind seems to have been an active, informed participant in managing the tour's finances. Saxon offers compelling evidence that it was the singer—not, as Barnum claims, himself—who insisted on altering in her favor the terms of their initial contract (*PTB* 173–74).

63. Saxon's effort to debunk the Lind myth is marred by this sexist double standard. While crediting Barnum for his determination, he ridicules Lind for her "obstinacy" (*PTB* 171).

64. *NYH* 24 Sept. 1850.

65. *HJ* 5 Oct. 1850.

66. *NYH* 7 Oct. 1850. For the attacks, see *NYH* 25, 26 Oct. 1850.

67. *NYTrib* 3 June 1851, 4.

68. See Fuller's comparison of Lind with a George Sand heroine in "Jenny Lind, the 'Consuelo' of George Sand" (Ossoli 241–49). Pascoe argues convincingly for the importance of Lind to Dickinson's "performance poems."

69. *NYH* 7 Sept. 1853. See the reports of Brown's experiences at the ironically titled World's Temperance Convention in E. Stanton 152–63, 506–12.

70. *NYH* 17 Sept. 1850.

71. A similar masculinization of the fair heroine occurs in *Uncle Tom's Cabin*, when Stowe contrasts the "Saxon" Eva (whose race makes her "prince-like") with the "Afric" Topsy (247).

72. *NYH* 17 Sept. 1850.

73. *NYH* 12 Sept. 1850. Neil Harris quotes more such comparisons (134–36). For a nongendered discussion of Lind's relation to "northern" European intellect and "southern" passion, see *New York Evening Post* 31 Oct. 1850. Sentimental novelist Caroline Lee Hentz may have drawn on the opposition of Lind and the Italians in *The Planter's Northern Bride* (1854). Her fair heroine Eulalia (who sings like a "nightingale" [99]) triumphs over the raven-haired, passionate Claudia, who was raised by her Italian parents as a street singer.

74. My reading of the Webster/Willis/Lind encounter is obviously indebted to Eve Sedgwick's discussion of homosocial desire in *Between Men*.

75. *HJ* 30 Nov. 1850. Compare Hawthorne's use of the same metaphor to express the triangle binding Holgrave, Clifford, and Phoebe in *The House of the Seven Gables*. Speaking of his desire to probe her cousin, Holgrave tells Phoebe, "Had I your opportunities, no scruples would prevent me from fathoming Clifford to the full depth of my plummet line!" (158).

76. For evidence of Lind's pre-Barnum celebrity, see the story on her London concert in *NYH* 13 May 1849 and the ad for "the burletta of JENNY LIND" at Burton's Theatre (*NYSun* 20 Aug. 1849). Joseph Roppolo lists productions of the "operatic burletta" *Jenny Lind Is [Has] Come* in New Orleans theaters beginning in March 1849 (103, 119–20).

77. Barrett was in England scouting for talent for the new Broadway Theatre, which would open in September 1847.

78. *Yankee Doodle* 14 Aug. 1847, 188.

79. In support of Barnum's claim, the *New York Herald* reported that the crowd at the wharf whispered, "'There is Barnum; watch him; she will be with him'" (2 Sept. 1850). The London *Times* later mocked this scene as "the instant when Jenny Lind was revealed to the 'cute gaze of the American world by her proximity to Barnum on the deck of the steamer"; reprinted in *NYH* 10 Oct. 1850.

80. Caroline Barnum writes of passing for Lind in New Orleans and Cincinnati in diary entries for 6 February and 11 April 1850. She mentions being mistaken for Lind on numerous other instances. The diary is in two parts: 4 December 1850 through 5 April 1851 is in the Bridgeport Public Library; 8–20 April 1851 is in the Manuscripts and Archives Collection of the Indiana Historical Society Library.

81. In her diary entry for 8 December 1850, Caroline Barnum writes of being mistaken for Jenny Lind at each of the three Baltimore churches she had visited that day. She does not mention singing at any of them.

82. *NYH* 6 Sept. 1850.

83. *NYH* 4 June 1851.

84. On the bribery of midcentury reviewers, see Grimsted *Melodrama* 42–44.

85. The blackmail letter was part of an exchange between Barnum and an anonymous writer that appeared on 11 Oct. 1850 in the Boston *Bee* and *Chronotype*. The alleged blackmailer was identified by the *Chronotype* as John M'Clenahan of the *New York Herald*. For the controversial letters and M'Clenahan's denial of the charges, see *NYH* 15 Oct. 1850; for an affidavit from Barnum on the scandal, see *NYH* 26 Oct. 1850. For stories that describe the letters as Barnum-created fakes, see *Boston Herald* 11, 12 Oct. 1850.

86. *National Era* 31 Oct. 1850, 175. For a discussion of Whitman's writings on the Lind tour and the identification of his pseudonym, see Rubin 256–57 and Silver. For Whitman's opposition to theatrical puffery, see Reynolds *Walt* 344.

87. *New York Evening Post* 1 Nov. 1850; *National Era* 21 Nov. 1850, 187.

88. *National Era* 21 Nov. 1850, 187.

89. For a report of Barnum being taunted by a crowd of children at the Princeton train station, see *NYH* 17 Oct. 1850. A postscript to the same story claims that some of the Philadelphia papers were downplaying their city's Lindomania "lest they should be charged with taking black mail."

90. Seeing the U.S. flag in the New York harbor, Lind reportedly declaimed, "There is the beautiful standard of Freedom, the oppressed of all nations worship it" (*NYTrib* 2 Sept. 1850, 1). *Punch* ironically credited Lind's effusion to "a sly sense of humor, no doubt, and a general recollection of all she had heard about the slave-trade, and the treatment of Mr. Frederic Douglas [*sic*]" (reprinted in *NYH* 22 Oct. 1850).

91. *NYH* 2 Sept. 1850.

92. *National Anti-Slavery Standard* 31 Oct. 1850, 90.

93. *NYTrib* 23 Sept. 1850.

94. The exchange between Thomas Ritchie and Barnum appears in the *Daily Union* [Washington] 18 Dec. 1850. For a witty parody of that exchange, see *National Anti-Slavery Standard* 16 Jan. 1851, 135.

95. For evidence of the antiabolitionist attacks on Bremer and Bull, see *National Anti-Slavery Standard* 26 Dec. 1850, 122 and *New York Clipper* 16 Aug. 1856, 134.

96. Stowe reprinted Jenny Goldschmidt's letter of 23 May 1852 in her 1878 introduction to *Uncle Tom's Cabin* (xxii).

97. Wilson documents Lind's contribution and Stowe's role in the Edmondson campaign (291–93).

98. *NYH* 18 May 1852. In *Struggles* Barnum blames Jay's "interference" for his own premature break with Lind (304).

99. For the details of the flight of Dudley (alias James P. Snowden), see *NYH* 18, 25 May 1852 and *NYTrib* 17 May 1852, 6. For an account of these events from an acquaintance of Jay, see Bright 81–85. Jay's involvement in an earlier New York City fugitive slave case is described in *NYTrib* 12 July 1847.

100. *Boston Times*; quoted in *NYH* 26 Sept. 1850. Yellin documents the 1 October 1850 protest meeting at Zion Chapel Street Church in her edition of *Incidents in the Life of a Slave Girl* (Jacobs 289–90 n. 5).

101. *Daily Picayune* [New Orleans] 11 Feb. 1851; *NYH* 20 Oct. 1850.

102. *Godey's Lady's Book* Dec. 1850, 388.

103. The egalitarian *New York Sun* claimed that the Jenny Lind Bonnets manufactured by East Side milliner Mrs. L. Isaacs were fully comparable to those available on Broadway. Yet, the paper observed, "Our aristocratic lady readers may, perhaps, turn up their noses at the thought of purchasing bonnets and hats in Division street" (12 Oct. 1850).

104. *Daily Union* [Washington] 8 Dec. 1850.

105. *Democratic Union* [Harrisburg] 27 Nov. 1850; quoted in Ware and Lockard 49.

106. *HJ* 9 Nov. 1850.

107. The cheapest promenade tickets were set at three dollars for Lind's first concerts, but later dropped to one dollar. There were exceptions to this, however. Just before the Providence concert, Barnum unloaded his remaining tickets for as little as twenty-five cents (*Boston Herald* 11 Oct. 1850).

108. In the days leading up to Lind's first concert, the *Brooklyn Daily Eagle* facetiously protested Barnum's prices by offering "tickets...at a price better suited to the means of the people. Our tickets will admit the bearers to the best places on the *Battery* (gates open at all hours,) and may be obtained for the moderate charge of fifty cents" (7 Sept. 1850).

109. *NYH* 21 Oct. 1850.

110. *NYH* 21 Oct. 1850; *Richmond Enquirer* 24 Dec. 1850.

111. *Missouri Republican* [St. Louis] 23 Mar. 1851.

112. *NYH* 25 Oct. 1850.

113. *NYH* 12 Sept. 1850. During this siege, a crowd of boys in boats tried to disrupt the concert by yelling and playing on drums and fifes (*NYTrib* 12 Sept. 1850, 1).

114. *Boston Herald* 9 Oct. 1850.

115. *Cincinnati Daily Enquirer* 16 Apr. 1851.

116. Rosenberg *Jenny Lind in America* 206.

117. For the violence at the Cincinnati concert, see *Daily Cincinnati Commercial* 15 Apr. 1851 and *Cincinnati Daily Enquirer* 16 Apr. 1851. Emerson is quoted in N. Harris 138. Charles Rosenberg recorded a Cincinnati policeman's prediction of what would have happened had the crowd not fled the warning shots: "We should have blazed away again, and, probably, a trifle lower" (*Jenny Lind in America* 210).

118. Rosenberg *Jenny Lind in America* 217.

119. *Post* [Pittsburgh], reprinted in *Cincinnati Daily Enquirer* 2 May 1851.

120. *Daily Commercial Journal* [Pittsburgh] 29 Apr. 1851. For refutation of the accounts of the crowd's disorder, see *Daily Commercial Journal* 2 May 1851 and *Pittsburgh Gazette* for 28 Apr. and 2, 3, 6 May 1851.

121. Rosenberg *Jenny Lind in America* 218.

122. *Pittsburgh Gazette* 28 Apr. 1851; *Post* [Pittsburgh], reprinted in *Cincinnati Daily Enquirer* 2 May 1851.

123. *Daily Commercial Journal* [Pittsburgh] 2 May 1851.

124. *Daily Commercial Journal* [Pittsburgh] 29 Apr. 1851.

125. Tensions between insiders and outsiders continued after Lind broke with Barnum: in Hartford, ill will over ticket speculation flared into a melee that prompted Lind to cut short her performance (Ware and Lockard 105–6).

126. *North American Miscellany* 31 May 1851, 236. I am indebted to Martha Dennis Burns for my references to this magazine.

127. The usual racial cast of Lind's audience was reversed in Natchez, where she sang for an audience that Julius Benedict later described as "a small number of planters and their families, the great bulk being colored people" (*Scribner's Monthly* May 1881, 132).

128. *NYH* 12, 25 Sept. and 2 Oct. 1850; *NYTrib* 18 Sept. 1850, 1; *Cummings' Evening Bulletin* [Philadelphia] 28 Nov. 1850; *Knickerbocker* Dec. 1850, 560; *New York Picayune* 31 Aug. 1850.

129. *NYH* 25 Oct. 1850.

130. *HJ* 12 Oct. 1850.

131. Max Maretzek, the manager of the Astor Place Opera House during the Lind tour, corroborated Willis's attack on the stinginess of the Upper Ten (6, 96–98).

132. *HJ* 12 Oct. 1850.

133. *NYH* 9 Sept. 1850.

134. For Ossian Dodge's rise from an artisanal temperance singer in the Washingtonian tradition to an entertainer of the middle class, see Tyrrell 178–79.

135. *Godey's Lady's Book* Dec. 1850, 388.

136. For press descriptions of Lind's hotel suites in New York and Boston, see Ware and Lockard 8–9, 35–36.

137. *HJ* 14 Sept. 1850.

138. The *Journal of Commerce* [New York] claimed that D. D. Howard paid Lind one thousand dollars to stay at his Irving House Hotel (5 Sept. 1850). For a letter from Howard denying this, see *NYTrib* 6 Sept. 1850, 1. The *New York Herald* repeated this charge as well as the rumor about the loaned furniture (*NYH* 7 Oct. 1850). For a satirical pamphlet that repeats these and other rumors about Barnum's intrigues during the tour, see *The Jenny Lind Mania in Boston* 14–17.

139. *National Anti-Slavery Standard* 3 Oct. 1850, 75.

140. For the anxieties raised by the middle-class female consumer, see Blumin 185–86.

141. *NYAtlas* 24 Nov. 1844.

142. *Godey's Lady's Book* Nov. 1850, 312.

143. On the elite affiliations of midcentury opera, see Buckley 249–50, 262 and McConachie "New York Operagoing."

144. For the press response to the Astor Place riot, see Buckley 19–20; on 23 May 1849, the *New York Herald* distributed blame for the riot between the socialists and the "exclusives."

145. *HJ* 14 Sept. 1850.

146. Ibid.

147. *Sartain's Union Magazine of Literature and Art* Mar. 1851, 215. Maretzek generally agreed with this assessment, depicting New York's elite as "a meagre and lazy mare who would not go ahead, in spite of corn and spurs" (6).

148. *NYTrib* 23 Sept. 1850, 1.

149. Ibid. For similar complaints, see *NYTrib* 14, 20 Sept. 1850.

150. *Holden's Dollar Magazine* Aug. 1851, 64. I am indebted to Martha Dennis Burns for this reference.

151. For attacks on "claptrap" in the concerts, see *NYH* 29 May 1852; *American Whig Review* Aug. 1852, 191; *Morning Courier and New-York Enquirer* 23 Sept. 1850.

152. *Putnam's Monthly* May 1853, 591. For an earlier endorsement, see *Putnam's Monthly* Jan. 1853, 119.

153. *Sartain's Union Magazine of Literature and Art* Sept. 1851, 231.

154. *North American Miscellany* 31 May 1851, 237.

155. *North American Miscellany* 14 June 1851, 335.

156. *North American Miscellany* 21 June 1851, 383.

## 3. Barnum's Long Arms: The American Museum

1. Prices went up to thirty cents for adults, fifteen for children, in 1864.

2. In addition to his American Museum, by 1855 Barnum had owned museums in Baltimore (1845–46) and Philadelphia (1849–51). In 1850 he also purchased the Chinese Museum in New York, which he soon folded into the collection of his American Museum.

3. For an account of Lind's visit to the Museum in the company of Giovanni Belletti and Julius Benedict, see *NYSun* 21 Nov. 1850. The reporter implies that the plebeian "sovereigns" in the crowd have not had the chance to hear her sing. Barnum had apparently hoped for a much earlier visit from Lind: one American Museum puff hinted at a visit in *Morning Courier and New-York Enquirer* 4 Sept. 1850.

4. In the following discussion, I use the term *American Museum* to signify collectively both of Barnum's New York halls.

5. Reprinted in *NYSun* 14 July 1865.

6. On Barnum's purchase of the Museum, see *Life* 215–22.

7. One sign of that continuity is Pintard's service as a trustee of Scudder's American Museum in the 1820s and early 1830s (Haberly 282–85).

8. On the origins of Tammany's American Museum, see Bender 47 and McClung and McClung 144–56.

9. On the Western Museum, see Dunlop and Tucker.

10. See, for example, Sellers and N. Harris 56.

11. On the Central Park Zoo, see Rosenzweig and Blackmar 341–49.

12. For an ad mentioning the Museum's original configuration, see *NYAtlas* 18 Apr. 1841.

13. For a floor-by-floor description of the Museum's contents, see *NYT* 14 July 1865, 1.

14. *The Nation* 27 July 1865, 113–14. For a sample of attacks on antebellum U.S. museums, see Bell 21–22.

15. *The Nation* 27 July 1865, 113.

16. Rosenzweig and Blackmar, it should be noted, credit the American Museum of Natural History with a friendlier stance toward the masses than the Metropolitan Museum of Art (355–58, 363).

17. *NYH* 25 Jan. 1864, 4.

18. The Museum announces it will be closed on Sundays on a bill for 16 Oct. 1848 (HTC).

19. The "What Can They Be?" were sham animals (one of them boasting two heads and one leg) supposedly discovered in an African cave. Barnum challenged scientists to identify them by any published work on natural history (Museum bill for 29 Sept. 1860; HTC).

20. *NYAtlas* 11 Apr. 1841.

21. The Agassiz letter is in *NYTrib* 5 Jan. 1861, 1. The praise for Barnum is in *NYAtlas* 11 Nov. 1860, 5.

22. For Peale's advertisement of his mastodon skeleton, see Sellers 142–47.

23. *NYT* 8 Nov. 1853, 4.

24. *NYH* 25 Jan. 1864, 4.

25. *NYH* 12 July 1866, 4.

26. *The Nation* had anticipated the *Herald* in rejecting the idea of a proprietary museum to replace Barnum's: "No individual or stock company which may undertake to form and manage a museum as a way of making money will be of any great or permanent service to the community" (27 July 1865, 114).

27. *The Nation* 10 Aug. 1865, 171.

28. See Saxon's account of this scheme in *PTB* 108–9.

29. *NYAtlas* 25 Aug. 1844.

30. For examples of the term *Barnumism* used as a synonym for advertisement, see Bobo 15 and *New York Picayune* 3 July 1852.

31. For examples of those stunts, see Barnum's anecdotes of the brick man and the plowing elephant (*ST* 121–23, 357–62).

32. For descriptions of the Museum's exterior, see James 165; Foster *New York* 8; Lewis 23–24; Thornbury 176; Bright 68.

33. Upon first approaching the Museum, Fanny Fern likewise suspected — wrongly, as it turned out — that "its internal will not equal its external appearance" (Parton 373).

34. On the Lincoln finger rings, see Ferguson 12.

35. For the jeweler's reminiscence, see *NYSun* 5 June 1910.

36. The Museum's bill for 7 July 1862 advertised panels for its curtain, as well as one in Barnum's Aquarial Gardens in Boston (HTC).

37. *The Nation* 7 Mar. 1867, 192. In its report on the Museum's 1868 fire, the *New York Tribune* sighed, "[W]hat a comfort it is to know that that abominable advertising drop-curtain has gone at last" (6 Mar. 1868, 8).

38. A bill for 23 Mar. 1863, for example, lists as panel holders the wine sellers "Dr. Underhill" and "The Bordeaux Wine Co." (Museum of the City of New York).

39. See the American Museum ad inside the back cover of Conway *Dred*.

40. See the American Museum ad inside the back cover of *Descriptive Pamphlet of the Celebrated Gorgeous Oriental Tableau of Cerean Sculpture*.

41. Later that year the showman was back onstage celebrating the fiftieth year of both the American Museum and Barnum. At each Lecture Room performance, he offered "BARNUM'S PICTORIAL ENTERTAINMENT," which consisted of a lecture accompanied by illustrations, "proving Barnum's success as a Manager, and EXACTLY HOW HE DID IT!!" (*NYAtlas* 9 Dec. 1860, 8).

42. There are copies of this poster, titled "Wonders of Barnum's Museum," in the New-York Historical Society and the Barnum Museum. For Barnum's role in the development of East Bridgeport, Connecticut, see *ST* chap. 35.

43. *NYH* 15 July 1865, 5.

44. On the display techniques at the American Museum of Natural History, see Rosenzweig and Blackmar 357.

45. *NYTrib* 9 Aug. 1861, 1.

46. For a story on Barnum's eighth and ninth whales, see *Frank Leslie's Illustrated Newspaper* 22 July 1865, 285. In advertising those belugas, Barnum made the most of their delicacy: "THEIR LIVES ARE UNCERTAIN, seven of the same species having died while being exhibited at this Museum" (*NYH* 2 July 1865, 7).

47. *NYH* 2 July 1865, 7.

48. See the critiques of Strong and Godkin discussed in chapter 1.

49. *NYH* 6 Aug. 1865, 1.

50. On the *Illustrated News*, see *PTB* 188–89; *Frank Leslie's Illustrated Newspaper* 15 Dec. 1855, 6; Everett 292.

51. For Leslie's biography, see Everett.

52. *Frank Leslie's Illustrated Newspaper* 5 Dec. 1857, 6.

53. *Frank Leslie's Illustrated Newspaper* 22 July 1865, 285.

54. As *Leslie's* put it approvingly, Barnum's "pictorial designs" were "suggestive of what might be seen inside" (29 July 1865, 295).

55. *NYH* 12 July 1866, 4.

56. *Atlantic Monthly* July 1893, 112–19.

57. *The Nation* 27 July 1865, 113. The founders of the American Museum of Natural History envisioned a library as part of their original plans (Hellman 19); on the ties between the Smithsonian Institution and libraries, see *Atlantic Monthly* July 1893, 113.

58. For the goals of the Tammany museum founders, see Bender 47.

59. *The Nation* 27 July 1865, 113. On the sacralization of late-nineteenth-century museums and libraries, see Levine 149–60.

60. For the Bowery milieu, see especially Buckley chap. 4; Wilentz 257–71; Lott chap. 3.

61. In the following discussion, I rely on the definitions of these categories developed by Laurie and by Dawley and Faler.

62. For Walt Whitman's 1842 impressions of the cross-class crowd visible from the American Museum's balcony, see Rubin and Brown 26–27.

63. *New York Commercial Advertiser* 7 Dec. 1848. On Benjamin Baker's "Mose" plays, see Stott 223–26 and Buckley 388–99.

64. *NYClip* 21 June 1856, 70.

65. *NYClip* 11 Feb. 1860, 342.

66. *Boston Courier* 4 Aug. 1855. The notorious Walsh represented the Bowery in the U.S. Congress; Isaiah Rynders headed a political gang.

67. For Barnum's citation of Channing, see *Life* 399–400.

68. On the "fistic prowess" of the Bowery politicians, see Stott 238.

69. After noting that his birthday is July 5, just after the Independence Day cannonades, Barnum observes: "This propensity of keeping out of harm's way has always stuck by me. I have often thought that were I forced to go to war, the first arms that I should examine would be my legs" (*Life* 12). The showman's pride in his self-control is especially evident in his account of his penny-pinching first year at the American Museum (*Life* 222–23).

70. *NYSun* 12 June 1843.

71. On the American and Mechanics Institutes, see Wilentz, especially 271–75.

72. In the summer, the Museum styled itself the American Museum, Garden and Perpetual Fair in honor of the plants and refreshment stand Barnum installed on the building's roof.

73. *NYH* 16 Aug. 1843. For a list of the exhibitors, see the bill for 23–28 Oct. 1843 (HTC).

74. *NYH* 26 Oct. 1843.

75. *NYAtlas* 19 Jan. 1845.

76. Ibid.

77. *NYH* 7 Aug. 1843.

78. Barnum to Kimball, 15 July 1843, in Moses Kimball, Letters received, 1840–78, Library of the Boston Atheneum.

79. Fordyce Hitchcock was running the Museum in Barnum's absence.

80. *NYSun* 12 June 1843.

81. On the entrepreneurialism of the institutes, see Wilentz 151–53, 271–76, 302–6.

82. On the Boweryites' contempt for middle-class decorum, see Stott 251–52.

83. On the middle-class identification of the loyalists, see Dawley and Faler 469. On the Christianity of the revivalists, see Laurie 34–52, 115–24, 140–47.

84. *Sights and Wonders in New York* 24.

85. For the Museum's depiction of blacks as lazy, see *An Illustrated Catalogue* 33 and T. D. Rice's minstrel playlet *O Hush! or, The Virginny Cupids* (this Lecture Room standard is reprinted in Engle 1–12). For an intemperate Indian, see Wahnotee in Boucicault's *The Octoroon*. In applying the concept of the industrial morality to popular cultural representations of the Irish, I have drawn upon Lott 147–49 and McConachie "Cultural Politics."

86. On the remaking of New York's working class, see Stott, especially chap. 3.

87. *Morning Courier and New-York Enquirer* 17 Mar. 1848. In Barnum's first year, he offered a "splendid model of the CITY OF DUBLIN" which would "positively be removed after St. Patrick's Day" (*NYTrib* 15 Mar. 1842).

88. The Museum's Irish performers included comedians W. O. Neil and J. L. Wallis and the famed actor Barney Williams.

89. My discussion of the stage Irishman is based largely on McConachie "Cultural Politics."

90. The Museum appealed to patrons to view American Republican parades from its balconies (*NYAtlas* 7 Apr. 1844; *Morning Courier and New-York Enquirer* 31 Nov. 1844). On the American Republicans' constituency, see Wilentz 316–24 and Laurie 140–41.

91. *Barnum's American Museum Illustrated* 25.

92. On the role of Protestant ministers as promoters of entrepreneurialism, see Wilentz 304–5 and Laurie 140–43.

93. *Sights and Wonders in New York* 24.

94. *Morning Courier and New-York Enquirer* 13 May 1848; *Sunday Mercury* [New York] 21 Aug. 1859.

95. American Museum bill for 6 Jan. 1862, in American Antiquarian Society. The Reverend T. W. Jones was scheduled to preach at the Barnum and Van Amburgh Museum when it was destroyed by fire (*NYTrib* 4 Mar. 1868, 8).

96. On the National and Bowery Theatres' Sunday services, see Birdoff 76.

97. McConachie *Melodramatic* 164–65, 168–69; Allen *Horrible* 63–65.

98. *NYH* 4 June 1855, 7.

99. *Morning Courier and New-York Enquirer* 4 May 1844.

100. *Morning Courier and New-York Enquirer* 14 Apr. 1860.

101. *Ten Thousand Things on China and the Chinese* 199.

102. For commentary on the American Museum's young patrons, see, for example, *Knickerbocker* Oct. 1850, 378 and *The Nation* 27 July 1865, 113. For memoirists who recalled visiting the Museum as children, see James 154–65 and C. Harris 2, 12–13.

103. See, for example, Alger's *Ragged Dick* 54, 58, 66 and *Slow and Sure; or, From the Street to the Shop* chap. 2.

104. This phrase appears on Barnum's American Museum stationery from the 1860s.

105. McConachie *Melodramatic* 164; Allen *Horrible* 64–65.

106. Bill for 25–28 June 1845 (HTC).

107. Barnum apparently took the idea for a baby show from an earlier exhibit in Springfield, Ohio (*Cincinnati Daily Enquirer* 24 Oct. 1855).

108. *NYT* 11 June 1855, 4.

109. *NYT* 7 June 1855, 3.

110. Barnum and Wood also advertised a show in Providence for 2–6 Oct. 1855, but I have found no evidence that it occurred. Wood was the proprietor of Colonel Wood's Great Museum of Living Wonders in Philadelphia.

111. *Putnam's Monthly* Aug. 1855, 139–43; *Democratic Review* Apr. 1855, 315–18; *Godey's Lady's Book* Dec. 1855, 570–71.

112. On the British baby shows, see *HJ* 10 Nov. 1855. On the Doylestown exhibit, see *Boston Evening Transcript* 28 Aug. 1855.

113. On later baby shows not sponsored by Barnum, see *NYT* 2 Aug. 1869, 2 and *Wheeling Register* 14 May 1883.

114. *Cincinnati Daily Commercial* 26 Oct. 1855.

115. On the overwhelmingly female crowds at the shows, see *New York Evening Post* 6 June 1855; *Boston Herald* 12 Sept. 1855; *Daily Pennsylvanian* [Philadelphia] 10 Oct. 1855.

116. *NYT* 6 June 1855, 1.

117. *Boston Herald* 5 Sept. 1855.

118. *NYTrib* 6 June 1855, 4.

119. *NYH* 12 May 1855, 7.

120. For a thorough study of the relationships among the various midcentury health reforms, see Nissenbaum.

121. *Providence Daily Journal* 25 Sept. 1855. For endorsements of baby shows from Lydia Fowler and another physician, see *NYTrib* 16 May 1855, 5. See also the defense of the shows by "Hygiene" (*Boston Herald* 13 Aug. 1855).

122. For the complete questionnaire, see *NYH* 7 June 1855, 1.

123. On Barnum's behavior at the shows, see *Daily News* [Philadelphia] 12 Oct. 1855. For an attack on the shows' rhetoric of health reform, see *Boston Daily Journal* 17 Sept. 1855.

124. Another judge at the 1855 American Museum baby show was the wife of Russell Trall, a temperance advocate and hydropathist, who founded a coeducational medical school. On Trall's career, see Davies 110–13; Nissenbaum 149–51; Brodie 147–49.

125. Hunt had been practicing medicine since the 1830s; Fowler was the second U.S. woman to earn an M.D. and the first appointed to a medical professor-

ship (Davies 47). Her husband, Lorenzo Fowler, was a partner in Fowlers & Wells, phrenologists and publishers (whom Barnum regarded as his "worthy friends" [*Life* 366]). In 1854 the firm published Barnum's temperance pamphlet, *The Liquor Business.*

126. *NYTrib* 8 June 1855, 5.

127. *New York Evening Post* 7 June 1855.

128. *NYH* 8 June 1855, 1.

129. *NYT* 8 June 1855, 3. For other feminists who made similar arguments, see the speeches of Ernestine Rose and Frances Gage at the Cincinnati Woman's Rights Convention (*Cincinnati Daily Commercial* 18, 19 Oct. 1855).

130. Saxon outlines Barnum's personal ties to the midcentury feminists in *PTB* 59–62.

131. *New York Evening Post* 7 June 1855.

132. On the prominence of immigrants among the exhibitors, see *NYH* 7 June 1855, 1.

133. *NYH* 10 June 1855, 1.

134. *NYTrib* 8 June 1855, 5. One thirteen-month-old boy was exhibited in an eagle-bedecked red, white, and blue "Native American costume" (*NYT* 6 June 1855, 1).

135. *NYH* 8 June 1855, 1.

136. On Scott's background, see *NYTrib* 6 June 1855, 5 and *New York Picayune* 16 June 1855.

137. *NYH* 2 June 1855, 7. For the full list of judges of the Museum's show, see *NYH* 7 June 1855, 1.

138. *Boston Courier* 12 Sept. 1855.

139. *Boston Daily Evening Transcript* 13 Sept. 1855.

140. See the letter by "Hygiene" that explains that the shows were meant not for the educated "few," but for the "mass" who lack information about physiology (*Boston Herald* 13 Aug. 1855).

141. American Museum bill for 28, 29 May 1855 (HTC).

142. On artisan republicanism, see Wilentz, especially chap. 2.

143. For the announcement of the one-hundredth contestant, see *NYH* 28 May 1855, 7.

144. *NYTrib* 2 May 1855, 6.

145. *NYTrib* 4 May 1855, 6.

146. On 1 March 1849, the American Museum welcomed "respectable COLORED PERSONS" from 8:00 a.m. to 1:00 p.m. For stories on this event, see *NYTrib* 27 Feb. 1849; *NYSun* 2 Mar. 1849; *National Anti-Slavery Standard* 26 Dec. 1850, 122.

147. *NYTrib* 4 May 1855, 6.

148. *NYH* 20 Feb. 1861, 7. Mark Twain observed "self-possessed groups of negroes and children at Barnum's Museum" in 1867 (*Mark* 84). An 1823 guidebook from Scudder's Museum attests to the different racial regime under which Barnum's predecessors operated. Among its "Rules of the American Museum" is the notice, "No coloured people admitted in the evening, except servants with their masters" (Scudder vi).

149. *NYH* 14 June 1855, 7.

150. *Boston Daily Evening Transcript* 10, 11, 12 Sept. 1855 and *Boston Herald* 14 Sept. 1855.

151. *Boston Daily Evening Transcript* 12 Sept. 1855.

152. *Daily News* [Philadelphia] 8 Oct. 1855.

153. *Providence Daily Journal* 25 Sept. 1855.

154. Barnum's fake contests included the 1836 juggling matches between Signor Vivalla and Roberts (*Life* 167–71), the 1843 "competition" between the American Museum and the New York Museum (which Barnum secretly owned), and the ostensible rivalry between the Barnum & London and Adam Forepaugh Circuses during their 1882–83 secret pact.

155. *North American and United States Gazette* [Philadelphia] 13 Oct. 1855.

156. *Boston Daily Advertiser* 15 Sept. 1855.

157. *Providence Daily Post* 29 Sept. 1855.

158. On white rioters' special hostility to bourgeois African Americans, see Lapsansky.

159. *Boston Daily Evening Transcript* 12 Sept. 1855; *Public Ledger* [Philadelphia] 11 Oct. 1855; *Boston Daily Courier* 12 Sept. 1855.

160. *Cincinnati Daily Commercial* 11 Oct. 1855.

161. See the letter from Barnum in *Cincinnati Daily Commercial* 22 Oct. 1855 and the one from "A LOVER OF PRETTY CHILDREN" in *Cincinnati Daily Enquirer* 23 Oct. 1855.

162. *Cincinnati Daily Commercial* 23 Oct. 1855.

163. On the Free Love Society, see Spurlock 153, 164–65. In November 1855, the American Museum commemorated the scandal with a play titled "Free Love; or, Passional Attraction" (bill for 26, 27 Nov. 1855 [HTC]).

164. *Cincinnati Daily Commercial* 20 Oct. 1855.

165. *Cincinnati Daily Commercial* 19 Oct. 1855.

166. For the rumors about the Nicholses' intentions and the couple's response, see *Cincinnati Daily Enquirer* 20, 23, 25 Oct. 1855. The Nicholses were associates of Brisbane, Stephen Pearl Andrews, and other New York free lovers. According to John Spurlock, Thomas Nichols traveled through Ohio and Michigan in 1855 proselytizing for free love (154).

167. *Cincinnati Daily Commercial* 19 Oct. 1855.

168. *Cincinnati Daily Commercial* 23 Oct. 1855; *Cincinnati Daily Enquirer* 24 Oct. 1855.

169. For Barnum's letter to Colonel Wood proposing the founding of a museum in Cincinnati, see *Cincinnati Daily Enquirer* 20 Oct. 1855. Barnum's suit against the *Cincinnati Daily Commercial* is described in the issue of 24 Oct. 1855.

170. *Albany Evening Journal* 22 Sept. 1855.

171. *Cincinnati Daily Enquirer* 24 Oct. 1855.

172. *NYTrib* 4 June 1862, 11 and 11 May 1863, 7.

173. On the uptown migration of Manhattan's middle and upper classes, see Spann 102–3, 107–12, 114–15.

174. *NYClip* 19 July 1856, 103.

175. *New York Evening Post* 20 Feb. 1860.

176. *NYTrib* 26 Mar. 1860, 7.

177. In a story on the 1865 fire, the *New York Times* observed that Barnum had been thinking for some time of moving the Museum "further up town, above Canal-street" (14 July 1865, 1).

178. *NYH* 15 July 1865, 5.

179. *Frank Leslie's Illustrated Newspaper* 30 Sept. 1865, 20. While recounting his experiences at the second Museum, Barnum recalls his abortive plans for a free national museum "farther up town" (*ST* 698).

180. *NYTrib* 26 Mar. 1860, 7.

181. For other references to the Museum's country patrons, see *ST* 142, 160.

182. On Barnum's country patrons, see also Haswell 470 and *Putnam's Monthly* Oct. 1856, 448.

183. *NYTrib* 4 Mar. 1868, 8.

184. See the interestingly titled verse ad "PELEG PETTINGHAME, IN TOWN, TO TIMOTHY TOUCHMENOT, IN THE COUNTRY" (*NYTrib* 1 Mar. 1861, 1) and the guidebook *Sights and Wonders in New York*, which narrates an American Museum visit by Timothy Find-Out and his two nephews who live in a "rural hermitage on the banks of the Passaic" (2).

185. See, for example, the bill for 28 Apr. 1860 (HTC).

186. Bill for 28 Apr. 1860 (HTC); Pfeiffer 465; *NYAtlas* 8 Apr. 1860, 5; *The Nation* 10 Aug. 1865, 171.

187. *NYH* 14 July 1865, 1.

188. *NYSun* 15 July 1865.

189. *NYH* 15 July 1865, 5.

190. *NYT* 4 Mar. 1868, 8.

191. *NYTrib* 11 May 1863, 7.

192. For Barnum's ties with the nation's public natural history museums, see *PTB* 95–96, 112, 278, 299–300, 308.

## 4. Barnum's Lecture Room: Excavating the Politics of the Moral Drama

1. Among the memoirists who recall childhood excursions to the Lecture Room, see especially James 154–65 and Haswell 12.

2. Although Barnum did not officially dedicate the Lecture Room to drama until 1850, it occasionally staged farce, pantomime, and light comedy in the 1840s.

3. On the relationship between Barnum's museums and the rise of vaudeville, see Allen "B. F. Keith."

4. In a pioneering chapter on the form, Bruce McConachie has shown how the museum owners staged plays that supported the dominant ideologies of their collections (*Melodramatic* chap. 6).

5. For a description of the Lecture Room's decorations, see *Barnum's American Museum Illustrated* 30–32. The *Herald* reported the Lecture Room's capacity as two thousand (*NYH* 16 June. 1850); the *Tribune* counted "[a]bout three thousand" (*NYTrib* 19 June 1850, 1). Barnum's figure of five thousand appears in an ad (*NYTrib* 17 June 1850, 5). Earlier enlargements of the Lecture Room occurred in May 1842 and December 1844.

6. *NYSun* 18 June 1850.

7. According to Claire McGlinchee, the unnamed fifth degree of crime in Hill's play was murder. See her discussion of Kimball's role in the formation of moral drama (23–27).

8. See, for example, Maretzek 200–201 and Northall 166–67.

9. *The Drunkard* appeared at the National on 14 June and at the Bowery in the first week of July. One sign of the competition between the Museum and the city's plebeian theaters was an ad for the Bowery's *Drunkard* that included thinly veiled attacks on Barnum and his revamped playhouse (*NYH* 4 July 1850).

10. See Bruce McConachie's discussion of the museums' revivals of these plays (*Melodramatic* 176–77).

11. *NYTrib* 19 June 1850, 1.

12. *NYH* 15 Dec. 1863, 7.

13. The genre lingered to haunt later defenders of the stage. In 1890, Joseph Jefferson still found it necessary to attack "[w]hat is called the moral drama" (336–37).

14. For a thorough discussion of the antitheater sentiment, see Grimsted *Melodrama* chap. 2.

15. *NYClip* 23 July 1853. In 1857, Henry W. Bellows claimed: "That disgusting and odious gallery once allotted to vice — formerly deemed inseparable from the theatre — has been almost universally abandoned" (39).

16. American Museum bill for 25–28 June 1845 (HTC). For reports of prostitutes in Barnum's Museum and Lecture Room, see Foster *New York* 8 and *NYH* 7 June 1855.

17. E. Porter Belden similarly advocated the "rational entertainment" at Barnum's, while condemning the city's theaters (118).

18. See McConachie's discussion of the productions of *Rosina Meadows* at Barnum's and Kimball's museums (*Melodramatic* chap. 6).

19. *NYSun* 12 June 1843.

20. On the Washingtonians, see Tyrrell chap. 7.

21. *NYAtlas* 10 July 1842.

22. On those later artisanal organizations, see Tyrrell 209–11.

23. After the first two nights at his refurbished Museum, Barnum wrote to Moses Kimball, "The Drunkard takes first rate & *must run*." 19 June 1850; P. T. Barnum Papers, Rare Books and Manuscripts Division, New York Public Library, Astor, Lenox and Tilden Foundations.

24. For the Washingtonians' experience meetings, see Wilentz 309 and Reynolds *Beneath* 67.

25. *NYTrib* 17 June 1850.

26. *NYTrib* 19 June 1850, 1.

27. William Dowton was also the name of a British comedian, whose lukewarm U.S. reception is discussed in Hodge chap. 7.

28. On the middle-class takeover of the Washingtonians, see Tyrrell 204–5.

29. *New York Morning Express* 4 Sept. 1850. According to Richard Moody, the Lecture Room's production of *The Drunkard* from 8 July to 7 October 1850 marked the first uninterrupted one hundred-performance run on the U.S. stage (277). Clarke's performances as Edward Middleton would eventually earn him the nickname "Drunkard."

30. My sense of the projection and identification that takes place across class and racial lines depends upon the model developed by Eric Lott. See especially Lott chap. 5.

31. *NYH* 23 Sept. 1850.

32. For an example of the opposition to the temperance women among male temperance advocates, see the reports of the 1853 Brick Church meeting in New York (E. Stanton 499–503). For the unrelated attacks on Barnum at that same meeting, see E. Stanton 503–5.

33. *NYH* 1 Apr. 1860, 1.

34. *NYAtlas* 20 Nov. 1853; *NYTrib* 15 Nov. 1853, 7.

35. The Museum's ads claimed that its production was "the only just and sensible Dramatic version of Mrs. Stowe's book that has ever been put upon the stage" (*New York Evening Post* 19 Nov. 1853).

36. For the origins of Conway's *Uncle Tom*, see McConachie "H. J. Conway's."

37. The record-breaking opening run of *Uncle Tom* at the National would end on 13 May 1854.

38. *New York Evening Post* 19 Nov. 1853.

39. Ibid. In similar vein, another Museum ad boasted that Conway's play makes "Virtue triumphant and Vice detestable, instead of permitting wickedness to prosper, and goodness to suffer, and thus leaving an untoward impression of the justice of Providence on the minds of the audience" (*NYT* 17 Nov. 1853, 1). In 1852, the National Theatre had staged C. W. Taylor's dramatization of *Uncle Tom*, which also ends with the hero's liberation.

40. In the following discussion, I rely on the script from Conway's dramatization in the Harry Ransom Humanities Research Center at the University of Texas at Austin. The third act of this script, it should be noted, is missing Conway's version of scenes 3 through 7. See McConachie's discussion of this flawed text in "Out" 25 n. 1.

41. The importance that Conway placed upon George's pledge is suggested by a letter he wrote to Kimball as he planned his dramatization. Among the chief difficulties that Conway foresaw was accounting for the time that George would need to grow into manhood. For the text of the letter, see McConachie "H. J. Conway's" 150–51.

42. See my discussion of this comparison in connection with Barnum's European Correspondence in chapter 1.

43. For a thorough discussion of Partyside's white "egalitarianism," see Lott 230–31.

44. Compare Stowe's St. Clare, who apologizes to Tom for getting drunk and is stabbed while peacefully intervening in a quarrel.

45. For the National Theatre's plebeian reputation, see Lott 227–28.

46. *New York Evening Post* 15 Nov. 1853. The antiabolitionist *New York Clipper* was less sanguine about Purdy's transformation of his theater: "We see but few of the *old patrons* at the National during these times" (3 Sept. 1853).

47. On Purdy's efforts to gentrify his theater, see MacDonald 273 and Birdoff 75–76, 95–96, 100–101. McConachie explains the class difference between pit and parquette (*Melodramatic* 200).

48. Lott acutely points out that Topsy's reply ("Does he live out South?" [5.2]) may be read as a dig at the southern sympathies of the Museum's *Uncle Tom* (226).

49. Partyside has come South to gather materials for "a book on human nature."

50. Legree is enraged at St. Clare for knocking him down in a brawl before being killed by a third party. After St. Clare's death, Legree explains his desire for Tom: "I couldn't kill his master—I can him" (4.1).

51. In Conway, Stowe's Emmeline is folded into the character of Eliza Harris, who escapes with George to Canada, whence she is kidnapped by Marks and sold to Legree.

52. *Liberator* 16 Dec. 1853, 198; *NYTrib* 15 Nov. 1853, 7. As Lott points out, Barnum altered the play to mollify his antislavery critics (275 n. 30). The *Tribune* praised the showman for cutting St. Clare's comparison of slaves and English workers and rewriting the auction scene (*NYTrib* 2 Dec. 1853, 7).

53. Conway's *Uncle Tom* reappeared in the Lecture Room from 23 February to 9 March 1855.

54. The Union Safety Committee provided a lawyer for the ex-owner of Henry Long and compensated planter Jonathan Lemmon, eight of whose slaves had been freed by the state of New York (P. Foner 60–63).

55. Conway wrote the play in June and July of 1852. See H. J. Conway to Moses Kimball, 1 June and 7 Aug. 1852, in Moses Kimball, Letters received, 1840–78, Library of the Boston Athenaeum. The former letter is reprinted and discussed in McConachie "H. J. Conway's."

56. The *Morning Courier and New-York Enquirer* acknowledged the rapid growth of antislavery sentiment in its review of Stowe's *Dred*: "[T]he people are now far beyond the point at which *Uncle Tom* found them" (17 Oct. 1856).

57. George L. Aiken was the cousin of Caroline (Fox) Howard, who performed at Barnum's Museum with her husband George L. Howard and daughter Cordelia.

58. On the popularity of the Howards' performances of *Uncle Tom* at the American Museum, see MacDonald 277. Caroline Howard was in the middle of a run as Topsy in Aiken's *Uncle Tom* when the Barnum and Van Amburgh Museum burned.

59. Speaking of the National Theatre's production of *Dred*, the *New York Clipper* condemned it as another playhouse "where our country cousins may go and have their previous prejudices [against slavery] made more deeply impervious to reason" (27 Sept. 1856, 182).

60. *Morning Courier and New-York Enquirer* 22 Sept. 1856.

61. *Morning Courier and New-York Enquirer* 18 Sept. 1856.

62. Conway's was the third version of *Dred* to be staged in New York in 1856. The National Theatre opened C. W. Taylor's dramatization on 22 September; one week later, the Bowery Theatre opened John Brougham's version, which starred blackface minstrel favorite T. D. Rice as Old Tiff.

63. For the details of Stowe's authorship of *Dred*, see Hedrick 258–60.

64. For the Republican critique of the South, see E. Foner *Free* chap. 2.

65. *New York Daily Express* 9 Oct. 1856; quoted inside the front cover of Conway's *Dred*.

66. My discussion of Conway's personalization of the slavery conflict in *Dred* draws heavily from David Grimsted's analysis of a similar dynamic in George Aiken's *Uncle Tom* ("*Uncle Tom*" 241, 244).

67. Nina Gordon dies two-thirds of the way through Stowe's novel.

68. The schoolchildren were played by white juveniles in blackface (*NYAtlas* 19 Oct. 1856).

69. For reviews of Tom Thumb's performance in *Dred*, see *NYTrib* 18 Oct. 1856, 7 and *NYAtlas* 19 Oct. 1856.

70. On white-on-white antebellum lynchings of supposed abolitionists, see Freehling chap. 6. The *New York Atlas* acknowledged those atrocities in protesting the antislavery speeches of Conway's Yankee: "Such a character would be lynched at a moment's notice any whereabouts of Mason & Dixon's line" (19 Oct. 1856).

71. For attacks on the supposed abolitionist sentiments of Conway's *Dred*, see *NYH* 17 Oct. 1856 and *NYAtlas* 19 Oct. 1856.

72. In the "comic" exception that proves the rule, Uncle John Gordon lives under the "petticoat government" of his stingy, nagging wife (Conway *Dred* 2).

73. The heroes also protect the feminized male ex-slave Tiff, who washes clothes while sporting a hoopskirt and bonnet.

74. In one phallic confrontation, Cute responds to a slave trader's "argument"—a brandished knife—by pulling a *very long pistol from his inside belt* and declaring, "'Tis but fair tew meet men with their own arguments" (3.4).

75. See Swerdlow for a discussion of Tappan's conservative female supporters.

76. On the participation of women in the American Museum's Test Vote, see *Morning Courier and New-York Enquirer* 15–19 Sept. 1856.

77. On the relationship between the tragic mulatta and the cult of True Womanhood, see Yellin 72. In the following discussion, I refer to female octoroons, quadroons, and mulattoes as mulattas.

78. The sexual fantasies of antebellum northerners about the South are discussed in Potter 252 and Walters.

79. *NYH* 1 Apr. 1860, 1.

80. *New York Evening Post* 8 Dec. 1859.

81. *NYH* 5 Dec. 1859, 6.

82. *NYH* 9 Dec. 1859, 6.

83. On the response of the Union Savers to Harper's Ferry, see P. Foner 162–68.

84. *New York Evening Post* 13 Dec. 1859.

85. For the noncommittal interpretation, see *NYT* 15 Dec. 1859, 4; for the southern reading, see the New York *Albion* (quoted in Kaplan 552).

86. *NYT* 15 Dec. 1859, 4 and 26 Dec. 1859, 4. The *New York Evening Post* also suspected that Boucicault and his manager were courting the attacks of anti-abolitionists (5 Dec. 1859).

87. The evidence emerged in the court battle between Boucicault and the management of the Winter Garden over the rights to *The Octoroon*. Boucicault and actress Agnes Robertson (his wife and the first Zoe) broke their contract with the Winter Garden after the first six performances of *The Octoroon*. The playwright then attempted to get an injunction to stop the performance of his play. In the course of the trial, Winter Garden manager William Stuart claimed that Boucicault had asked him "to use his influence with certain newspapers to attack [*The Octoroon*] as an *Abolition piece*, and thus draw public attention to it" (*NYT* 26 Dec. 1859, 3). For an account of Boucicault's legal battles over his play, see Faulkner.

88. *NYH* 7 Dec. 1859, 5.

89. *NYT* 9 Feb. 1860, 2. Disgusted by this letter, the *Sunday Mercury* [New York] ranked Boucicault among the "toadies of the theatrical profession" (12 Feb. 1860).

90. Joan Steele points out that Reid publicly charged Boucicault with plagiarizing *The Quadroon* (27). In 1874 Barnum and Reid talked of producing dramatizations of several of Reid's novels in Barnum's Great Roman Hippodrome, but nothing seems to have come of this scheme (*Spirit of the Times* [New York] 16 May 1874, 326; Steele 28).

91. *NYTrib* 7 Dec. 1859, 5.

92. John Brown was a hot theatrical property in December 1859, when the Old Bowery Theatre challenged the Winter Garden with *The Insurrection; or, Kansas and Harper's Ferry* (Odell 7:230).

93. The dates of Boucicault's composition of *The Octoroon* were revealed in his court battle with the Winter Garden. An affidavit filed by Winter Garden trustee Thomas Fields makes clear that the play was written between 22 October and 23 November 1859 (*NYT* 26 Dec. 1859, 2).

94. For contemporary attempts to construct Brown as a Puritan, see Thoreau "A Plea" 113–14 and Phillips "Harper's" and "The Puritan."

95. For the text of Brown's last message to his country, see Oates 351.

96. *Spirit of the Times* [New York] 17 Dec. 1859, 529.

97. For recent examples of this reading of the tragic mulatta, see Yellin 71 and Richardson 133.

98. On the American school, see Fredrickson chap. 3 and W. Stanton.

99. *NYT* 15 Dec. 1859, 4.

100. See Faulkner on the battle between Boucicault and Winter Garden Theatre manager William Stuart.

101. Museum bill for 24 Feb. 1860 (HTC).

102. *NYTrib* 23 Apr. 1860, 2.

103. *NYAtlas* 12 Feb. 1860, 5.

104. *NYTrib* 16 Mar. 1860, 1.

105. Barnum "secured" the "What Is It?" after hearing of his exhibition in Philadelphia (*SL* 104).

106. Saxon discusses Barnum's role in the 1846 London exhibition of Hervey Leach as a "What Is It?" (*PTB* 98). In 1845 and 1846 the American Museum exhibited orangutans as "connecting link[s] between the human and brute creation" (*NYSun* 2 May 1846).

107. For a sampling of such comparisons, see the American Museum ad in *NYTrib* 1 Mar. 1860, 2.

108. *NYClip* 31 Mar. 1860, 398.

109. *NYTrib* 29 Feb. 1860, 7.

110. *NYTrib* 16 Mar. 1860, 1; *NYTrib* 9 Feb. 1860, 6. Despite the fact that Wahnotee does speak a word here and there, the *New York Times* also referred to the part as "a non-speaking one" (8 Dec. 1859, 1). The "What Is It?" likewise got in the occasional word in his early performances. The *New York Sun* observed: "[S]ometimes short words spoken by its keeper are repeated with considerable distinctness" (reprinted in *NYTrib* 1 Mar. 1860, 2).

111. See American Museum bills for 10 and 17 Mar. 1860 (HTC).

112. *New York Morning Express* 19 Mar. 1860.

113. *NYH* 28 Feb. 1860, 2.

## 5. "A Stupendous Mirror of Departed Empires": The Barnum Hippodromes and Circuses

1. For illustrations and stories on the elephant-hunting expedition, see *Gleason's Pictorial Drawing-Room Companion* 21 June 1851, 116–17, 124–25, and 28 June 1851, 132–33.

2. When the show disbanded after four years, Barnum put the Cingalese and one of the elephants to work plowing on a lot adjacent to the New York and New Haven railroad. See his account of this publicity stunt in *ST* 356–62.

3. *NYSun* 3 July 1845 and 6 Jan. 1848.

4. Bill for Barnum's Asiatic Caravan, Museum and Menagerie (CWM).

5. For whatever reason, Barnum failed to mention his plan for a Congress of Nations in *Life*; in revising that book to create *Struggles*, he inserted this passage at the beginning of his chapter "The Jenny Lind Enterprise."

6. The titles appear in an undated letter from Barnum (though in someone else's hand) to an unidentified correspondent in the P. T. Barnum Papers, Rare

Books and Manuscripts Division, New York Public Library, Astor, Lenox and Tilden Foundations. In it, the showman requests help in locating and transporting to the United States "specimens" for his exhibition. See also Barnum's 1856 letter referring to Circassian women as potential members of a "Congress of Nations" (*SL* 91–92).

7. *Philadelphia Evening Bulletin* 24 Aug. 1874, 6.

8. *Boston Daily Globe* 17 Aug. 1874, 1. One Cincinnati reviewer obviously took the Congress at face value: "The costuming not only delights the looker-on, but affords interesting information to the student of men and manners, for it is true to fact. One sees Turks and Celestials just as if he had taken a voyage to Constantinople or Shanghai" (*Cincinnati Daily Gazette* 14 Oct. 1874, 8).

9. *Philadelphia Evening Bulletin* 24 Aug. 1874, 6.

10. For the definitive discussion of Orientalism, see Said.

11. *P. T. Barnum's Roman Hippodrome Advance Courier* 2 (CWM).

12. *NYH* 28 Apr. 1874, 9.

13. *NYTrib* 2 Nov. 1874, 12.

14. *Boston Daily Globe* 14 Aug. 1874, 8.

15. *NYT* 6 June 1874, 7; *Spirit of the Times* [New York] 23 May 1874, 352.

16. *NYH* 28 Apr. 1874, 9; *Boston Daily Globe* 4 Aug. 1874, 5.

17. One Hippodrome ad declared: "WANTED—IMMEDIATELY—NINE HUN-DRED MEN TO TAKE part in the grand CONGRESS OF NATIONS" (*Pittsburgh Daily Dispatch* 28 Sept. 1874).

18. For a discussion of the logistics of the Hippodrome's five-city 1874 tour, see Dahlinger 29.

19. *Boston Daily Globe* 4 Aug. 1874, 5.

20. Ibid.

21. For a discussion of the racialization of class differences in journalistic and reformist discourses of the 1870s, see Slotkin chap. 14.

22. For a discussion of the tramp as a new category of bourgeois social analysis arising from Gilded Age class strife, see Denning chap. 8.

23. *P. T. Barnum's Roman Hippodrome Advance Courier* 21 (CWM).

24. *Boston Daily Globe* 14 Aug. 1874, 8.

25. *NYT* 17 May 1874, 11.

26. *Philadelphia Evening Bulletin* 21 Aug. 1874, 6.

27. *NYT* 5 Nov. 1874, 4.

28. Barnum's partner in the Great Roman Hippodrome, W. C. Coup, later acknowledged the contrasting class affiliations of those two bonus attractions of the nineteenth-century circus, the after-concert and the sideshow: "The circus of the present day is not complete without the side shows and after concerts.... all classes of show-goers must be pleased, and there is one class which demands the concert and another class that wants the side shows" (127).

29. *Philadelphia Evening Bulletin* 29 Aug. 1874, 8.

30. *Philadelphia Evening Bulletin* 18 Aug. 1874, 6.

31. *Boston Daily Globe* 14 Aug. 1874, 8; *NYTrib* 3 Nov. 1874, 7.

32. *Boston Daily Globe* 14 Aug. 1874, 8. As Neil Harris points out, testing gender conventions proved fatal to at least one of the Hippodrome's equestriennes (246). When the Hippodrome returned to New York after its first tour, the *Times* noted approvingly that "[t]he surface of the [track] has been leveled so as to prevent the recurrence of accidents to equestriennes, so frequent formerly" (*NYT* 5 Nov. 1874, 4).

33. *NYH* 28 Apr. 1874, 9.

34. *Cincinnati Daily Gazette* 20 Oct. 1874, 8.

35. For the Walsh-Colton nuptials, see *Frank Leslie's Illustrated Newspaper* 7 Nov. 1874, 133, 135.

36. *Republican and Leader* [La Crosse] 23 Aug. 1875.

37. *Philadelphia Evening Bulletin* 24 Aug. 1874, 6; *Boston Daily Globe* 11 June 1884, 7.

38. D. S. Thomas, the Barnum & London Circus's press agent, explained the financial advantages of ethnological authenticity: "It pays better to have the genuine article.... For instance, there are those Nubian Arabs. Nobody doubts they are genuine. Of course we could hire darkies in New York to dress, look, and act like them, but they would want $6 or $8 every week, while these fellows are satisfied with half of that" (*Chicago Tribune* 2 Sept. 1884, 5).

39. On African Americans masquerading as non-Westerners, see Lindfors 11–13.

40. *P. T. Barnum's Greatest Show on Earth Combined with the Great London Circus* [1884] 6 (CWM).

41. For the correspondence of Barnum and his associates regarding the Ethnological Congress, see *PTB* 307–8 and *SL* 226–29.

42. In this passage Barnum mistakenly claims that both "civilized and savage" peoples were on view in the Ethnological Congress — an interesting mistake that may derive from his original conception of the exhibit (*ST* 1889, 349).

43. *NYTrib* 15 Mar. 1885, 11.

44. *P. T. Barnum's Greatest Show on Earth Combined with the Great London Circus* [1884] 10 (CWM).

45. *Philadelphia Evening Bulletin* 21 Apr. 1881, 3.

46. In this same vein was a reporter's account of Chang as "a good-natured curiosity" who enjoyed the attentions of a group of orphaned circus patrons (*Philadelphia Evening Bulletin* 27 Apr. 1881, 7).

47. *P. T. Barnum's Greatest Show on Earth, Sanger's Royal British Menagerie Consolidated The Great London Circus, & Grand International Allied Shows* 7 (CWM).

48. *NYH* 9 Mar. 1884, 20.

49. *NYH* 12 Mar. 1884, 10.

50. *Louisville Courier Journal* 16 Oct. 1884, 5.

51. *NYH* 11 Sep. 1860, 3.

52. *NYH* 12 Mar. 1884, 10.

53. *Chicago Tribune* 4 June 1883, 7.

54. Ibid.

55. *Chicago Tribune* 6 June 1883, 8.

56. *NYH* 9 Mar. 1884, 20.

57. See the descriptions of the Todars and Patagonian giants in *P. T. Barnum's Greatest Show on Earth Combined with the Great London Circus* [1885] 8–9.

58. Ibid., 8, 10.

59. As the Congress began coming together in 1883, its representatives were grouped with the other human curiosities in the museum tent. By May 1883, however, the non-Westerners were already being displayed in the menagerie tent (*Wheeling Register* 15 May 1883). For a description of the Congress arrayed around the cages in the menagerie tent, see *St. Louis Post-Dispatch* 16 Sept. 1884, 5.

60. *P. T. Barnum's Greatest Show on Earth Combined with the Great London Circus* [1884] 6 (CWM).

61. *P. T. Barnum & Co.'s United* 4 (CWM).

62. Ibid., 3.

63. My sense of U.S. white males' psychic investment in the bodies of non-whites is heavily indebted to Lott chap. 5.

64. For the roots of the late-nineteenth-century crisis of white manhood, see Rotundo chaps. 9, 10; Kimmel 143–53; and Bederman 6–9. For the period's critique of the concept of the autonomous self, see Lears chap. 1.

65. *NYTrib* 27 Mar. 1887, 7.

66. *Philadelphia Evening Bulletin* 15 Apr. 1884, 5.

67. *NYTrib* 24 Mar. 1889, 11.

68. *The Barnum & Bailey 15 New United Shows* 9 (CWM).

69. *P. T. Barnum's Greatest Show on Earth Combined with the Great London Circus* [1884] 7 (CWM).

70. Ibid., 6.

71. For late-nineteenth-century predictions of the extinction of Native Americans and African Americans, see Gossett *Race* 235, 243–44, 281–82 and Fredrickson 232–33, 235–39, 244–52.

72. As David Levin has shown, there was a precedent for such cross-cultural comparisons in the work of antebellum U.S. historians (150–59).

73. African Americans did appear in the Barnum & London and Barnum & Bailey shows as jubilee singers and jockeys.

74. For a discussion of a comparable sympathy for the victims of Euro-American imperialism among antebellum U.S. historians, see Levin 126–59.

75. *P. T. Barnum's Greatest Show on Earth Combined with the Great London Circus* [1884] 8 (CWM).

76. *Boston Daily Globe* 20 June 1887, 2.

77. *NYClip* 12 May 1883, 123.

78. *Philadelphia Evening Bulletin* 22 Apr. 1884, 8.

79. On Barnum's upscale circus patronage, see *Springfield Daily Republican* 10 June 1884, 8; *Providence Journal* 12 June 1884, 8; *Boston Post* 17 June 1884.

80. *St. Louis Post-Dispatch* 16 Sept. 1884, 5.

81. For references to the staleness and conservatism of the Barnum & London Circus, see *NYH* 14 Mar. 1882, 4 and 1 Apr. 1886, 10.

82. *NYTrib* 31 Mar. 1884, 2.

83. *Chicago Tribune* 6 June 1883, 8.

84. *Boston Daily Globe* 12 June 1885, 2.

85. *NYH* 24 Mar. 1889, 14.

86. It is important to note that Barnum & Bailey continued to mine popular interest in anthropology by reviving the Ethnological Congress for its 1894 and 1895 seasons.

## Conclusion. "A Transient Disease": Barnumism at the World's Columbian Exposition

1. *NYT* 19 June 1893, 9.

2. Ibid. *The Barnum & Bailey Official Route Book* (1894) claimed that the Ethnological Congress "may, perhaps, have suggested the very idea upon which the now celebrated Midway Plaisance of the Fair was founded." I am indebted to Fred Dahlinger for this reference.

3. Saxon argues that the article was actually ghostwritten from ideas supplied by the showman (*PTB* 322).

4. *North American Review* Mar. 1890, 401.

5. On imperialist spectacles in Buffalo Bill's Wild West Show, see Blackstone 70–72. For discussion of similar displays in the turn-of-the-century U.S. circus, see the forthcoming dissertation by Janet Davis from the University of Wisconsin's History Department.

6. On the fair's financial woes and the directors' response, see Burg 169–70; *The Dial* 1 Sept. 1893, 105–7; *Chicago Tribune* 19 Aug. 1893, 2.

7. *The Dial* 1 Sept. 1893, 106; *Chicago Tribune* 19 Aug. 1893, 2.

8. On the effect of the outdoor amusements on attendance, see *Chicago Tribune* 20 Aug. 1893, 12.

9. Ibid.

10. See the discussion of Warner's speech in Burg 252–54.

11. *The Dial* 16 July 1893, 30.

12. Ibid. For the full text of Warner's speech, see *Chicago Tribune* 14 July 1893, 8.

13. For recent examples—both of them unjust—of Barnum's name used as an epithet by cultural critics, see Stanley Crouch on Toni Morrison (209) and Stanley Fish on Henry Louis Gates Jr. (in Carby 7).

# Works Cited

*Advance Courier of P. T. Barnum's Greatest Show on Earth and the Great London Circus.* Buffalo: Courier, [1881].

Aiken, George L. *Uncle Tom's Cabin. Dramas from the American Theatre, 1762–1909.* Ed. Richard Moody. Cleveland: World, 1966. 360–96.

Alger, Horatio, Jr. *Ragged Dick and Mark, the Match Boy.* New York: Collier-Macmillan, 1962.

———. *Slow and Sure; or, From the Street to the Shop.* New York: Hurst, n.d.

Allen, Robert C. "B. F. Keith and the Origins of American Vaudeville." *Theatre Survey* 21 (1980): 105–15.

———. *Horrible Prettiness: Burlesque and American Culture.* Chapel Hill: University of North Carolina Press, 1991.

Aptheker, Herbert. *Abolitionism: A Revolutionary Movement.* Boston: Twayne, 1989.

Arnold, Matthew. *Culture and Anarchy: An Essay in Political and Social Criticism* [1869]. Indianapolis: Bobbs-Merrill, 1971.

———. *Letters of Matthew Arnold.* Ed. George W. E. Russell. Vol 2. New York: Macmillan, 1895.

———. *Philistinism in England and America.* Ed. R. H. Super. Ann Arbor: University of Michigan Press, 1974.

Ashworth, John. *'Agrarians' & 'Aristocrats': Party Political Ideology in the United States, 1837–1846.* London: Royal Historical Society, 1983.

Baker, Jean H. *Affairs of Party: The Political Culture of Northern Democrats in the Mid–Nineteenth Century.* Ithaca, N.Y.: Cornell University Press, 1983.

Banner, Lois W. *American Beauty.* New York: Knopf, 1983.

Barnum, P. T. *The Life of P. T. Barnum, Written by Himself.* New York: Redfield, 1855.

———. *Struggles and Triumphs; or, Forty Years' Recollections of P. T. Barnum, Written by Himself* [1869]. n.p.: Arno, 1970.

———. *Struggles and Triumphs; or, Forty Years' Recollections of P. T. Barnum, Written by Himself*. Buffalo: Warren, Johnson, 1873.

———. *Struggles and Triumphs; or, Forty Years' Recollections of P. T. Barnum, Written by Himself*. Buffalo: Courier, 1875.

———. *Struggles and Triumphs; or, Forty Years' Recollections of P. T. Barnum, Written by Himself*. Buffalo: Courier, 1882.

———. *Struggles and Triumphs; or, Fifty Years' Recollections of P. T. Barnum, Written by Himself*. Author's ed. Buffalo: Courier, 1884.

———. *Struggles and Triumphs; or, Sixty Years' Recollections of P. T. Barnum, Including His Golden Rules for Money-Making, Illustrated and Brought up to 1889, Written by Himself*. Buffalo: Courier, 1889.

*The Barnum & Bailey 15 New United Shows*. Buffalo: Courier, [1889].

*The Barnum & Bailey Official Route Book*. Buffalo: Courier, [1894].

*Barnum's American Museum Illustrated*. n.p.: William Van Norden & Frank Leslie, 1850.

Bederman, Gail. "'Civilization,' the Decline of Middle-Class Manliness, and Ida B. Wells's Antilynching Campaign (1892–94)." *Radical History Review* 52 (1992): 5–30.

Belden, E. Porter. *New-York: Past, Present, and Future*. New York: Putnam, 1849.

Bell, Whitfield J., Jr. "The Cabinet of the American Philosophical Society." *A Cabinet of Curiosities: Five Episodes in the Evolution of American Museums*. Charlottesville: University Press of Virginia, 1967. 1–34.

Bellows, Henry W. *The Relation of Public Amusements to Public Morality, Especially of the Theatre to the Highest Interests of Humanity*. New York: Francis, 1857.

Bender, Thomas. *New York Intellect: A History of Intellectual Life in New York City, from 1750 to the Beginnings of Our Own Time*. Baltimore: Johns Hopkins University Press, 1987.

Bercovitch, Sacvan. "The Problem of Ideology in American Literary History." *Critical Inquiry* 12.4 (1986): 631–53.

Berger, Max. *The British Traveller in America, 1836–1860*. New York: Columbia University Press, 1922.

Bernstein, Iver. *The New York City Draft Riots: Their Significance for American Society and Politics in the Age of the Civil War*. New York: Oxford University Press, 1990.

Betts, John Rickards. "P. T. Barnum and the Popularization of Natural History." *Journal of the History of Ideas* 20 (1959): 353–68.

Birdoff, Harry. *The World's Greatest Hit*. New York: Vanni, 1947.

Blackstone, Sarah J. *Buckskins, Bullets, and Business: A History of Buffalo Bill's Wild West.* New York: Greenwood, 1986.

Blumin, Stuart M. *The Emergence of the Middle Class: Social Experience in the American City, 1760–1900.* Cambridge: Cambridge University Press, 1989.

[Bobo, William M.] *Glimpses of New-York City.* Charleston, S.C.: McCarter, 1852.

Bogdan, Robert. *Freak Show: Presenting Human Oddities for Amusement and Profit.* Chicago: University of Chicago Press, 1988.

Borrett, George Tuthill. *Letters from Canada and the United States.* London: Adlard, 1865.

Boucicault, Dion. *The Octoroon; or, Life in Louisiana. Plays.* Ed. Peter Thomson. Cambridge: Cambridge University Press, 1984. 133–69.

Brace, Charles Loring. *The Dangerous Classes of New York, and Twenty Years' Work among Them* [1872]. Washington, D.C.: NASW Classic Series, 1973.

Brasher, Thomas L. *Whitman as Editor of the Brooklyn Daily Eagle.* Detroit: Wayne State University Press, 1970.

Bright, Henry Arthur. *Happy Country This America: The Travel Diary of Henry Arthur Bright.* Ed. Anne Henry Ehrenpreis. Columbus: Ohio State University Press, 1978.

Brodhead, Richard H. *Cultures of Letters: Scenes of Reading and Writing in Nineteenth-Century America.* Chicago: University of Chicago Press, 1993.

Brodie, Janet Farrell. *Contraception and Abortion in Nineteenth-Century America.* Ithaca, N.Y.: Cornell University Press, 1994.

Brougham, John. *Temptation; or, The Irish Emigrant.* New York: French, 1856.

[Browne, Charles Farrar]. *Artemus Ward: His Works, Complete.* New York: Carleton, 1876.

Buckley, Peter George. "To the Opera House: Culture and Society in New York City, 1820–1860." Doctoral dissertation, State University of New York at Stony Brook, 1984.

Buell, Lawrence. "Autobiography in the American Renaissance." *American Autobiography: Retrospect and Prospect.* Ed. Paul John Eakin. Madison: University of Wisconsin Press, 1991.

*Buffalo Bill's Wild West and Congress of Rough Riders of the World.* Buffalo: Courier, n.d.

Bulman, Joan. *Jenny Lind: A Biography.* London: Barrie, 1956.

Burg, David F. *Chicago's White City of 1893.* Lexington: University Press of Kentucky, 1976.

Carby, Hazel V. "The Multicultural Wars." *Radical History Review* 54 (1992): 7–18.

Cawelti, John G. *Apostles of the Self-Made Man.* Chicago: University of Chicago Press, 1965.

Clapp, William W., Jr. *A Record of the Boston Stage*. Boston: Munroe, 1853.

Conway, H. J. *Dred; A Tale of the Great Dismal Swamp*. New York: Amerman, 1856.

———. *Uncle Tom's Cabin* [1852]. Script in Harry Ransom Humanities Research Center, University of Texas-Austin.

Coup, W. C. *Stardust and Spangles: Stories and Secrets of the Circus*. Chicago: Stone, 1901.

Crouch, Stanley. *Notes of a Hanging Judge: Essays and Reviews, 1979–1989*. New York: Oxford University Press, 1990.

Cunliffe, Marcus. *Chattel Slavery and Wage Slavery: The Anglo-American Context, 1830–1860*. Athens: University of Georgia Press, 1979.

Dahlinger, Fred, Jr. "The Development of the Railroad Circus: Part 3." *Bandwagon* 28.2 (1984): 28–36.

Davies, John D. *Phrenology: Fad and Science; A 19th-Century American Crusade*. New Haven, Conn.: Yale University Press, 1955.

Dawley, Alan, and Paul Faler. "Working-Class Culture and Politics in the Industrial Revolution: Sources of Loyalism and Rebellion." *Journal of Social History* 9.4 (1976): 466–80.

Denning, Michael. *Mechanic Accents: Dime Novels and Working-Class Culture in America*. New York: Verso, 1987.

*Descriptive Pamphlet of the Celebrated Gorgeous Oriental Tableau of Cerean Sculpture, (Each Figure Moving as if Alive,) Entitled "Lord Byron and the Greeks; or, The Suliot Conspiracy," [D. Andrews, Principal Artist.] Now Exhibiting at Barnum's Museum, with such Unparalleled Applause*. New York: Cunningham, 1852.

Dippie, Brian W. *Catlin and his Contemporaries: The Politics of Patronage*. Lincoln: University of Nebraska Press, 1990.

Dublin, Thomas. *Women at Work: The Transformation of Work and Community in Lowell, Massachusetts, 1826–1860*. New York: Columbia University Press, 1979.

Dunlop, M. H. "Curiosities Too Numerous to Mention: Early Regionalism and Cincinnati's Western Museum." *American Quarterly* 36.4 (1984): 524–48.

Emerson, Ralph Waldo. "The American Scholar." *Selections from Ralph Waldo Emerson*. Ed. Stephen E. Whicher. Boston: Houghton, 1957.

———. *The Journals and Miscellaneous Notebooks of Ralph Waldo Emerson*. Ed. William H. Gilman et al. Vol. 13. Cambridge: Harvard University Press, 1977.

———. "Success." *The Complete Works of Ralph Waldo Emerson*. Centenary edition [1904]. Vol. 7. New York: AMS, 1979.

———. *The Topical Notebooks of Ralph Waldo Emerson*. Ed. Ralph H. Orth et al. Vol. 1. Columbia: University of Missouri Press, 1990.

Engle, Gary D., ed. *This Grotesque Essence: Plays from the American Minstrel Stage.* Baton Rouge: Louisiana State University Press, 1978.

Epstein, Barbara Leslie. *The Politics of Domesticity: Women, Evangelism and Temperance in Nineteenth-Century America.* Middletown, Conn.: Wesleyan University Press, 1980.

Everett, George. "Frank Leslie." *Dictionary of Literary Biography.* Ed. Perry J. Ashley. Vol. 43. Detroit: Brucolli-Gale, 1985. 290–303.

Faulkner, Seldon. "The *Octoroon* War." *Educational Theatre Journal* 15.1 (1963): 33–38.

Ferguson, Robert. *America during and after the War.* London: Longmans, Green, Reader, and Dyer, 1866.

F. J. N. *Barnum's Baby Show; a Satire, Written with a View to Prove the Wickedness and Immorality of that Ungracious Exposition of Humanity, and its Tendency to Corrupt the Manners and Virtue of the Rising Generation.* Boston: Damrell & Moore, [1855].

[Flanders, Mrs. G. W.] *The Ebony Idol.* New York: Appleton, 1860.

Foner, Eric. *Free Soil, Free Labor, Free Men: The Ideology of the Republican Party before the Civil War.* New York: Oxford University Press, 1970.

———. *Reconstruction: America's Unfinished Revolution, 1863–1877.* New York: Harper, 1988.

Foner, Philip S. *Business and Slavery: The New York Merchants and the Irrepressible Conflict* [1941]. New York: Russell, 1968.

Ford, Thomas. *A Peep behind the Curtain by a Supernumary.* Boston: Redding, 1850.

Foster, George G. *Memoir of Jenny Lind.* New York: Dewitt and Davenport, 1850.

———. *New York by Gas-Light: With Here and There a Streak of Sunshine.* New York: Dewitt and Davenport, 1850.

Fredrickson, George M. *The Black Image in the White Mind: The Debate on Afro-American Character and Destiny, 1817–1914.* New York: Harper, 1971.

Freedley, Edwin T. *A Practical Treatise on Business: or, How to Get, Save, Spend, Give, Lend, and Bequeath Money: with an Inquiry into the Chances of Success and Causes of Failure in Business.* Philadelphia: Lippincott, Grambo, 1855.

Freehling, William W. *The Road to Disunion: Secessionists at Bay, 1776–1854.* Vol. 1. New York: Oxford University Press, 1990.

Gorn, Elliott J. *The Manly Art: Bare-Knuckle Prize Fighting in America.* Ithaca, N.Y.: Cornell University Press, 1986.

Gossett, Thomas F. *Race: The History of an Idea in America.* Dallas: Southern Methodist University Press, 1963.

———. *Uncle Tom's Cabin and American Culture.* Dallas: Southern Methodist University Press, 1985.

Greenwood, Grace [Sara Jane Lippincott]. *Haps and Mishaps of a Tour in Europe*. Boston: Ticknor, Reed, and Fields, 1854.

Grimsted, David. *Melodrama Unveiled: American Theater and Culture, 1800–1850.* Chicago: University of Chicago Press, 1968.

———. "*Uncle Tom* from Page to Stage: Limitations of Nineteenth-Century Drama." *Quarterly Journal of Speech* 56.3 (1970): 235–44.

Haberly, Loyd. "The American Museum from Baker to Barnum." *New-York Historical Society Quarterly* 43.3 (1959): 273–87.

Haines, George W. *Plays, Players and Playgoers! Being Reminiscences of P. T. Barnum and his Museums. Also, a Graphic Description of the Great Roman Hippodrome and Lives of Celebrated Players.* New York: Bruce, Haines, 1874.

Hall, Stuart. "New Ethnicities." *Black Film/British Cinema.* Ed. Kobena Mercer. London: ICA, 1988. 27–31.

Halttunen, Karen. *Confidence Men and Painted Women: A Study of Middle-Class Culture in America, 1830–1870.* New Haven, Conn.: Yale University Press, 1982.

Hamm, Charles. *Music in the New World.* New York: Norton, 1983.

Harris, Charles Townsend. *Memories of Manhattan in the Sixties and Seventies.* New York: Derrydale, 1928.

Harris, Neil. *Humbug: The Art of P. T. Barnum.* Chicago: University of Chicago Press, 1973.

Haswell, Charles H. *Reminiscences of an Octogenarian of the City of New York.* New York: Harper's, 1897.

Hawthorne, Nathaniel. *The House of the Seven Gables* [1851]. New York: Signet, 1961.

Hedrick, Joan D. *Harriet Beecher Stowe: A Life.* New York: Oxford University Press, 1994.

Hellman, Geoffrey. *Bankers, Bones and Beetles: The First Century of the American Museum of Natural History.* Garden City, N.Y.: Natural History, 1968.

Hentz, Caroline Lee. *The Planter's Northern Bride.* Philadelphia: Peterson, 1854.

Herz, Henri. *My Travels in America.* Trans. Henry Bertram Hill. Madison: State Historical Society of Wisconsin, 1963.

Hingston, Edward P. *The Genial Showman: Being the Reminiscences of the Life of Artemus Ward.* Barre, Mass.: Imprint Society, 1971.

*History of the $200,000 Sacred White Elephant. Ethnological Congress of Savage and Barbarous Tribes and Book of Jumbo.* Buffalo: Courier, [1884].

Hodge, Francis. *Yankee Theatre: The Image of America on the Stage, 1825–1850.* Austin: University of Texas Press, 1964.

Hoh, LaVahn, and William Rough. *Step Right Up! The Adventure of the Circus in America.* White Hall, Va.: Betterway, 1990.

Holland, Henry Scott, and W. S. Rockstro. *Jenny Lind the Artist, 1820–1851: A Memoir of Madame Jenny Lind Goldschmidt, Her Art-Life and Dramatic Career: From Original Documents, Letters, MS. Diaries, &c., Collected by Mr. Otto Goldschmidt.* Abr. ed. New York: Scribner's, [1893].

Holt, Michael F. *The Political Crisis of the 1850s.* New York: Norton, 1978.

[Hurlbert, William Henry]. "Barnum's and Greeley's Biographies." *Christian Examiner and Religious Miscellany* 58 (Mar. 1855): 245–64.

Hutchinson, John Wallace. *Story of the Hutchinsons (Tribe of Jesse)* [1896]. Vol. 1. New York: Da Capo, 1977.

*An Illustrated Catalogue and Guide Book to Barnum's American Museum.* New York: Wynkoop, Hallenbeck & Thomas, 1863.

*In Grand Combination. P. T. Barnum and Company's Greatest Show on Earth and the Great London Circus and Adam Forepaugh's New and Greatest All Feature Show.* New York: Fox, [1887].

Jackson, Andrew. "A Political Testament." *Social Theories of Jacksonian Democracy.* Ed. Joseph L. Blau. Indianapolis: Bobbs-Merrill, 1954.

Jacobs, Harriet. *Incidents in the Life of a Slave Girl; Written by Herself.* Ed. Jean Fagan Yellin. Cambridge: Harvard University Press, 1987.

James, Henry. *A Small Boy and Others.* New York: Scribner's, 1913.

Jefferson, Joseph. *The Autobiography of Joseph Jefferson.* Ed. Alan S. Downer. Cambridge: Harvard University Press, 1964.

*The Jenny Lind Mania in Boston; or, A Sequel to Barnum's Parnassus.* Boston: n.p., 1850.

Johnson, Claudia D. "That Guilty Third Tier: Prostitution in Nineteenth-Century American Theaters." *American Quarterly* 27.2 (1975): 575–84.

Kaplan, Sidney. "*The Octoroon*: Early History of the Drama of Miscegenation." *Journal of Negro Education* 20.4 (1951): 547–57.

Kasson, John F. *Amusing the Million: Coney Island at the Turn of the Century.* New York: Hill-Farrar, 1978.

Kelley, Mary. *Private Woman, Public Stage: Literary Domesticity in Nineteenth-Century America.* New York: Oxford University Press, 1984.

Kimmel, Michael S. "The Contemporary 'Crisis' of Masculinity in Historical Perspective." *The Making of Masculinities: The New Men's Studies.* Ed. Harry Brod. Boston: Allen, 1987. 121–53.

Koch, Donald A. "Introduction." *Ten Nights in a Bar-Room, And What I Saw There.* By Timothy Shay Arthur. Cambridge: Harvard University Press, 1964. v–lxxxiii.

Lakier, Aleksandr Borisovich. *A Russian Looks at America: The Journey of Aleksandr Borisovich Lakier in 1857.* Trans. Arnold Schrier and Joyce Story. Chicago: University of Chicago Press, 1979.

Lapsansky, Emma Jones. "'Since They Got Those Separate Churches': Afro-Americans and Racism in Jacksonian Philadelphia." *American Quarterly* 32.1 (1980): 54–78.

Laurie, Bruce. *Working People of Philadelphia, 1800–1850.* Philadelphia: Temple University Press, 1980.

Lears, T. J. Jackson. *No Place of Grace: Antimodernism and the Transformation of American Culture, 1880–1920.* New York: Pantheon, 1981.

Lerner, Gerda. *The Majority Finds Its Past: Placing Women in History.* New York: Oxford University Press, 1979.

Levin, David. *History as Romantic Art: Bancroft, Prescott, Motley and Parkman* [1959]. New York: Harcourt, 1963.

Levine, Lawrence W. *Highbrow/Lowbrow: The Emergence of Cultural Hierarchy in America.* Cambridge: Harvard University Press, 1988.

[Lewis, John Delaware]. *Across the Atlantic.* London: George Earle, 1851.

*The Life of Joice Heth, The Nurse of Gen. George Washington, (The Father of our Country,) Now Living at the Astonishing Age of 161 Years, and Weighs only 46 Pounds.* New York: n.p., 1835.

Lindberg, Gary. *The Confidence Man in American Literature.* New York: Oxford University Press, 1982.

Lindfors, Bernth. "Circus Africans." *Journal of American Culture* 6.2 (1983): 9–14.

Lott, Eric. *Love and Theft: Blackface Minstrelsy and the American Working Class.* New York: Oxford University Press, 1993.

MacDonald, Cordelia Howard. "Memoirs of the Original Little Eva." *Educational Theatre Journal* 8.4 (1956): 267–82.

Maretzek, Max. *Revelations of an Opera Manager in 19th-Century America.* New York: Dover, 1968.

Mathews, Cornelius. *A Pen-and-Ink Panorama of New-York City.* New York: Taylor, 1853.

McCabe, James D. *Great Fortunes and How They Were Made; or, The Struggles and Triumphs of Our Self-Made Men.* Cincinnati: Hannaford, 1871.

McClung, Robert M., and Gale S. McClung. "Tammany's Remarkable Gardiner Baker: New York's First Museum Proprietor, Menagerie Keeper, and Promoter Extraordinary." *New-York Historical Society Quarterly* 42.2 (1958): 143–69.

McConachie, Bruce A. "The Cultural Politics of 'Paddy' on the Midcentury American Stage." *Studies in Popular Culture* 10 (1987): 1–13.

———. "H. J. Conway's Dramatization of *Uncle Tom's Cabin*: A Previously Unpublished Letter." *Theatre Journal* 34.2 (1982): 149–54.

———. *Melodramatic Formations: American Theatre and Society, 1820–1870.* Iowa City: University of Iowa Press, 1992.

———. "New York Operagoing, 1825–50: Creating an Elite Social Ritual." *American Music* 6.2 (1988): 181–92.

———. "Out of the Kitchen and into the Marketplace: Normalizing *Uncle Tom's Cabin* for the Antebellum Stage." *Journal of American Drama and Theatre* 3 (1991): 5–28.

McGlinchee, Claire. *The First Decade of the Boston Museum*. Boston: Humphries, 1940.

Melville, Herman. *The Piazza Tales and Other Prose Pieces, 1839–1860*. Ed. Harrison Hayford et al. Evanston, Ill.: Northwestern-Newberry, 1987.

Miller, Perry. *The Raven and the Whale: The War of Words and Wits in the Era of Poe and Melville*. New York: Harcourt, 1956.

Moody, Richard, ed. *Dramas from the American Theatre, 1762–1909*. Cleveland: World, 1966.

Morantz-Sanchez, Regina Markell. *Sympathy and Science: Women Physicians in American Medicine*. New York: Oxford University Press, 1985.

Mulvey, Laura. "Visual Pleasure and Narrative Cinema." *Women and the Cinema: A Critical Anthology*. Ed. Karyn Kay and Gerald Peary. New York: Dutton, 1977. 412–28.

Nasaw, David. *Going Out: The Rise and Fall of Public Amusements*. New York: Basic Books-HarperCollins, 1993.

Nissenbaum, Stephen. *Sex, Diet, and Debility in Jacksonian America: Sylvester Graham and Health Reform*. Westport, Conn.: Greenwood, 1980.

Northall, William Knight. *Before and Behind the Curtain; or, Fifteen Years' Observations among the Theatres of New York*. New York: Burgess, 1851.

Oates, Stephen B. *To Purge This Land with Blood: A Biography of John Brown*. 2d ed. Amherst: University of Massachusetts Press, 1984.

Odell, George C. D. *Annals of the New York Stage*. 15 vols. New York: Columbia University Press, 1927–49.

Odom, Herbert H. "Generalizations on Race in Nineteenth-Century Physical Anthropology." *Isis* 58.1 (1967): 5–18.

Ossoli, Margaret Fuller. *Woman in the Nineteenth Century, and Kindred Papers Relating to the Sphere, Condition, and Duties of Woman* [1874]. New York: Greenwood, 1968.

*P. T. Barnum & Co.'s United*. Buffalo: Courier, [1887].

*P. T. Barnum's Greatest Show on Earth Combined with the Great London Circus*. Buffalo: Courier, [1884].

*P. T. Barnum's Greatest Show on Earth Combined with the Great London Circus*. Philadelphia: Morrell, [1885].

*P. T. Barnum's Greatest Show on Earth, Sanger's Royal British Menagerie Consolidated The Great London Circus, & Grand International Allied Shows*. n.p., [1882].

*P. T. Barnum's Roman Hippodrome Advance Courier.* Buffalo: Courier, [1875].

Pairpoint, Alfred. *Uncle Sam and his Country; or, Sketches of America, in 1854–55–56.* London: Simpkink, Marshall, 1857.

[Parton, Sara Payson (Willis)]. *Fern Leaves from Fanny's Portfolio.* 2d series. Auburn, N.Y.: Miller, Orton and Mulligan, 1854.

Pascoe, Judith. "'The House Encore Me So': Emily Dickinson and Jenny Lind." *Emily Dickinson Journal* 1.1 (1992): 1–18.

Pessen, Edward. *Jacksonian America: Society, Personality, and Politics.* Rev. ed. Urbana: University of Illinois Press, 1985.

Pfeiffer, Ida. *Lady's Second Journey Round the World.* New York: Harper, 1856.

Phillips, Wendell. "Harper's Ferry." *Speeches, Lectures, and Letters* [1863]. 1st series. Boston: Lee and Shepard, 1894. 263–88.

———. "The Puritan Principle and John Brown." *Speeches, Lectures, and Letters* [1863]. 2d series. Boston: Lee and Shepard, 1894. 294–308.

Pilgrim, James. *The Limerick Boy; or, Paddy's Mischief.* New York: French, n.d.

Potter, David M. *The Impending Crisis, 1848–1861.* Completed and ed. Don E. Fehrenbacher. New York: Harper, 1976.

Pratt, William W. *Ten Nights in a Bar-Room* [1858]. *Hiss the Villain: Six English and American Melodramas.* Ed. Michael Booth. New York: Blom, 1964. 146–202.

Presbrey, Frank. *The History and Development of Advertising.* Garden City, N.Y.: Doubleday, Doran, 1929.

Raleigh, John Henry. *Matthew Arnold and American Culture.* Berkeley: University of California Press, 1961.

Read, Allen Walker. "The World of Joe Strickland." *Journal of American Folklore* 76 (1963): 277–308.

Reid, Captain Mayne. *The Quadroon; or, Adventures in the Far West* [1856]. Ridgewood, N.J.: Gregg, 1967.

Reynolds, David S. *Beneath the American Renaissance: The Subversive Imagination in the Age of Emerson and Melville.* New York: Knopf, 1988.

———. *Walt Whitman's America: A Cultural Biography.* New York: Knopf, 1995.

Richardson, Gary A. *American Drama from the Colonial Period through World War I: A Critical History.* New York: Twayne, 1993.

Roediger, David R. *The Wages of Whiteness: Race and the Making of the American Working Class.* London: Verso, 1991.

Rogin, Michael Paul. *Subversive Genealogy: The Politics and Art of Herman Melville.* New York: Knopf, 1983.

Roppolo, Joseph Patrick. "Local and Topical Plays in New Orleans, 1806–1865." *Tulane Studies in English* 4 (1954): 91–124.

Rosenberg, C[harles] G. *Jenny Lind: Her Life, Her Struggles, and Her Triumphs.* New York: Stringer and Townsend, 1850.

———. *Jenny Lind in America.* New York: Stringer and Townsend, 1851.

Rosenzweig, Roy, and Elizabeth Blackmar. *The Park and the People: A History of Central Park.* Ithaca, N.Y.: Cornell University Press, 1992.

Ross, Joel H. *What I Saw in New-York; or, A Bird's Eye View of City Life.* Auburn, N.Y.: Derby and Miller, 1851.

Rotundo, E. Anthony. *American Manhood: Transformations in Masculinity from the Revolution to the Modern Era.* New York: Basic Books, 1993.

Rubin, Joseph Jay. *The Historic Whitman.* University Park: Pennsylvania State University Press, 1973.

Rubin, Joseph Jay, and Charles H. Brown, eds. *Walt Whitman of the New York Aurora: Editor at Twenty-Two.* State College, Pa.: Bald Eagle, 1950.

Ryan, Mary P. *Cradle of the Middle Class: The Family in Oneida County, New York, 1790–1865.* Cambridge: Cambridge University Press, 1981.

Rydell, Robert W. *All the World's a Fair: Visions of Empire at American International Expositions, 1876–1916.* Chicago: University of Chicago Press, 1984.

Said, Edward W. *Orientalism.* New York: Vintage, 1978.

Saxon, A. H., comp. *Barnumiana: A Select, Annotated Bibliography of Works by or Relating to P. T. Barnum.* Fairfield, Conn.: Jumbo's Press, 1995.

———. *P. T. Barnum: The Legend and the Man.* New York: Columbia University Press, 1989.

———, ed. *Selected Letters of P. T. Barnum.* New York: Columbia University Press, 1983.

Saxton, Alexander. *The Rise and Fall of the White Republic: Class Politics and Mass Culture in Nineteenth-Century America.* London: Verso, 1980.

Scudder, John. *A Companion to the American Museum.* New York: Hopkins, 1823.

Sedgwick, Eve Kosofsky. *Between Men: English Literature and Male Homosocial Desire.* New York: Columbia University Press, 1985.

Sellers, Charles Coleman. *Mr. Peale's Museum: Charles Willson Peale and the First Popular Museum of Natural Science and Art.* New York: Norton, 1980.

*Sights and Wonders in New York; Including a Description of the Mysteries, Miracles, Marvels, Phenomena, Curiosities, and Nondescripts Contained in that Great Congress of Wonders, Barnum's Museum; Also, A Memoir of Barnum Himself, With a Description of his Oriental Villa at Bridgeport, Conn., General Tom Thumb, His Reception by Queen Victoria and the Principal Crowned Heads of Europe, Etc., Etc.* New York: Redfield, 1849.

Silver, Rollo G. "Whitman in 1850: Three Uncollected Articles." *American Literature* 19.4 (1948): 301–17.

Sketchley, Arthur [George Rose]. *The Great Country; or, Impressions of America.* London: Tinsley Brothers, 1868.

Sklar, Kathryn Kish. "'Women Who Speak for an Entire Nation': American and British Women Compared at the World Anti-Slavery Convention, London, 1840." *Pacific Historical Review* 59.4 (1990): 453–99.

Slotkin, Richard. *The Fatal Environment: The Myth of the Frontier in the Age of Industrialization, 1800–1890.* Middletown, Conn.: Wesleyan University Press, 1985.

Smith, Matthew Hale. *Sunshine and Shadow in New York.* Hartford, Conn.: Burr, 1869.

Smith, W. H. *The Drunkard; or, The Fallen Saved* [1844]. *Dramas from the American Theatre, 1762–1909.* Ed. Richard Moody. Cleveland: World, 1966. 281–307.

Smith-Rosenberg, Carroll. *Disorderly Conduct: Visions of Gender in Victorian America.* New York: Knopf, 1985.

Spann, Edward K. *The New Metropolis: New York City, 1840–1857.* New York: Columbia University Press, 1981.

Spurlock, John C. *Free Love: Marriage and Middle-Class Radicalism in America, 1825–1860.* New York: New York University Press, 1988.

Stansell, Christine. *City of Women: Sex and Class in New York, 1789–1860.* Urbana: University of Illinois Press, 1982.

Stanton, Elizabeth Cady, et al., eds. *History of Woman Suffrage,* 2d ed. Vol. 1. Rochester, N.Y.: Mann, 1889.

Stanton, William R. *The Leopard's Spots: Scientific Attitudes toward Race in America, 1815–1859.* Chicago: University of Chicago Press, 1960.

Steele, Joan. *Captain Mayne Reid.* Boston: Twayne, 1978.

Stewart, Susan. *On Longing: Narratives of the Miniature, the Gigantic, the Souvenir, the Collection.* Baltimore: Johns Hopkins University Press, 1984.

Still, Bayrd. *Mirror for Gotham: New York as Seen by Contemporaries from Dutch Days to the Present.* New York: New York University Press, 1956.

Stott, Richard B. *Workers in the Metropolis: Class, Ethnicity, and Youth in Antebellum New York City.* Ithaca, N.Y.: Cornell University Press, 1990.

Stowe, Harriet Beecher. *Dred: A Tale of the Great Dismal Swamp* [1856]. 2 vols. Grosse Pointe, Mich.: Scholarly Press, 1968.

———. *Uncle Tom's Cabin; or, Life among the Lowly* [1852]. New York: Harper, 1965.

Strong, George Templeton. *Diaries.* Ed. Allan Nevins and Milton H. Thomas. Vol. 4. New York: Macmillan, 1952.

Swerdlow, Amy. "Abolition's Conservative Sisters: The Ladies' New York City Anti-Slavery Societies, 1834–1840." *The Abolitionist Sisterhood: Women's Political Culture in Antebellum America.* Ed. Jean Fagan Yellin and John C. Van Horne. Ithaca, N.Y.: Cornell University Press, 1994.

Takaki, Ronald T. *Iron Cages: Race and Culture in Nineteenth Century America.* Seattle: University of Washington Press, 1979.

*Ten Thousand Things on China and the Chinese: Being a Picture of the Genius, Government, History, Literature, Agriculture, Arts, Trade, Manners, Customs, and Social Life of the People of the Celestial Empire, as Illustrated by the Chinese Collection, 539 Broadway.* New York: Redfield, 1850.

Thoreau, Henry D. "The Last Days of John Brown." *Reform Papers.* Ed. Wendell Glick. Princeton, N.J.: Princeton University Press, 1973. 145–53.

———. "A Plea for Captain John Brown." *Reform Papers.* Ed. Wendell Glick. Princeton, N.J.: Princeton University Press, 1973. 111–38.

Thornbury, Walter. *Criss-Cross Journeys.* Vol. 1. London: Hurst and Blackett, 1873.

Tompkins, Jane. *Sensational Designs: The Cultural Work of American Fiction, 1790–1860.* New York: Oxford University Press, 1985.

*Too White for Barnum; Forepaugh's Reply to Barnum; Forepaugh's Sacred White Elephant "Light of Asia" Proved by the Highest Scientific Authority to be Genuine and Barnum's "Sacred White?" Elephant and All its Surroundings a Rank Fraud.* Buffalo: Courier, [1884].

*The True Lamplighter, and Aunt Mary's Cabin.* Boston: Cushing, Perkins & Fay, 1854.

Tucker, Louis Leonard. "'Ohio Show-Shop': The Western Museum of Cincinnati, 1820–1867." *A Cabinet of Curiosities: Five Episodes in the Evolution of American Museums.* Charlottesville: University Press of Virginia, 1967. 73–105.

Twain, Mark. *A Connecticut Yankee at King Arthur's Court* [1889]. London: Penguin, 1971.

———. *Mark Twain's Travels with Mr. Brown.* Ed. Franklin Walker and G. Ezra Dane. New York: Knopf, 1940.

Tyrrell, Ian R. *Sobering Up: From Temperance to Prohibition in Antebellum America, 1800–1860.* Westport, Conn.: Greenwood, 1979.

Wallis, Severn Teackle. *Writings of Severn Teackle Wallis.* Vol. 2. Baltimore: Murphy, 1896.

Walters, Ronald G. "The Erotic South: Civilization and Sexuality in American Abolitionism." *American Quarterly* 25.2 (1973): 177–201.

Ware, W. Porter, and Thaddeus C. Lockard Jr. *P. T. Barnum Presents Jenny Lind: The American Tour of the Swedish Nightingale.* Baton Rouge: Louisiana State University Press, 1980.

Watkins, Harry. *One Man in His Time: The Adventures of H. Watkins, Strolling Player, 1845–1863; From His Journal.* Ed. Maud Skinner and Otis Skinner. Philadelphia: University of Pennsylvania Press, 1938.

Welter, Barbara. "The Cult of True Womanhood 1820–1860." *American Quarterly* 18.2 (1966): 151–74.

Wilentz, Sean. *Chants Democratic: New York City and the Rise of the American Working Class, 1788–1850.* New York: Oxford University Press, 1984.

Wilks, Thomas Egerton. *State Secrets: or, The Tailor of Tamworth.* New York: Samuel French, n.d.

Willis, Nathaniel Parker. *Hurry Graphs; or, Sketches of Scenery, Celebrities and Society, Taken from Life.* New York: Scribner's, 1851.

———. *Memoranda of the Life of Jenny Lind.* Philadelphia: Peterson, 1851.

Wilson, Forrest. *Crusader in Crinoline: The Life of Harriet Beecher Stowe.* Philadelphia: Lippincott, 1941.

Wyllie, Irvin G. *The Self-Made Man in America.* New Brunswick, N.J.: Rutgers University Press, 1954.

Yellin, Jean Fagan. *Women and Sisters: The Antislavery Feminists in American Culture.* New Haven, Conn.: Yale University Press, 1989.

# Index

**Bluford Adams** is an assistant professor in the Department of English at the University of Iowa, where he teaches U.S. cultural studies and literature.

| DATE DUE | | |
|---|---|---|
| MAY 04 2006 | | |
| | | |
| | | |
| | | |
| | | |
| | | |
| | | |
| | | |
| | | |
| | | |